REACTIONS

MULTICULTURAL R
WRITING M(

D0118341

Roni Lebauer
Saddleback College

Robin Scarcella
University of California, Irvine

with the assistance of
Susan Stern
Irvine Valley College

Prentice Hall Regents

Library of Congress Cataloging--in--Publication Data

Lebauer, Roni.
    Reactions : multicultural reading-based writing modules / Roni
Lebauer, Robin Scarcella : with the assistance of Susan Stern.
      p.   cm.
    ISBN 0-13-756214-4
    1. English language -- Textbooks for foreign speakers.   2. Pluralism
(Social Sciences) --Problems, exercises, etc.   3. Ethnic groups-
-Problems, exercises, etc.   4. Readers--Pluralism (Social sciences)
5. English language--Rhetoric.   6. Readers--Ethnic groups.
7. College readers.   I. Scarcella, Robin C.   II. Stern, Susan.
III. Title.
PE1128.L39   1992
    428.2 ' 4--dc20   92-16414
                                                                CIP

Acquisitions editor: Nancy Leonhardt
Editorial/production supervision and interior
  design: Kala Dwarakanath and Noël Vreeland Carter
Cover design: Ben Santura
Cover art: ©Richard Fukuhara, Westlight
Photo research: Rhoda Sydney
Art illusrations: Don Martinetti, D.M. Graphics, Inc.
Pre-press buyer: Ray Keating
Manufacturing buyer: Lori Bulwin
Scheduler: Leslie Coward

© 1993 by Prentice Hall Regents

Photo Credits: Page 2, Children's Bureau, Dept. of Health and Human Services;
Pages 6, 181, James Carroll; Pages 21, 31, 42, 117, 187, 216, Ken Karp; Page 73, Levi
Strauss & Co.; Pages 77, 80, 104, 191, 268, Laimute Druskis; Page 90, Marc Anderson;
Page 176, Shirley Zeiberg; Page 202, The Library of Congress; Page 237, PhotoFest;
Page 271, Oklahoma Tourism Photo; Page 275, United Nations; Page 281, Quintana
Roo Dunne.

Permissions appear on page x which constitutes a continuation of the Copyright page.

Printed in the United States of America
20 19 18 17 16 15 14 13 12

ISBN 0-13-756214-4

CONTENTS

PREFACE

TO THE INSTRUCTOR

Reactions is a writing text which uses as its base thematically grouped readings emphasizing a multicultural perspective. It is designed to improve the writing of high intermediate and advanced university ESL students, permanent residents as well as immigrants. The book is also appropriate for freshman writing courses or preuniversity writing courses which are specifically geared to nonnative speakers.

The key features of *Reactions* are that it

- allows flexibility in content and room for teacher and student creativity;
- permits teachers to follow a process approach to the teaching of writing;
- allows students to obtain insights into writing concepts through their own experiences;
- contains sufficient numbers of readings from a variety of genres keyed to high intermediate and advanced ESL learners' English proficiency levels (so that students receive comprehensible input and can gather ideas for their writing on related topics);
- provides students with a suitable number and variety of writing tasks including journals, short writings, and essay assignments;
- includes numerous peer writing samples to be discussed and edited;
- includes authentic examples of peer composing processes, from brainstorming through peer feedback and multiple drafts to a final version;
- leads students to discover meaning through their spoken and written interactions;
- fits in well with a writing curriculum which sees grammar instruction as only one part of writing — at a later editing stage in the composing process;
- fits in with the notion that grammar instruction should stem from students' needs and abilities as demonstrated by their own writing and second language acquisition research;
- emphasizes vocabulary development; and
- stimulates students with diverse interests.

Theoretical Underpinnings

Research into the writing process of native and nonnative speakers has found that writers do not have a linear writing process, but rather that the process of writing (for both native and nonnative writers) is nonlinear—a constant interaction between idea generation, rhetorical and lexical "shaping," and mechanical revision. This view of writing as an idiosyncratic process which requires multiple revisions at both a global and local level is a central theoretical basis of this book.

Another important theoretical basis for this book is the idea that reading is necessary for writing improvement. This concept is supported by language teaching theory. Reading (at an appropriate English proficiency level) is considered to be necessary input for the acquisition of writing skills, vocabulary, and grammar. Proponents of a communicative approach to language teaching emphasize that reading and writing skills should be connected and taught in a realistic context, one possible context being works of literature. This "reading-writing connection" is an essential feature of this text; the reading selections provide students with an opportunity to acquire academic grammar, vocabulary, and discourse through comprehensible input. Multiple readings on a single topic are provided in each module, thereby recycling the vocabulary, grammar structures, and discourse and providing reexposure to these forms in varying contexts. In addition, the use of literary texts allows teachers to introduce the basics of literary analysis. (For example, Appendix A contains journal excerpts from famous writers.)

Grammar is an important part of writing competence; however, it is not the only component. This book is a writing text with editing exercises. It focuses on editing for specific grammar mistakes which ESL students actually make and which second language acquisition research suggests can be corrected. The grammar exercises do not interfere with the composing process. They focus on just a few grammatical mistakes at a time and provide illustrations from student writing samples. (Appendix B contains rules, explanations, and exercises for some of the most common grammar problem areas of high intermediate to advanced students.)

Another key element of this book is the integration of speaking and writing. Linguists have argued that there are important connections between speaking and writing, and that these two modes of communication must be integrated in college classrooms. Activities in the textbook which enrich the integration of speaking and writing include discussions and peer group work.

Finally, *Reactions* has been written with a multicultural audience in mind. Reading requires background knowledge, which varies among cultures. Writing requires a knowledge of culturally shared information and culturally expected rules of discourse. *Reactions* provides the students with the cultural information needed to comprehend the readings and to integrate ideas from these readings into their writing. This text is also sensitive to the difficulties which both immigrants and international students encounter when acquiring a second language and adapting to life in the United States. *Reactions* includes materials which are explicitly designed to address these difficulties.

Methodological Approach

A primary feature of this textbook is its use of modules. The book is made up of three modules (Learning a Second Language, Education, and Stereotypes). Teachers will be able to choose which modules to use and, within the module, which readings and exercises to use. Sequencing of activities is entirely up to the teacher. Thus, teachers have great flexibility in adapting the course to their own and students' needs and in varying the course from quarter to quarter or semester to semester. Each module has the following design:

- Journal topics that relate to the general topic of the module;
- Four or five key readings (from a variety of genres, some adapted or abridged), each followed by a vocabulary gloss, comprehension questions, an interaction activity, a vocabulary acquisition chart, short writing topics (dealing with responding to ideas in the article, responding as or to characters in a story, varying a point of view), peer writing samples and peer editing exercises for each short writing topic, and additional journal questions focusing specifically on that reading;
- Two possible essay topics, designed to allow students to use ideas gathered from the readings, class discussions, and short writings;
- Sample composing processes of essays written in response to the assigned topics (each containing multiple drafts, teacher comments, peer comments, and a discussion sheet to guide students in an examination of the process);
- Exercises focusing on a rhetorical feature relevant to the module;
- A checklist for editing and revising essays; and
- Supplemental readings related to the module (to be used for variety or for additional information on the topic, as desired).

Readings have been chosen to stimulate readers to see an issue from different perspectives and to help them relate the issue to their own lives. Comprehension checks that follow the readings take the form of statements to be marked "true" or "false"; these are designed to insure that the reader has understood the basic facts of the story. Once the true-false exercises are done, the student has an overview of the story or article, which can serve to confirm or revise his or her initial comprehension.

Vocabulary development is an important part of writing improvement. Vocabulary is best learned through reading and seeing words in a variety of contexts. A vocabulary acquisition checklist is provided after each reading. This checklist allows the students to choose which of the many new words in the reading they want to learn. Students do not need to learn every word in the vocabulary gloss; the stories or articles can be understood even if all the words are not known. The checklist activity asks students to choose ten words from each reading that they want to learn, words that seem to be of personal use to them. Students then are more "invested" in these words and are more likely to remember them.

Students need numerous opportunities to write and to vary the type of writing and the circumstances under which they write. *Reactions* offers students a variety of writing assignments: journal writing, short in-class writings (without multiple revisions), and longer pieces requiring multiple revisions (two or more drafts). Students are encouraged to keep a daily journal in which they include personal writing as well as writing in reaction to questions that are given to them at the beginning of each module and after each key reading. (Journal writing can be a source of ideas and a chance for the writer to learn the pleasure of writing for oneself without the pressure of others' opinions or grades.)

Short writing assignments in the book serve to encourage students to respond to ideas and think more deeply about the readings. They require more grammatical accuracy than the journal entries, yet do not require the multiple drafting and revising of the major essay. Students should be encouraged to spend no more than an hour on each of these assignments, striking a balance between fluency and accuracy.

The essay writing assignment unifies all of the activities in each module. Ideas from journal entries, readings, and short writing assignments can be used as stimuli and resources for the writing of the longer multidraft assignment. Prior to writing the first draft, students should be given suggestions for shaping their ideas but should not be given "cookie-cutter rhetorical forms." Rather, students should be encouraged to look at what they are trying to say and to discover the organization that best communicates those ideas. Exercises designed to help students improve the organization and unity of their essays are also contained in Appendix C. Student papers are included in the essay section of each module so that students can look at their "peers' work" and learn from these examples. During the first drafts of the essay assignment, content and organization should be stressed. During later drafts, grammar and mechanics should be stressed.

Grammar instruction should stem from your students' own work. Student samples that need grammatical editing are included because they contain errors typical of students at the high intermediate to advanced level. (These student samples are original pieces of work done in classes at the University of California, Irvine. The author's initials follow each piece of student work.)

As the title suggests, *Reactions* is designed to encourage interest and involvement in writing through reacting to the ideas of others, whether discovered through the written word (by reading the works of professional authors and peers) or the spoken word (by listening to and participating in classroom discussions). We hope this book contributes to this type of enthusiasm in your classroom.

TO THE STUDENT

This book is designed to improve your academic writing; however, we hope that it will also encourage you to enjoy writing. The title, *Reactions*, was chosen because that is what you will do in this book: react to readings by professional authors, react to writing samples done by your peers at the University of California, Irvine[1], and react to your classmates during discussions of the readings and of your own writings. Being able to express and communicate your ideas on paper is what makes writing enjoyable to many; perhaps you, too, will discover that enjoyment as you use this book.

While using this book, you will do many kinds of writings. You will be asked to keep a journal in which you will write your thoughts about events in your life, occurrences around you, and readings that you do inside and outside your class. Writing a journal should be a relaxing activity. It should give you the opportunity to write without the pressure of a grade and focus on what you want to say, not how you say it. Writing in a journal every day will increase your fluency, your ability to write freely. In addition, you will also be asked to write numerous short writings in which you react to ideas in the readings, in which you vary the point of view of a story, and in which you respond to a character in a story. Finally, you will use all of the ideas that

---

[1]These samples end with the initials of the student who wrote them.

you have gathered in your journal, through your readings of the articles and other students' papers, and through your classroom discussions to write a main essay with multiple drafts and revisions.

While doing all of this writing, you will have the opportunity to improve your reading, vocabulary, and grammar skills. Each reading is followed by a vocabulary gloss[2], comprehension and discussion questions, vocabulary acquisition charts (in which you select the vocabulary that you want to learn), peer writing samples, and peer editing exercises (in which you will practice editing for common grammar errors.)

Read, react, write . . . and in the process discover more about yourself and others.

ACKNOWLEDGMENTS

We are grateful to the following people for the special contributions they have made to this textbook: Lorraine Kumpf and Wendy Maccoun generously contributed their ideas and insights. Ronald Albright, Katherine Watson, Susan Earle-Carlin, and Susan Stern took time out of busy schedules to comment on the text and pilot it with their students. Thanks also go to the students at the University of California at Irvine, Saddleback Community College, and Irvine Valley Community College, who through their questions and comments, shaped the development and revision of this book. Finally, we would like to extend heartfelt thanks to Michelle Ryan and Lou Scarcella for their ongoing encouragement, understanding, and support.

PERMISSIONS AND SOURCES

"Why Couldn't My Father Read?" by Enrique Lopez: From *The Cleveland Plain Dealer*, September 1, 1979.

"The Misery of Silence": Adapted and abridged excerpt from *The Woman Warrior: Memoirs of a Girlhood Among Ghosts,* Copyright ©1975, 1976 by Maxine Hong Kingston, courtesy of John Schaffner Agency, Inc. Reprinted by permission of Alfred A. Knopf, Inc.

"Not Forever Blowing Bubbles": Adapted and abridged excerpt from "Swimming the English Channel: A Gradual Approach" by Robin Scarcella and Leroy Perkins in Gaikokugo Kyoiku Kiyo #20 (1989). Reprinted by permission.

"Successful Language Learners: What Do We Know About Them?": Adapted from an article by Alice Omaggio originally published in the ERIC/CLL News Bulletin, May, 1978. Reprinted by permission.

"America and I": Abridged excerpt from *Children of Loneliness* by Anzia Yezierska. Copyright ©1923 by Funk & Wagnall Company, Inc. Reprinted by permission of HarperCollins Publishers, Inc.

"Cultural Patterns and Rhetoric": Essay by Dale Johnson, written as part of a Linguistics course assignment at the University of California at Irvine.

"Contrastive Rhetoric: An American Writing Teacher in China": Adapted and abridged from an article by Carolyn B. Matalene in *College English,* December, 1985. Copyright ©1985 by the National Council of Teachers of English. Reprinted with permission.

"College Pressures": Abridged version of an article by William Zinsser originally published in Blair & Ketchum's Country Journal, Vol. VI, No. 4, April, 1979. Copyright ©1979 by William K. Zinsser. Reprinted by permission of the author.

"Fresh Start": By Evelyn Herald.

"What is College For?": Abridged version of an article by Ezra Bowen *Time* November 10, 1986. Copyright ©Time Inc. Reprinted with permission.

---

[2]The gloss uses the following abbreviations for grammatical parts of speech:

noun	(n.)
verb	(v.)
adjective	(adj.)
adverb	(adv.)
preposition	(prep.)
prepositional phrase	(p.p.)

Module 1:

Learning a Second Language

CONTENTS

Learning English can be a challenging task. In this module, you will be reading about others' ideas concerning second language learning. In addition, you will be examining your own experiences learning English and exploring your personal opinions about second language acquisition. Some of the questions you will consider in this module include:

- What are the consequences of growing up illiterate in the United States?
- How can teachers help second language learners develop their writing skills?
- What are the characteristics of successful second language learners?

In this module, your final task will be to write an essay with multiple drafts on one aspect of your own experience acquiring a second language. Specific assignments are given on pages 51–52. All the readings and activities in this module are designed to prepare you for this final task by providing you with appropriate ideas and language.

KEEPING A JOURNAL

There are many different types of writing and many different reasons to write. One type of writing is journal writing. This writing is for the writer, not for an audience (although the journals of many people have been published). You will be asked to keep a journal while you use this book. Keep the following guidelines in mind when writing your journal:

1. Write at least one page a day.
2. Do not write a list of events. Your journal will be more meaningful if you see it as a place to put your thoughts and reactions. Rather than writing everything that happened in a day, perhaps you might write about one thought that really struck you or about something you read or saw.
3. Your journal is for you. Do not be overly concerned with grammar or style. Your goal should be to get your ideas down. Your journal will not be checked for grammar.
4. In your journal, approximately half of your entries will be "free," that is, on the topic of your choice. The other half will be in response to questions in this book or additional questions that your teacher gives you.

Enjoy writing in your journal. Enjoy the conversation with yourself. (Refer to Appendix A to read reflections by two famous authors on their own journals.)

JOURNAL TOPICS

The general topic for this module is your own experience in learning English, and more specifically, learning to write in English. Here are some suggested topics. (As part of this module's journal writing assignment, choose three of the following topics to discuss in your journal each week.)

1. What is your writing process like? How do you go about doing a written assignment? (Describe, in detail, what goes through your mind as you get ready to write, as you write, as you finish writing. Describe what someone would see if they were watching you.)

2. In what ways, if any, have teachers' corrections helped you to improve your writing?

3. What is most important in good writing?

4. What is your writing ability in your native language?

5. How do you feel about English and writing in English?

6. Are writing classes a waste of time for you, considering your major? What will you need writing for in college? What about after college?

7. Have your writing classes in college and high school been different? Better or worse?

8. Does grammar instruction help you improve your writing ability?

9. What are your biggest problems with writing?

10. What is the best way to learn how to be a good writer?

Reading Unit 1A

Why Couldn't My Father Read?

Enrique Lopez

In this story, Lopez describes his childhood experiences dealing with his illiterate father. Before reading his story, consider the following questions: In what ways does reading make a person more powerful? Do you know any adults who are unable to read? In what ways do they rely on others for help? How would you feel if one of your parents was unable to read?

(1) Recent articles on immigration and education remind me of my father, who was an <u>articulate</u>, fascinating storyteller but totally <u>illiterate</u>. By the time I entered fourth grade in Denver, I was a proud, <u>proficient</u> reader—and painfully aware of my father's inability to read a single word in either Spanish or English. Although I'd been told there were no schools in his native village of Bachimba Chihuahua, I found it hard to accept the fact that he didn't even know the alphabet.

(2) Consequently, every night as I watched my mother read to him, I would feel a surge of <u>resentment</u> and shame. Together they bent over *La Prensa* from San Antonio—the only available Spanish language newspaper. "How can he be so dumb?" I would ask myself. "Even a little kid can read a damned newspaper." Of course many adults in our barrio[1] couldn't read or write, but that was no comfort to me. Nor did it <u>console</u>

---

[1]*Barrio* is Spanish for a subdivision of a city or neighborhood.

me that my hero Pancho Villa was also illiterate. After all, this was my own father, the man I considered to be smarter than anyone else, who could answer questions not even my mother could answer, who would take me around the ice factory where he worked and show me how all the machinery ran, who could make huge cakes of ice without any air bubbles, who could fix any machine or electrical appliance, who could tell me all those wonderful stories about Pancho Villa.

(3) But he couldn't read. Not one damned word!

(4) Whenever I saw my mother reading to him—his head thrust forward like a dog waiting for a bone—I would walk out of the kitchen and sit on the back porch, my stomach churning with a swelling anger that could easily have turned to hatred. So bitter was my disappointment, so deep was my embarrassment, that I never invited my friends into the house during that after-dinner hour when my mother habitually read to him. And if one of my friends had <u>supped</u> with us, I would hastily herd them out of the kitchen when my mother reached for *La Prensa*.

(5) Once, during a period of deepening frustration, I told my mother that we ought to teach him how to read and write. And when she said it was probably too late to teach him—that it might hurt his pride—I <u>stomped</u> out of the house and ran furiously down the back alley, finally staggering behind a trash can to vomit everything I'd eaten for supper.

(6) Standing there in the dark, my hand still clutching the rim of the can, I simply couldn't believe that anyone as smart as my dad couldn't learn to read, couldn't learn to write "cat" or "dog" or even "it." Even I, who could barely understand the big words he used when he talked about Pancho Villa (revolucion,[2] libertad[3]), even I, at the mere age of ten, could write big words in both English and Spanish. So why couldn't he?

(7) Eventually, he did learn to write two words—his name and surname. Believing that he would feel less <u>humble</u> if he could sign his full name rather than a mere "X" on his weekly paycheck, my mother wrote "José Lopez" on his Social Security card and taught him to copy it letter by letter. It was a slow, painstaking process that usually required two or three minutes as he drew each separate letter with solemn tight-lipped determination, pausing now and then as if to make sure they were in the proper sequence. Then he would carefully connect the letters with short hyphen-like lines, sometimes failing to close the gaps or overlapping letters.

(8) I was with him one Friday evening when he tried to cash his paycheck at a furniture store owned by Frank Fenner, a red-faced German with a bulbous nose and <u>squinty</u> eyes. My father usually cashed his check at Alfredo Pacheco's corner grocery store, but that night Pacheco had closed

---

[2]*Revolucion* is Spanish for revolution.
[3]*Libertad* is Spanish for freedom.

the store to attend a cousin's funeral, so we had crossed the street to Fenner's place.

(9) "You cambiar⁴ this?" asked my father, showing him the check.

(10) "He wants you to cash it," I added, annoyed by my father's use of the word *cambiar*.

(11) "Sure, Joe," said Fenner. "Just write your signature on the back of it."

(12) "Firme su nombre atrás," I told my father, indicating that Fenner wanted him to sign it.

(13) "Okay, I put my name," said my father, placing his Social Security card on the counter so he could copy the "José Lopez" my mother had written for him.

(14) With Fenner looking on, a <u>smirk</u> building on his face, my father began the ever-so-slow copying of each letter as I literally <u>squirmed</u> with shame and hot resentment. Halfway through "Lopez," my father paused, nervously licked his lips, and glanced <u>sheepishly</u> at Fenner's <u>leering</u> face. "No write too good," he said. "My wife teach me."

(15) Then, concentrating harder than before, he wrote the final "e" and "z" and slowly connected the nine letters with his jabby little scribbles. But Fenner was not satisfied. Glancing from the Social Security card to the check, he said, "I'm sorry, Joe, that ain't the same signature. I can't cash it."

(16) "You bastard!" I yelled. "You know who he is! And you just saw him signing it."

(17) Then suddenly grabbing a can of furniture polish, I threw it at Fenner's head but missed by at least six inches. As my father tried to restrain me, I twisted away and screamed at him, "Why don't you learn to write, goddamn it! Learn to write!"

(18) He was trying to say something, his face <u>blurred</u> by my angry tears, but I couldn't hear him, for I was now backing and stumbling out of the store, my temples throbbing with the most awful <u>humiliation</u> I had ever felt. My throat dry and sour, I kept running and running down Larimer Street and then north on 30th Street toward Curtis Park, where I finally flung myself on the recently watered lawn and wept myself into a state of complete exhaustion.

(19) Hours later, now <u>guilt-ridden</u> by what I had yelled at my dad, I came home and found him and my mother sitting at the kitchen table, writing tablet between them, with the alphabet neatly penciled at the top of the page.

(20) "Your mother's teaching me how to write," he said in Spanish,

⁴*Cambiar* is Spanish for change.

his voice so <u>wistful</u> that I could hardly bear to listen to him. "Then maybe you won't be ashamed of me."

(21) But for reasons too complex for me to understand at that time, he never learned to read or write. Somehow, the multisyllabic words he had always known and accurately used seemed confusing and totally beyond his grasp when they appeared in print or in my mother's handwriting. So after a while, he quit trying.

Vocabulary Gloss

The definitions given next are intended to aid your comprehension. Numbers in parentheses refer to the paragraphs in which the words appear. (Since you are not expected to understand each word in the preceding reading passage, not all the words you do not know are glossed. You will need to guess the meaning of other words you do not understand.)

articulate	(1)	(adj.)	expressing or able to express thoughts and feelings clearly, especially in words
illiterate	(1)	(adj.)	unable to read and write
proficient	(1)	(adj.)	thoroughly skilled; well-practiced in an art, science, skill, or branch of study
resentment	(2)	(n.)	a feeling of anger or bitterness about bad treatment
to console	(2)	(v.)	to give comfort or sympathy to someone in times of disappointment or sadness
to sup	(4)	(v.)	(slang) to eat supper
to stomp	(5)	(v.)	to walk or dance with a heavy step
humble	(7)	(adj.)	low in rank or position; unimportant; not held in high regard by society
squinty	(8)	(adj.)	looking with almost closed eyes, as at a bright light
to smirk	(14)	(v.)	to smile in a false or too satisfied way
to squirm	(14)	(v.)	to twist the body nervously about, as from discomfort, shame or nervousness
sheepishly	(14)	(adv.)	awkwardly, as from being slightly ashamed or fearful of others
leering	(14)	(adj.)	looking with an unpleasant smile expressing cruel enjoyment or rudeness

blurred	(18)	(adj.)	having a shape that is not clearly seen
humiliation	(18)	(n.)	the feeling of losing the respect of others
guilt-ridden	(19)	(adj.)	doing something with the knowledge or belief that one has done something wrong
wistful	(20)	(adj.)	having thoughts of a wish that may not be satisfied

Comprehension Check

Fill in the blanks on the left with a "T" if the statement is true or an "F" if the statement is false. Write the number of a paragraph (¶) which includes information to support your answer if the answer is explicitly found in this story.

1. _____ Enrique's father was illiterate.   (¶ ___)

2. _____ Enrique's father was proficient in written Spanish.   (¶ ___)

3. _____ Enrique resented the fact that his father could not read.   (¶ ___)

4. _____ Enrique's father only went to school through the fifth grade.   (¶ ___)

5. _____ Enrique knew that some famous people were illiterate.   (¶ ___)

6. _____ Enrique wanted his friends to know that his father was illiterate.   (¶ ___)

7. _____ Enrique's mother read to his father after dinner.   (¶ ___)

8. _____ Enrique's mother thought that teaching Enrique's father to read might hurt his father's pride.   (¶ ___)

9. _____ Enrique wanted his father to learn to read and write.   (¶ ___)

10. _____ Enrique's father used big words when he spoke Spanish.   (¶ ___)

11. _____ Enrique's mother taught Enrique's father how to write his name, address, and telephone number.   (¶ ___)

12. _____ Writing was a time-consuming process for Enrique's father.   (¶ ___)

13. _____ Enrique's father usually went to Frank Fenner's furniture store to cash his paycheck. (¶ ___)

14. _____ Frank Fenner was able to cash workers' checks. (¶ ___)

15. _____ Frank Fenner was happy to cash Enrique's father's check. (Inference)

16. _____ Enrique thought that Frank Fenner was a kind man. (¶ ___)

17. _____ Enrique's father tried to prevent Enrique from hurting Frank Fenner. (¶ ___)

18. _____ Enrique threw a bottle of perfume at Frank Fenner. (¶ ___)

19. _____ Enrique's father knew that Enrique was ashamed of him. (¶ ___)

20. _____ It took Enrique's father a few years to learn how to write. (¶ ___)

Interaction Activity

Work in groups of three to answer the following questions. Try to reach a consensus; that is, discuss your different opinions and see if you can reach an agreement about your answer.

1. Look at the following list of adjectives.[5]

___ dumb	___ embarrassed; ashamed	___ angry
___ resentful	___ confused	___ respectful
___ scared	___ empathetic	___ guilty
___ intolerant	___ image conscious	___ intelligent
___ condescending	___ impatient	___ prejudiced
___ unhappy	___ frustrated	___ hostile

[5]You may not know the following words:

resentful (adj.)	angry feeling occurring as a result of a real or imagined offense
intolerant (adj.)	narrow-minded; not able to understand different views
condescending (adj.)	arrogant or snobbish; tending to look down on others
empathetic (adj.)	sensitive to others' feelings and beliefs
image conscious (adj.)	sensitive about and aware of one's own appearance
hostile (adj.)	unfriendly and antagonistic

a. Which of the adjectives describe Enrique, the son? Which events in the narrative allow you to make this choice?

b. Which of the adjectives describe José, the father? Which events in the narrative allow you to make this choice?

c. Which of the adjectives describe the shopkeeper? Which events in the narrative allow you to make this choice?

2. What emotions do you feel as you read this narrative? How does the author make you feel these emotions?

3. What does this narrative demonstrate about the interrelationship of the four skills—speaking, listening, reading, and writing? Are any or all of these skills independent of each other? Are any or all of them dependent on each other?

Vocabulary Acquisition

One way to learn vocabulary is to make a commitment to yourself to learn a certain number of words per week. In this chapter, you will use a certain form to learn words of your own choosing.

Your page will be divided into four columns. In the first column, you will list the word you want to learn. In the second column, you will copy the context (or sentence) in which you found the word. In the third column, you will copy a short dictionary definition of the word. In the fourth column, you will use the word in your own sentence.

EXAMPLE

WORD	CONTEXT	DEFINITION	OWN SENTENCE
articulate	Recent articles on immigration and education remind me of my father, who was an articulate, fascinating storyteller but totally illiterate.	(adj.) (of a person) able to express thoughts clearly	She was so articulate that she was asked to give a speech at her graduation.

Choose ten words that you would like to learn from "Why Couldn't My Father Read?" and fill in the following chart.

WORD	CONTEXT	DEFINITION	OWN SENTENCE
1.			
2.			
3.			
4.			
5.			
6.			
7.			
8.			
9.			
10.			

SHORT WRITING: VARYING THE POINT OF VIEW

The narrator of this story is clearly Enrique. He is speaking from the point of view of an adult looking back at his behavior when he was a child. Enrique, the adult, remembers how Enrique, the child, felt and acted. Enrique, the adult, is telling the story the way Enrique, the child, experienced it.

Write from someone else's point of view: the mother? the father? a neighbor? a school friend of Enrique's? The events will remain the same, but the experience of these events will change. (Do not just rewrite the story and substitute pronouns. When we change the point of view, everything can change!) Before starting this assignment, read the peer writing sample and do the peer editing exercises which follow.

Peer Writing Sample

Read the following student writing sample and determine whose point of view is discussed.

> *Being able to read opens the door to the world. I wouldn't know. I can't read or write. I try, but I am old and it seems impossible to teach an old dog new tricks.*
>
> *My son, Enrique Lopez, on the other hand, is what I can't be: a literate person. He is a great kid. He is really smart. He knows how to read and write in English as well as in Spanish. I love him. I know that's not the way he feels toward me at times. But who can blame him? He has the right to be embarrassed about my disorder. Other fathers read stories to their kids. I can't! I know I should have learned to read and write when I was young. The thought of how Enrique would feel about me being illiterate never crossed my mind at that time. I am the one to blame for his embarrassment.*
>
> *When Enrique was young, he looked up to me. He thought I was the best father in the world. To him, I was everything. It wasn't until the fourth grade or so that he discovered the truth about my illiteracy, and the reality disappointed him. It hurt me to see him that way. I tried to read. I just couldn't. (R.B.)*

Peer Editing

1. In the following student writing sample, there are six verb tense errors. Read the sample and try to correct the errors.

    So many memories flash back as I sit here in my living room once again. Every table, every chair, every piece of furniture has its own story to tell. Everything seemed the way it used to be. The only difference is that I'm in a different time frame and my husband has gone to another world.

    Oh, I still can clearly picture those happy evenings when my husband and I sit near the warm fireplace. Outside, the rain would knock against our windows beckoning us to come out. But no, I prefer taking out the only Spanish magazine we have, La Prensa, and reading to my husband who listened attentively to every word I say. You see, he doesn't know how to read or write. (T.P.Q.)

    In what "time frame" is this taking place?

2. In the next student sample, there are a number of different types of grammar errors. Before correcting the sample, complete the exercises that follow.

    Avoiding Double Negatives   Correct the following sentences:

    a.   I don't want nothing.

    b.   I don't see no one.

    c.   I can't go nowhere.

    too + Adjective + to   Correct the following sentences:

    a.   She's short to reach the blackboard.

    b.   She's too young that she can't go see that movie.

    c.   He's too strong to move that box.

to see + Simple Verb Form or Gerund   Correct the following sentences:

a. I didn't see her went.

b. I saw the man leaves.

c. I've seen John studied.

My husband and I immigrated to America a long time ago. My husband could not read nothing in Spanish or English. When my son was a little child, he used to listen to his father tell him stories. My husband has always been a great storyteller. At that time, my son, Enrique, was young to realize that his father was illiterate. As Enrique grew older, I began to fear that he might discover his father's illiteracy and feel ashamed of it. Despite my efforts to prevent Enrique from discovering his father's inability to read or write, eventually Enrique did learn the truth.

Once Enrique asked me if I could teach his father how to read and write, but I told Enrique that it was too late to teach him and that it might hurt his pride. Then, I saw my son runs out of the house furiously down the back alley. As a mother, I was frustrated and devastated to see him ran out. I was very confused. (A.Y.H.C.)

SHORT WRITING: RESPONDING TO A CHARACTER

Write a letter of advice to one of the characters in Lopez' article, "Why Couldn't My Father Read?" You can write to Enrique (as a child), José (Enrique's father), Enrique's mother, or even Frank Fenner! Before writing your letter, read the peer writing samples and do the peer editing activities which follow.

Peer Writing Samples

Read the following letters and discuss the advice given. Would you give the same advice?

> Dear Enrique,
>
> After reading your article, I feel sorry for your dad because of the way you treat him just because he does not know how to read or write. Your behavior shows that you are prejudiced against your father. I don't blame you for being embarrassed or angry, but don't show your emotions in front of him. You make your father feel bad about himself. If I were you, instead of getting upset with your father, I would sit down with him and teach him how to read and write. For example, I would help Mom read *La Prensa* to him and, while reading it to him, teach him how to read.
>
> I know that your father doesn't want to be illiterate so try to understand him. After all, he is your father. I hope that this advice will help you in some way.
>
> Sincerely,
>
> L.K.L.

> Dear José,
>
> I feel very sorry about how your son feels about your illiteracy. I understand how much you want to learn to read and write just to make your son feel better in front of his friends. But let me tell you, this really shouldn't be the reason that you're learning to read and write. You must feel you're learning because it is for your own benefit.
>
> I understand it is more difficult for you to learn to read and write at your age than it was for your son who accomplished this in his youth. However, it is never too late to start learning. Despite the fact that you have to work and lack the time to learn, why did you quit studying after only a couple of days? It takes

time to learn to read and write. Look how many years it has been since your son started school. You must devote the same amount of time or even more in order to read and write as well as your son.

Let me tell you a story which explains why you are having difficulty learning. In India, people use elephants to help them carry logs or other heavy material. While their masters are away, only a very fragile rope is tied to the elephants' legs to prevent them from running away. Of course, they can break that rope very easily using just a little of their strength. Then, why don't they just stretch their legs and break the rope? The reason is that those fragile ropes exist in their minds as hard steel chains. In their youth, the elephants were tied with strong chains to big trees; the elephants tried to escape by pulling away from the trees day after day and year after year. They had no success. Finally, they gave up trying to break their chains. From that time on, only a fragile string was necessary to keep them in place.

José, don't you think you are exactly like those elephants? Like the elephants, a negative attitude has built up in you that prevents you from trying. If the elephants make any effort to escape, they will surely break free from the restraints. It's the same with you. Mind power is very important. If you think you are beaten by illiteracy, then you absolutely *are* since you won't even try. I have to admit that learning is a difficult task but really, the hardest part of this task is acquiring the belief that you'll be successful.

Sincerely,

D.C.

Peer Editing

1. In the next student sample, there are four run-on sentences and one sentence fragment. Before correcting the sample, practice correcting run-on and fragment errors by doing the following exercises.

Run-on Sentences Rewrite the following run-on sentences so that they are grammatical by using appropriate transitions or punctuation, or by dividing them into two sentences.

a. You shouldn't be so upset about getting a B in your English class, after all, you got A's in all your other classes!

b. Give me a call when you've finished your homework, if it's early enough we can still go out to dinner.

c. She didn't have to pay anything for legal advice about the accident, her father is a lawyer.

Sentence Fragments   Make complete sentences out of these sentence fragments:

a. I'd like to go to the movies with you tonight. But I've already made other plans and I really can't break them.

b. I can't help you out with a ride today. Although I would really like to be able to help you.

c. The committee couldn't come up with any solution to the problem. So they decided to hire a consultant to help them out.

Dear Enrique,

I am writing to you as a man. I want you to understand that your father is old and many times it is hard for him to catch on to things that you easily understand, I guess all I'm saying is don't be so hard on your father, try to put yourself in your father's situation. I know your father wants to be able to read and write just like anyone else. But he just can't. It is not that he is dumb or stupid. One time you yourself said that your father was an intelligent man. If your father was as stupid and worthless as you now think, would he be able to tell all those great stories? I don't think a dumb person would be able to tell exciting stories like your father. Your father is an old-fashioned man, he has never had a chance to learn like you did. I bet if he was given a chance when he was younger, he would be just like anyone else to you. Take it easy on your father, instead of trying to put him down, maybe you should try to help him learn how to read and write. Try your best to understand his situation, and don't make the matter worse.

(P.R.S.)

2. In the following student letter, there are three relative clause errors. Before correcting the sample, practice correcting relative clause errors by doing the exercise below.

Relative Clauses   Correct the following sentences:

a. She served us a wonderful meal, which it was nutritious as well as delicious.

b. I am waiting for my sister to arrive, who I haven't seen her for five years.

c. The university is in a large city which I want to attend.

Dear Enrique,

I have read your story which it was very interesting to me and truly understand your feeling about your father's illiteracy. If my father could not read or write his name, I would feel the same way. However, you must understand that your father might be disappointed in himself. Because of his age, it is hard for him to learn to read as easily as we do. Although it bothers you all the time, you should not show your resentment. Moreover, if your mother accepts the fact that your father is illiterate, why don't you? I know that it is difficult for you, but it is that truth which you have to cope with it. Perhaps you can give him a little time to overcome his problems. Empathizing with your father will improve your relationship which is very hard to do.

Sincerely,

Your friend, John (J.C.)

ADDITIONAL JOURNAL TOPIC

Your journal will continue on the topic of writing and learning a second language; however, you may want to go into greater depth and focus specifically on issues raised in the readings in this module. Following is the suggested journal topic for "Why Couldn't My Father Read?"

> *Lopez' story is about illiteracy and its effect on the literate son. What is the importance of literacy in your native culture? Is literacy connected with social class? wealth? prestige? How common is illiteracy? for men? for women? Would the story of José and his son be possible in your native culture? Why or why not?*

Reading Unit 1B

The Misery of Silence
Maxine Hong Kingston

Hong Kingston is a Chinese-American author, well-known for her dealing with the Chinese experience in the United States. The following abridged excerpt is from *The Woman Warrior*. Before you read the story, consider the following questions: What problems might a newcomer to the United States face in participating in American schools? Have you ever been in a situation in which you were afraid to speak your mind? How did you feel? How do you feel when you give an oral report and you are not prepared? Why?

(1) When I went to kindergarten and had to speak English for the first time, I became silent. A dumbness—a shame—still cracks my voice in two, even when I want to say "hello" casually, or ask an easy question in front of the check-out counter, or ask directions of a bus driver. I stand frozen, or I hold up the line with the complete, grammatical sentence that comes squeaking out at impossible length. "What did you say?" says the cab driver, or "Speak up," so I have to perform again, only weaker the second time. A telephone call makes my throat bleed and takes up that day's courage. It spoils my day with self-disgust when I hear my broken voice. It makes people <u>wince</u> to hear it. I'm getting better, though. Recently I asked the postman for special-issue stamps; I've waited since childhood for postmen to give me some <u>of their own</u> <u>accord</u>. I am making progress, a little every day.

(2) My silence was thickest—total—during the three years that I cov-

ered my school paintings with black paint. I painted layers of black over houses and flowers and suns, and when I drew on the blackboard, I put a layer of chalk on top; I was making a stage curtain, and it was the moment before the curtain parted or rose. The teachers called my parents to school, and I saw they had been saving my pictures, curling and cracking, all alike and black. The teachers pointed to the pictures and looked serious, talked seriously too, but my parents did not understand English. ("The parents and teachers of criminals were executed," said my father.) My parents took the pictures home. I spread them out (so black and full of possibilities) and pretended the curtains were swinging open, flying up, one after another, sunlight underneath, mighty operas.

(3) During the first silent year I spoke to no one at school, did not ask before going to the <u>lavatory</u>, and <u>flunked</u> kindergarten. My sister also said nothing for three years, silent in the playground and silent at lunch. There were other quiet Chinese girls not of our family, but most of them got over it sooner than we did. I enjoyed the silence. At first it did not occur to me I was supposed to talk or to pass kindergarten. I talked at home and to one or two of the Chinese kids in class. I made motions and even made some jokes. I drank out of a toy saucer when the water spilled out of the cup, and everybody laughed, pointing at me, so I did it some more. I didn't know that Americans don't drink out of saucers.

(4) I liked the Negro students (Black Ghosts)[1] best because they laughed the loudest and talked to me as if I were a <u>daring</u> talker too. One of the Negro girls had her mother coil braids over her ears Shanghai-style like mine; we were Shanghai twins except that she was covered with black like my paintings. Two Negro kids enrolled in Chinese school, and the teachers gave them Chinese names.

(5) It was when I found out I had to talk that school became a misery, that the silence became a misery. I did not speak and felt bad each time that I did not speak. I read aloud in first grade, though, and heard the barest whisper with little squeaks come out of my throat. "Louder," said the teacher, who scared the voice away again. The other Chinese girls did not talk either, so I knew the silence had to do with being a Chinese girl.

(6) Reading out loud was easier than speaking because we did not have to make up what to say, but I stopped often, and the teacher would think I'd gone quiet again. I could not understand "I." The Chinese "I" has seven strokes, <u>intricacies</u>. How could the American "I," assuredly wearing a hat like the Chinese, have only three strokes, the middle so straight? Was it out of politeness that this writer left off strokes the way a Chinese [girl] has to write her own name small and crooked? No, it was not politeness;

---

[1]Hong Kingston regarded all non-Chinese as ghosts because they seemed so threatening and "unreal."

"I" is a capital and "you" is lower-case. I stared at that middle line and waited so long for its black center to resolve into tight strokes and dots that I forgot to pronounce it.

(7) When my second grade class did a play, the whole class went to the auditorium except the Chinese girls. The teacher, lovely and Hawaiian, should have understood about us, but instead left us behind in the classroom. Our voices were too soft or nonexistent, and our parents never signed the permission slips anyway. They never signed anything unnecessary. We opened the door a crack and peeked out, but closed it again quickly. One of us (not me) won every spelling bee, though.

(8) I remember telling the Hawaiian teacher, "We Chinese can't sing 'land where our fathers died.' "[2] She argued with me about politics, while I meant because of curses. But how can I have that memory when I couldn't talk? My mother says that we, like the ghosts, have no memories.

(9) After American school, we picked up our cigar boxes, in which we had arranged books, brushes, and an inkbox neatly, and went to Chinese school, from 5:00 to 7:30 P.M. There we chanted together, voices rising and falling, loud and soft, some boys shouting, everybody reading together, reciting together and not alone with one voice. When we had a memorization test, the teacher let each of us come to his desk and say the lesson to him privately, while the rest of the class practiced copying or tracing. Most of the teachers were men. The boys who were so well behaved in the American school played tricks on them and talked back to them. The girls were not mute. They screamed and yelled during recess, when there were no rules; they had fistfights. Nobody was afraid of children hurting themselves or of children hurting school property. The glass doors to the red and green balconies with the gold joy symbols were left wide open so that we could run out and climb the fire escapes. We played capture-the-flag in the auditorium, where Sun Yat-sen and Chiang Kai-shek's pictures hung at the back of the stage, the Chinese flag on their left and the American flag on their right. We climbed the teak ceremonial chairs and made flying leaps off the stage. One flag headquarters was behind the glass door and the other on stage right. Our feet drummed on the hollow stage. During recess the teachers locked themselves up in their office with the shelves of books, copybooks, inks from China. They drank tea and warmed their hands at a stove. There was no play supervision. At recess we had the school to ourselves, and also we could roam as far as we could go—downtown, Chinatown stores, home—as long as we returned before the bell rang.

(10) At exactly 7:30 the teacher again picked up the brass bell that sat on his desk and swung it over our heads, while we charged down the

[2]This line is from a patriotic song called "My Country 'Tis of Thee" that is customarily sung in public schools in the United States after the "Pledge of Allegiance."

stairs, our cheering <u>magnified</u> in the stairwell. Nobody had to line up.

(11) Not all of the children who were silent at American school found voice at Chinese school. One new teacher said each of us had to get up and <u>recite</u> in front of the class, who was to listen. My sister and I had memorized the lesson perfectly. We said it to each other at home, one chanting, one listening. The teacher called on my sister to recite first. It was the first time a teacher had called on the second-born to go first. My sister was scared. She glanced at me and looked away; I looked down at my desk. I hoped that she could do it because if she could, then I would have to. She opened her mouth and a voice came out that wasn't a whisper, but it wasn't a proper voice either. I hoped that she would not cry, fear breaking up her voice like twigs underfoot. She sounded as if she were trying to sing through weeping and strangling. She did not pause or stop to end the embarrassment. She kept going until she said the last word, and then she sat down. When it was my turn, the same voice came out, a crippled animal running on broken legs. You could hear splinters in my voice, bones rubbing jagged against one another. I was loud, though. I was glad I didn't whisper.

Vocabulary Gloss

The definitions given here are intended to aid your comprehension. Numbers in parentheses refer to the paragraphs in which the words appear. (Since you are not expected to understand each word in the preceding reading passage, not all the words you do not know are glossed. You will need to guess the meaning of other words you do not understand.)

to wince	(1)	(v.)	to move suddenly, as if drawing the body away from something unpleasant
of their own accord	(1)	(prep.)	(done) willingly; (done) without being asked
lavatory	(3)	(n.)	bathroom
to flunk	(3)	(v.)	to fail
daring	(4)	(adj.)	very brave
intricacies	(6)	(n.)	something containing many detailed parts and thus difficult to understand
curse	(8)	(n.)	a word or sentence asking God, heaven, a spirit, etc. to bring evil or harm to someone or something
to chant	(9)	(v.)	to repeat in time

mute	(9)	(adj.)	silent; without speech
recess	(9)	(n.)	a pause for rest or recreation during the school day or year
supervision	(9)	(n.)	the act of keeping watch over others as the person in charge
to roam	(9)	(v.)	to wander with no very clear aim
to magnify	(10)	(v.)	to make something appear larger than it is
to recite	(11)	(v.)	to say (something learned) aloud from memory

Comprehension Check

Fill in the blanks on the left with a "T" if the statement is true or an "F" if the statement is false. Write the number of a paragraph (¶) which includes information to support your answer if the answer is explicitly found in this story.

1. _____ Hong Kingston used the term *ghosts* to refer to Chinese immigrants whom she considered frightening. (¶ ___)

2. _____ When Hong Kingston went to kindergarten, she frequently spoke to her classmates. (¶ ___)

3. _____ During Hong Kingston's first year at school, she failed to speak to anyone at school except for one or two Chinese children. (¶ ___)

4. _____ As an adult, Hong Kingston now feels confident about speaking English in front of others. (¶ ___)

5. _____ As an adult, Hong Kingston likes to speak English on the telephone. (¶ ___)

6. _____ Hong Kingston's teachers were concerned when they saw that Hong Kingston's pictures were covered with paint. (Inference)

7. _____ Hong Kingston's parents could speak English well. (¶ ___)

8. _____ Hong Kingston failed kindergarten. (¶ ___)

9. _____ When Hong Kingston drank out of a toy saucer at school, everyone laughed. (¶ ___)

10. _____ Hong Kingston liked the Black students the best because they talked to her as if she could talk like they did. (¶ ___)

11. _____ At first, Hong Kingston enjoyed silence, but later, when she found out that she had to talk in school, silence became a misery. (¶ ___)

12. _____ Hong Kingston was silent throughout the first grade. (¶ ___)

13. _____ After school, Hong Kingston always went home to play by herself. (¶ ___)

14. _____ Many of the children who were silent at the American school were talkative at the Chinese school. (Inference)

15. _____ In Chinese school, Hong Kingston was not afraid to talk in front of the class. (Inference)

Interaction Activity

Discuss the following questions in groups of three. Try to reach a consensus; that is, discuss your different opinions and see if you can reach an agreement about your answer.

1. How do people in your culture view silence? Does this view conflict with American cultural expectations?

2. Silence was not always a "misery" for Hong Kingston. When did it become a misery? Why?

3. Hong Kingston describes her paintings which she covered with black paint. How did her teachers interpret the paintings? How did Hong Kingston interpret these paintings?

4. Hong Kingston describes her problems with reading. The teacher interprets the problem differently than Hong Kingston. Why does Hong Kingston think she has a problem reading certain words? Why does the teacher think she has this problem?

5. Contrast the American public school and the Chinese school described by Hong Kingston. Consider the students' behavior, the teachers' behavior, the classroom environment, and the activities. Why do you think students behave so differently in the two schools?

6. When Hong Kingston describes her voice when reading aloud in Chinese class, she uses words which are not usually used to describe a voice. For instance, she describes her voice as "a crippled animal running on broken legs." She says you "could hear splinters in my voice, bones rubbing jagged against one another." How do you imagine her voice

sounded? Create your own images to describe your voice when you were first learning English.

7. What could Hong Kingston's parents, friends, and teachers have done to help her get through "the misery of silence"?

Vocabulary Acquisition

One way to learn vocabulary is to make a commitment to yourself to learn a certain number of words per week. In this chapter, you will use a certain form to learn words of your own choosing.

Your page will be divided into four columns. In the first column, you will list the word you want to learn. In the second column, you will copy the context (or sentence) in which you found the word. In the third column, you will copy a short dictionary definition of the word. In the fourth column, you will use the word in your own sentence.

Choose ten words that you would like to learn from "The Misery of Silence."

EXAMPLE

WORD	CONTEXT	DEFINITION	OWN SENTENCE
faltering	Most of us eventually found some voice, however faltering.	moving unsteadily as through weakness, fear or disrepair	The baby's first steps were faltering, but she was on her way to learning how to walk.

SHORT WRITING: RESPONDING TO A CHARACTER

Write a letter of advice to Maxine in Hong Kingston's "The Misery of Silence." You can write to Maxine (as a child) or Ms. Hong Kingston (as an adult). Before writing your letter, read the peer writing sample and do the peer editing exercises that follow.

Peer Writing Sample

Read the following letter and discuss the advice given. Would you give the same advice?

Dear Maxine,

As I read your last letter, I realized that you are going through some very difficult times communicating with others using your second language. I understand that you have problems speaking English in front of people, and therefore, you have developed a fear of using English. I would like to share this personal story with you.

I came to the United States six years ago. When I first came here, I didn't know a single word of English. It was very hard for me. But after about a year of hardship, I finally realized that to master my second language, I needed to use it constantly. At first, I was afraid of communicating in English because I was intimidated by all the native speakers around me, and I kept my mouth shut. After a period of silence, I found out that keeping quiet wasn't helping me to learn at all. I became more outspoken.

The consequences of my decision were striking. I made many new friends, I obtained first-hand experience using English, and I learned much faster. These changes have helped me to gain faith and trust in myself. My fear went away, and I became my "loud mouth" self again.

From my personal experience, I would like to advise you to be more outspoken. I know it will be very hard at first, but once you pass through that unavoidable stage of "silence," your whole life will become easier; you will meet more friends with whom you can communicate and encounter help whenever you need it. Through the assistance of your new friends, you will automatically gain self-confidence. Therefore, put away your "silence," and be yourself again.

Sincerely,

Your friend,

J.C.

Peer Editing

1. The following student letter contains ten article errors (a/an/the). Read the letter and try to correct these errors.

Dear Ms. Hong Kingston:

I am very glad I read your article. After reading your article, I realize that I am not only one who suffered the misery of silence. Perhaps because we are both Asians, my experience resembles yours. I came here when I was just thirteen years old. My younger brother and sister seemed to have much easier time learning the English. Sometimes I regret fact that I came here so late, but at least now I have acquired English. When I was reading your story, I was surprised that my experience was exactly same as yours. During my first years in United States, all I thought about was the last year in my country. Everything I saw seemed so strange to me. Everyone I met seemed so different. I sought places where I couldn't be seen. I was so scared on first day of school. Looking for classes frustrated me. I wished that there was way I could go back to my country. My dad stayed at my school whole day helping me. The other days I hung around with my sister. Whenever I saw my sister, I felt like crying, realizing that she was only one I could talk to. In my classes, I rarely opened my mouth. Perhaps the only time I spoke one word was once a day during attendance.

Sincerely,

A.C.

2. The following letter contains six errors of tense and verb form. (These are underlined.) Read the letter and correct the errors.

Dear Ms. Hong Kingston,

My name is J.Y.H. and I am attending the University of California at Irvine. A while ago, I read your story about your experience of learning English and how it affected your personality. I was very touched; that story reminded me of my past years. I went through most of the things that you have been through and I am still have some problems with learning English.

However, after I have lived through all those difficult times, I realized that I should have had more strength to speak out instead of keeping to myself. Maybe it was because of my character, but if I had been a little smarter then, I would have overcame all the hard times that I <u>have</u>. Instead of being quiet all the time, I should <u>speak</u> <u>out</u> and <u>try</u> to get along with everybody around me.

Sincerely,

J.Y.H.

3. In the following student sample, there are five errors of word form; for example, a noun may be used in place of an adverb, or an adjective may be used in place of an adverb. Try to find and correct these errors.

Dear Maxine,

I would like to advice you to overcome your fear of speaking. You cannot remain in a state of "silent" all your life. Besides, speaking up will give you self-confident which in turn will bring you happiness. I hope you follow this advise and become success in learning your second language.

Your friend,

Q.T.

ADDITIONAL JOURNAL TOPIC

Your journal entries will continue on the topic of writing and learning a second language; however, you may want to go into greater depth and focus specifically on issues raised in the readings in this module. Following is the suggested topic for "The Misery of Silence."

> *Hong Kingston demonstrates in her story how her "voice" in Chinese and in a Chinese-speaking environment was very different from her "voice" in English and in an English-speaking environment. (By "voice," she means more than just speaking sound; she means the ability to express her personality.) Do you feel that you have a different "voice" in English than you do in your native language? Explain.*

Reading Unit 1C

Not Forever Blowing Bubbles
Robin Scarcella and Leroy Perkins

In this article, Scarcella and Perkins, two applied linguists, are writing suggestions for teachers to help them teach writing to nonnative English speakers. Before reading the article, reflect on your own experiences learning to write in English. What obstacles did you have to overcome in learning to write English? How did you overcome these obstacles? Did any teachers guide (or interfere with) your development of effective writing skills? What were these teachers like? How helpful did you find grammar instruction, corrective feedback on your essays, and interesting reading materials?

(1) Christopher is three years old and learning to swim. His first lesson is in blowing bubbles: <u>exhaling</u> under water, <u>inhaling</u> with every bob above the surface. He will later incorporate blowing bubbles and taking breaths into his swimming stroke,[1] which will permit Christopher to swim far beyond the distance he might be able to cover in just one breath. The inefficient alternative is to dog paddle, that is, swim without putting his head in the water.

(2) Christopher's teacher knows that blowing bubbles leads to bigger things—like maybe swimming the English Channel—but for now it's enough

---

[1] A variety of swimming strokes are mentioned in this article, including the dog paddle, the overhand sidestroke, and the crawl.

for Christopher to blow bubbles and become comfortable with his head in the water. As she puts it, "Don't worry. With time Christopher's arm/leg coordination will develop." When that happens, he'll be swimming laps with the other children. For now, he can pop up for air. That will save him in an emergency.

(3) Perhaps Christopher's swimming instructor should talk to ESL writing instructors. How many of us are asking our students to swim the English Channel before they are ready? ESL writing instruction (let's go further: any writing instruction in any language, whether first, second or fiftieth) must start by encouraging students to talk to themselves on paper, that is, record their thoughts in a way that is meaningful to them. We suggest that students' "thoughts" in the target language gradually take shape through sufficient and appropriate input, namely, enough interesting listening and reading material that they can understand. But writing activities cannot be postponed until students have sufficient mastery of the language to write grammatically and rhetorically correct essays, any more than babies should be discouraged from talking until they can utter complete and connected sentences. One of the first lessons in a swim class is blowing bubbles. Blowing bubbles does not look like swimming, and ungrammatical, rhetorically inept scribbles do not look like compositions. But just as knowing how to blow bubbles and come up for air is essential if swimmers are to progress to more complex tasks of physical coordination, ESL writers—and their teachers—should not initially concern themselves with grammatical rules and rhetorical forms, which are probably best acquired subconsciously through meaningful interaction with "comprehensible input." At the risk of taking the swimming analogy too far, it's worth noting that just as Christopher's instructor gets into the water with him to show him to blow bubbles, second language instructors need to be in the water with their students, modeling the target language at levels which are appropriate to the students' proficiency levels. Instructors should trust that students will improve the grammatical and rhetorical aspects of their essays as they develop the content and get help on revising their drafts from fellow students and the instructor in pair and group work.

(4) We must remember that writing is thinking or, more precisely, writing is a record of thought. It's a conversation first between the writer and him or herself, and then a conversation between the writer and his or her audience. Until ESL writers can "speak their minds" in writing, grammatical and rhetorical considerations are premature and will likely inhibit students' progress by intimidating them with the complexities of written English.

(5) Odd, isn't it, how so many well-meaning teachers in our profession have assumed that the place to start is with what they call "the basics": grammatical and rhetorical rules. In our view, grammatical and

rhetorical <u>competence</u> are connected and necessarily "taught" together, though we believe such teaching is best done by example rather than by rule, by modeling the correct grammatical usage and effective rhetorical strategies in meaningful contexts, rather than giving students <u>cookie cutter</u> <u>rhetorical</u> <u>forms</u> as containers for shaping the expression of their ideas. Before grammatical and rhetorical modeling and practicing, however, come <u>fluency</u>, and modeling fluency is perhaps the best way to start any writing classroom, whether ESL or not.

(6) By "fluency" we mean the student's ease in filling the page with meaningful scribbles in the target language, even if the scribbles are comprehensible only to the second language learner. First things first. We believe that formal grammatical and rhetorical considerations interfere with the early stages of the writing process. Grammar and rhetoric belong to the fine tuning stages. The real "basics" of writing are the marks on the page we make with the intent to communicate. Our students need both content and fluency. Without content, there's nothing to say, and without some degree of fluency, there's no way to say it.

(7) ESL instructors who accept the premise that the primary function of language is to communicate understand that communication need not be strictly shaped into a <u>culturally</u> <u>sanctioned</u> form to be effective. We want our students to be able to ask for directions downtown or to write a note explaining why they missed class on Friday. These are survival skills, similar to Christopher's learning to blow bubbles and take a breath. Just as Christopher is capable of blowing bubbles without the arm/leg coordination necessary to swim the crawl, so too are second language students capable of communicating their thoughts and improving essay content and organization without specific instruction in grammatical rules and rhetorical form in the early stages of composing. The grammatically correct, <u>cohesive</u>, <u>coherent</u> essays that we are all waiting for will come eventually, given sufficient time, student motivation and appropriate input, as the students revise their drafts with the help of each other and their instructor. But to stress grammar and rhetoric in the early stages is to put things backwards. Let our students blow bubbles first; the overhand sidestroke will come along when they're ready for it.

(8) Our thesis is in agreement with the profession's emerging <u>consensus</u> that grammatical correctness comes naturally, given sufficient modeling (another way of saying "comprehensible input") and opportunities for the students to use this modeling. As far as rhetoric goes, it's far better to let students <u>flail</u> around for themselves for a while than to give them rhetorical forms for their essays. These forms may satisfy a teacher's desire for cohesiveness and coherence while actually delaying the students' progress toward letting their thoughts determine the essay's form.

(9) For now, Christopher has developed what we'll call <u>coping</u> strategies

to get him to the other side of the pool. While more advanced children propel themselves through the water by kicking and rotating their arms, Christopher gets across the pool by first pushing off from the side (which is good for about 10 feet) and then dog-paddling as fast as he can. When he gets tired—and that doesn't take long when he's dog-paddling—he just floats. There's nothing wrong with floating for survival. And there's nothing wrong with second language learners (who have many learning demands placed on them all day long) floating on a sea of formless pieces of writing until they acquire the degree of comfort with their writing in the target language to enable them to keep trying and learn the grammatical and rhetorical niceties that native speakers gradually acquire as a consequence of communicating in their culture. Since the communication of ideas and feelings, no matter how ineptly done, is what writing is about in any language, we tell students who are just beginning to write their essays just to fill pages. We never mention grammatical or rhetorical considerations until the final drafts. We have red pens, but we only use them to write words like "Good" and "Yes" in response to our students' writing. Of course we try to be more specific when we can, going on to explain why a passage of student writing is effective and providing students with models of alternative means of expressing themselves. We ignore mistakes until the final draft.

(10) Similarly, Christopher's instructor allows him to make lots of mistakes in a playful, supportive environment, but never lets him fail a task. Her estimation of his capability and her subsequent assignment of appropriate tasks (that challenge Christopher to do only what she is reasonably sure that he can accomplish) constitute a large portion of the art of teaching anything: knowing when and how and what to ask from students. She knows that pushing swimmers to reach goals they are not yet ready to achieve only causes swimmers to become dependent on coping strategies or to fail. Encouraging second language speakers to produce essays far beyond their linguistic competence may be like putting a child who does not yet know how to come up for air in the deep end of the pool. Christopher's instructor provides him with both abundant modeling of "correct" form and abundant opportunities to use this modeling, thus indirectly enhancing his "form" while building stamina and confidence.

(11) While Christopher's instructor is working on what he is developmentally capable of doing (blowing bubbles), she is simultaneously working on his arm/leg coordination. Though she never pushes Christopher to move his arms and legs in a particular way, she provides him with a goal which requires such movement and models to show him how it is done. The goal is getting across the pool. The models are the other students and the teacher. When Christopher is ready, he will know what to do with his arms and legs. So too will second language learners gradually acquire the

linguistic refinements of correct grammar and a grasp of the rhetorical forms they need for communication in a meaningful context. In the meantime, they learn to blow bubbles in that often perplexing pool of communication we call "English."

Vocabulary Gloss

The definitions given here are intended to aid your comprehension. Numbers in parentheses refer to the paragraphs in which the words appear. (Since you are not expected to understand each word in the preceding reading passage, not all the words you do not know are glossed. You will need to guess the meaning of other words you do not understand.)

to exhale	(1)	(v.)	to breathe out
to inhale	(1)	(v.)	to breathe in
lap	(2)	(n.)	a single journey around the track
to postpone	(3)	(v.)	to delay; to move to some later time
mastery	(3)	(n.)	skill in doing something
rhetorically correct	(3)	(adj.)	having correct organization and content
to utter	(3)	(v.)	to speak
inept	(3)	(adj.)	totally unable to do things
scribble	(3)	(n.)	a meaningless written mark; writing which is careless and hard to read
subconsciously	(3)	(adv.)	present only at a hidden level of the mind
comprehensible input	(3)	(n.)	language that can be easily understood
target language	(3)	(n.)	the language which the language learner is trying to learn
to revise	(3)	(v.)	to read through a paper carefully, making improvement on content and organization
premature	(4)	(adj.)	developing or happening before the natural or proper time
to inhibit	(4)	(v.)	to prevent (from doing something)

to intimidate	(4)	(v.)	to make someone afraid or feel threatened
complexity	(4)	(n.)	that which is complex or difficult
competence	(5)	(n.)	skill; ability to do what is needed
cookie cutter rhetorical forms	(5)	(n.)	organizational forms such as the "five paragraph essay" which can be easily taught, memorized, and used
fluency	(5)	(n.)	the quality of writing smoothly and readily
culturally sanctioned	(7)	(adj.)	supported or encouraged by the culture
cohesive	(7)	(adj.)	tending to stick together
coherent	(7)	(adj.)	easily understood; being reasonably connected
consensus	(8)	(n.)	a general agreement; collective or group opinion
to flail	(8)	(v.)	to wave violently
to cope	(9)	(v.)	to deal successfully with something
to float	(9)	(v.)	to stay at the top of liquid or be held up in the air without sinking
abundant	(10)	(adj.)	more than enough; plentiful; many
to enhance	(10)	(v.)	to increase (good things such as value, power or beauty)
refinement	(11)	(n.)	improvement
perplexing	(11)	(adj.)	confusing

Comprehension Check

Fill in the blanks on the left with a "T" if the statement is true or an "F" if the statement is false. Write the number of a paragraph (¶) which includes information to support your answer if the answer is explicitly found in the article.

1. _____ The authors believe that learning to swim is like learning to write. (¶ ___)

2. _____ Christopher's swimming teacher thinks that, in the early stages, Christopher should try to learn how to incorporate blowing bubbles, taking breaths, and using his swimming stroke at the same time.   (¶ ___)

3. _____ According to Scarcella and Perkins, the first step in learning to write is simply writing.   (¶ ___)

4. _____ Scarcella and Perkins do not believe that writers should wait until they've achieved mastery of the grammar before they start to write.   (¶ ___)

5. _____ Scarcella and Perkins think that memorizing grammatical rules will significantly improve a writer's ability to produce good writing.   (¶ ___)

6. _____ Scarcella and Perkins encourage writers to consider grammar and rhetoric when they first sit down to write.   (¶ ___)

7. _____ According to the authors, writers can compose effective messages which are ungrammatical.   (¶ ___)

8. _____ Swimmers are capable of swimming across the pool without perfect arm and leg coordination.   (¶ ___)

9. _____ For Scarcella and Perkins, the real meaning of writing is the use of correct forms.   (¶ ___)

10. _____ Scarcella and Perkins believe that teachers can help their students improve their writing by editing all of their students' grammar mistakes on their first drafts. (Inference)

11. _____ Christopher's swim instructor allows him to make mistakes in a supportive environment.   (¶ ___)

12. _____ Scarcella and Perkins believe that students should not be pushed to complete writing assignments that are too hard for them.   (¶ ___)

13. _____ Scarcella and Perkins believe that students need many opportunities to write.   (¶ ___)

14. _____ The authors argue that grammar mistakes should always be ignored.   (¶ ___)

15. _____ Although Christopher's teacher doesn't force him to move his arms in a certain way, she creates goals for him which require specific movements.   (¶ ___)

Interaction Activity

Work in small groups to do the following exercise.

The Scarcella and Perkins article provides an analogy between Christopher's learning to swim and students' learning to write. Clarify that analogy in chart form. An example is given for you. Write as many examples as you can find.

LEARNING TO SWIM	LEARNING TO WRITE
The teacher doesn't expect Christopher to look like a swimmer immediately.	Teachers shouldn't expect students' writing to look like perfect writing immediately.

Vocabulary Acquisition

One way to learn vocabulary is to make a commitment to yourself to learn a certain number of words per week. In this chapter, you will use a certain form to learn words of your own choosing.

Your page will be divided into four columns. In the first column, you will list the word you want to learn. In the second column, you will copy the context (or sentence) in which you found the word. In the third column, you will copy a short dictionary definition of the word. In the fourth column, you will use the word in your own sentence.

Choose ten words that you would like to learn from "Not Forever Blowing Bubbles."

EXAMPLE

WORD	CONTEXT	DEFINITION	OWN SENTENCE
incorporate	He will incorporate blowing bubbles and taking breaths into his swimming stroke, which will permit Christopher to swim far beyond the distance he might be able to cover in just one breath.	(verb) to join with something else; to make a part of a group	The dancer likes to incorporate a variety of styles into her dance routines.

SHORT WRITING: RESPONDING TO IDEAS IN AN ARTICLE

In a paragraph, react to one of Scarcella and Perkins's suggestions. Discuss this suggestion in relation to your own language learning experiences. Before writing your response, read the peer writing samples and do the peer editing exercises that follow.

Peer Writing Samples

Read the following student writing samples and discuss whether your own views match the writers' views.

1. *Scarcella and Perkins ask teachers, "how many of us are asking our students to swim the English Channel before they are ready?" I would like to ask ESL students a similar question: how many of you are asking yourselves to write a grammatically and rhetorically correct essay when you know that you are not ready to do this? Often we ESL students expect so much from ourselves that we get easily discouraged when we cannot write a perfect paper. For example, I used to get so frustrated when I couldn't find the exact words to use that I would throw out my night's work and not turn in my writing assignments. I have learned a valuable lesson from Scarcella and Perkins. I learned to adopt a positive attitude toward writing and practice writing even when I am unable to write perfectly. Let me emphasize this point to all ESL students. Not everyone can write a model essay. You're not the only one! (Y.H.)*

2. *As Scarcella and Perkins explain, we ESL students should remember that "writing is thinking" or, more precisely, "writing is a record of thought. It's a conversation first between the writer and him or herself, and then a conversation between the writer and his or her audience." My experience has taught me that writing a journal or a diary everyday develops writing skills. When I recorded my thoughts in my journal, I became more interested in writing instead of hating and fearing it. After I started recording my thoughts consistently, I actually felt comfortable and at ease about writing. I suggest that ESL students use journals as a tool to help them open the door to writing, to lessen the*

fear of failure, and not to force themselves to write beyond their writing ability. (T.A.)

Peer Editing

1. In the following student writing sample, there are three word form errors. Read the sample and try to correct the errors.

According to Perkins and Scarcella, "until ESL writers can speak their minds" in writing, "grammatical and rhetorical considerations are premature and will likely inhibit students' progress by intimidating them with the complexities of written English." This idea is absolute correct. If ESL students have to concentrate on grammar rules and organization instead of ideas, they will not be able to express themselves fluent. I experienced this situation myself when I was a freshman in high school. All I learned were grammar rules and patterns for organizing my essays. I was very frustrating all the time. Beginning writers need to free themselves from an over-emphasis on grammar and organization so that they can get their ideas to flow on paper. (A.R.)

2. In the following student writing sample, there are five errors involving singular and plural noun forms. Read the sample and try to correct the errors.

Scarcella and Perkins believe that students need many opportunities to write. I agree with them. There are several reason why I have the same points of view. First, frequent writing helps build the students' fluency. Second, it gives them many ideas. For example, when people don't write a lot about specific topics, they don't have the opportunity to think about these topic. Finally, when students write a lot, they develop their vocabularies and improve their gram-

mars. (P. Q. T.)

3. In the following student writing sample, the five underlined words and expressions are used inappropriately in formal writing. Read the sample and try to replace the words with more appropriate words or expressions.

> *I disagree with one point in Scarcella and Perkins' ar-*
>
> *ticle. I think we should be pushed to complete writing as-*
>
> *signments that are very difficult. We have already learned*
>
> *to blow bubbles before coming to the university. We wrote*
>
> *lots of easy stuff in our high school English classes and now*
>
> *we need to write real challenging essays. We need to be*
>
> *given a ton of homework so we can learn from our mistakes.*
>
> *By the way, the guys in college I know attend this place to*
>
> *obtain knowledge, not to waste their time completing easy*
>
> *essay assignments. (L. K.)*

ADDITIONAL JOURNAL TOPIC

Your journal will continue on the topic of writing and learning a second language; however, you may want to go into greater depth and focus specifically on issues raised in the readings in this module. Following is the suggested journal topic for "Not Forever Blowing Bubbles."

> *Scarcella and Perkins make a lot of suggestions about how teachers should teach students to write. Which suggestions do you agree with? Which suggestions do you disagree with?*

Reading Unit 1D

Successful Language Learners: What Do We Know About Them?

Alice Omaggio

In this article, Omaggio, an applied linguist, describes the characteristics of successful second language learners. Consider your own experiences learning English as a second language. What strategies did you use to learn English? Which strategies were useful and which ones were not? Which of your own personality characteristics helped you to acquire English? (You may want to consider such characteristics as your curiosity, friendliness, ability to get along with others, and politeness.) Which of your own personality characteristics interfered with your ability to acquire English?

(1) Almost everyone agrees with the statement that most people learn their native language with a fair degree of success. Although some people seem to have more verbal skills than others, almost everyone can acquire his or her first language easily and well. Why is it, then, that the success record for acquiring skill in a second or foreign language in a classroom setting is so poor for so many students? What makes some foreign language learners succeed (regardless of the teacher, textbook, or classroom situation) while others fail (even with the best teacher, textbook, or classroom situation)?

(2) Several researchers have been curious about these questions in recent years and have designed studies to find out what makes the "good"

language learner good. The researchers suggest that if we knew more about what successful learners did, we might be able to teach these strategies to poorer learners and, in this way, increase their chances of success. The studies have typically focused on three aspects of the problem:

1. What personality characteristics are more frequently associated with good language learners?
2. What specific strategies and techniques do good language learners tend to use when learning languages?
3. Are these techniques teachable? If so, how?

PERSONALITY CHARACTERISTICS

(3) Researchers have done many studies to try to isolate personality characteristics that are associated with successful language learners. Their findings are preliminary and limited; however, some tentative conclusions are listed below:

(4) A. *Tolerance of Ambiguity*   Researchers suggest that the successful language learner is someone who can tolerate a certain amount of frustration and uncertainty while completing second language tasks. Therefore, a successful language learner remains calm even when he or she is confused or unsure of the answer. In contrast, more intolerant learners may react to this kind of ambiguity in the language learning situation with dislike, depression, or avoidance behaviors.

(5) B. *Extroversion.*   Several researchers have found a significant relationship between oral fluency and extroversion. Extroverted people often are willing to express their own ideas openly and take risks in life—two characteristics which may be related to successful language learning.

STRATEGIES AND TECHNIQUES

(6) The following language learning strategies have been collected from a variety of sources: interviews, direct observations, research experiments, insights from experienced language learners and teachers, and theoretical discussions about how the language is learned. These strategies are frequently associated with good language learning experiences.

(7) A. *Successful language learners have insight into their own language learning styles and preferences.*   They have a personal style or positive learning strategy that fits their needs and preferences. They can adapt to various methods and materials and know how to make sense of the linguistic information that is presented to them. Poor learners, in contrast, do not have insight into their own learning difficulties. They are often frustrated by methods that are not appropriate for them. It is difficult for them to organize their linguistic input into a coherent system; instead, they see the

input as an unconnected, untidy collection of individual items.

(8) B. *Successful learners take an active approach to the learning task.* They select learning goals for themselves and find ways to use the second language. They try to find opportunities to communicate in the second language and to truly understand this communication. The poor learner, on the other hand, often relies too heavily on the teacher and has a <u>passive</u>, uninvolved attitude.

(9) C. *Good language learners are willing to take risks.* They are willing to appear foolish sometimes in order to communicate and will use their imagination to find creative ways to communicate, (for example, using "body language," creating new words such as making a verb into a noun).

(10) D. *Good language learners are good guessers.* They constantly search for clues to meaning and skillfully use these clues to make reasonable guesses. For example, successful reading comprehension strategies that involve guessing include using the context around the word and using grammar clues to determine the meaning of unknown words.

(11) E. *Good language learners are aware of form as well as content,* that is, they refer to the form of the word or sentence (its grammar, spelling, pronunciation, etc.) as well as its meaning. Good language learners constantly look for patterns in the language and try to figure out rules for forming the language. They look for and use correction that is given to them.

(12) F. *Successful learners actively try to develop the second language into a separate reference system;* that is, they try to think of the second language as separate from their first language. They try to think in the second language as soon as possible rather than continually translating from one language to another.

(13) G. *Good language learners generally have a tolerant and outgoing approach to the new language and its speakers.* They have a positive and accepting view of the native speakers of the new language and look for opportunities to use the language with native speakers.

Vocabulary Gloss

The definitions given here are intended to aid your comprehension. Numbers in parentheses refer to the paragraphs in which the words appear. (Since you are not expected to understand each word in the preceding reading passage, not all the words you do not know are glossed. You will need to guess the meaning of other words you do not understand.)

to acquire (a language)	(1)	(v.)	to gain proficiency in (a language)
regardless of	(1)	(prep.)	without worrying about

strategy	(2)	(n.)	particular plan for winning success in a particular activity
to isolate	(3)	(v.)	to separate one substance from others for examination
preliminary	(3)	(adj.)	as a preparation for
tentative	(3)	(adj.)	not certain; made or done only as a suggestion to see the effect
tolerance	(4)	(n.)	the quality of allowing others to behave in different ways without becoming annoyed
ambiguity	(4)	(n.)	something that is understood in more than one way; uncertain or unclear
depression	(4)	(n.)	a feeling of sadness and hopelessness
extroversion	(5)	(n.)	personality characteristic of people who like to spend time in activities with others
insight	(6)	(n.)	the understanding which results from using one's mind to comprehend something deeply without help from outside information
to adapt	(7)	(v.)	to change so as to make suitable for new needs, different conditions, etc.
linguistic input	(7)	(n.)	language that is heard
coherent	(7)	(adj.)	being naturally or reasonably connected; easily understood
passive	(8)	(adj.)	not active; influenced by outside influences, but not reacting in return

Comprehension Check

Fill in the blanks on the left with a "T" if the statement is true or an "F" if the statement is false. Write the number of a paragraph (¶) which includes information to support your answer if the answer is explicitly found in the article.

1. _____ Most people learn a second language easily in classroom situations.   (¶ ___)

2. _____ Researchers are not interested in what makes a successful second language learner.   (¶ ___)

3. _____ Research indicates that the successful language learners can handle a certain amount of frustration and uncertainty. (¶ __)

4. _____ Successful language learners do poorly when the teaching style does not match their own learning styles. (¶ __)

5. _____ Omaggio suggests that extroverts are better language learners then introverts. (¶ __)

6. _____ According to Omaggio, risk-takers are good language learners. (¶ __)

7. _____ Research about good language learners comes from a variety of sources including research experiments and observations. (¶ __)

8. _____ Successful language learners are unaware of their personal learning styles. (¶ __)

9. _____ Successful language learners take a passive approach toward language learning. (¶ __)

10. _____ Successful language learners never set goals for themselves. (¶ __)

11. _____ Poor language learners do not understand how the linguistic input they receive is related to the knowledge that they already have. (¶ __)

12. _____ Good language learners try to guess the meaning of words. (¶ __)

13. _____ It is important to good language learners to understand the precise meaning of all words. (¶ __)

14. _____ Good language learners are concerned with the grammar of their second language. (¶ __)

15. _____ Good language learners try to translate words from their first language whenever possible. (¶ __)

Interaction Activity

Discuss the following questions in small groups.

1. The Omaggio article focuses on the following two questions:
   - What personality characteristics are associated with good language learners?
   - What specific strategies and techniques do good language learners tend to use in approaching various language learning tasks?

One way to check your reading comprehension is to tell someone about your interpretation of a concept without looking at the reading. Read the article and take turns telling each other what you understand about each concept. Other members of the group may add or correct as they see fit.

a. What personality characteristics are associated with good language learners? According to Omaggio, good language learners have a high degree of tolerance of ambiguity and are extroverts.

b. What specific strategies and techniques do good language learners tend to use in approaching various language learning tasks? Good language learners

- have insight into their own language learning styles
- take an active approach to the learning task
- are willing to take risks
- are good guessers
- attend to form as well as content
- develop the target language into a separate reference system
- have a tolerant and outgoing approach to speakers of the target language

2. Omaggio states that one personality characteristic associated with successful language learning is extroversion. However, more recent research has shown that introverts who carefully observe others' interaction are also excellent learners. Which of these ideas is more consistent with your own experiences as a language learner?

Vocabulary Acquisition

One way to learn vocabulary is to make a commitment to yourself to learn a certain number of words per week. In this chapter, you will use a certain form to learn words of your own choosing.

Your page will be divided into four columns. In the first column, you will list the word you want to learn. In the second column, you will copy the context (or sentence) in which you found the word. In the third column, you will copy a short dictionary definition of the word. In the fourth column, you will use the word in your own sentence.

Choose ten words that you would like to learn from "Successful Language Learners: What Do We Know About Them?"

EXAMPLE

WORD	CONTEXT	DEFINITION	OWN SENTENCE
tolerate	Researchers suggest that the successful language learner is someone who can tolerate a certain amount of frustration and uncertainty while completing second language tasks.	(verb) to endure or put up with someone or something without complaining	She was used to living in a cold climate, so it was difficult for her to tolerate the extreme heat of the desert.

SHORT WRITING: RESPONDING TO IDEAS IN AN ARTICLE

Omaggio suggests strategies that she considers important for a language learner. Think about a strategy—good or bad—that you used in learning English. Write from your own experience. Here are some strategies to consider:

- didn't say anything; just listened (a silent period)
- watched TV; listened to the radio
- memorized dialogues; relied on memorized routines
- relied on friends who speak my native language
- relied on friends who speak English natively
- socialized a lot
- did exercises in grammar books
- read a lot
- memorized vocabulary
- pretended I knew what was being said even when I didn't
- translated in my head

Peer Writing Samples

Read the following student writing samples and discuss whether you use or used the strategies with the same results.

> 1. *My first English instruction came from the television. When I first came to this country, I used to sit in front of the TV from morning until night, only taking an oc-*

casional break for meals. I watched cartoon after cartoon. Although I didn't understand all the language used by the characters in the cartoons, I managed to gain a fair idea of what they said by observing their actions. Soon, I began to acquire the expressions I heard from the TV. I remember seeing a friend and asking, "What's up, Doc?". While admittedly, it was embarrassing for an eighth grader to use "cartoon talk," this talk enabled me to convey simple thoughts. This, in turn, allowed me to make friends who provided me with more sophisticated English instruction. (G.C.)

2. I was always involved in classroom discussions. I think that active approach played a significant role in developing my fluency in English and was an effective strategy for helping me to learn the language quicker. Even though it was tough to communicate, I kept trying. Sometimes, I even drew pictures or made gestures with my hands in order to communicate my meaning. I didn't mind looking foolish to others if I knew that I would be rewarded with better understanding. (R.B.)

3. What helps me to write in English? My tendency to think in English rather than in my native language. Whenever I'm in the process of planning a paper, organizing it, or actually composing it, I talk to myself in English. This strategy enables me to avoid language errors which are caused by using a word or grammatical structure from the first language when writing in the second. (P.G.)

Peer Editing

1. The following writing sample contains three agreement errors. Read the sample and correct the errors.

I have learned to analyze the meanings of words through their context. Reading difficult materials require guess work, and I have developed the habit of guessing rather than going directly to a dictionary to look up an unknown word. I try to analyze what the word is trying to suggest and makes possible guesses. Then, I look up the word to confirm my guess. Continuing to practice this method *enable me to discover relationships between words and meanings. (A.L.)*

2. The following paragraph is incoherent. Instead of switching between pronouns and nouns, as the reader expects, the writer uses nouns where pronouns are expected. Revise the following paragraph by replacing nouns with pronouns where appropriate so that the paragraph becomes more coherent.

> *I used the dictionary constantly when I was learning English. My dictionary was compact enough so that my dictionary fit right into my backpack and I could carry my dictionary around wherever I went. Whenever there was a word that I didn't know, the dictionary did the translation for me. However, since I was so dependent on the dictionary, I experienced some difficulty when taking tests and reading. For instance, I discovered the meaning of a word by looking it up in a dictionary, but I forgot it as soon as I put the dictionary away. This experience taught me that the dictionary was only good for looking up words. However, without practicing words, I just couldn't store words in my brain. (M.G.)*

 # ADDITIONAL JOURNAL TOPIC

Your journal will continue on the topic of writing and learning a second language; however, you may want to go into greater depth and focus specifically on issues raised in the readings in the module. Following is the suggested journal topic for "Successful Language Learners: What Do We Know About Them?"

> *Omaggio, in "Successful Language Learners: What Do We Know About Them?" creates a "profile" of the successful language learner. In this profile are personality characteristics, cognitive styles, as well as strategies and techniques. Consider your own language learning experiences and discuss how you fit (or don't fit) into Omaggio's "profile."*

ESSAY WRITING: TOPICS

Select one of the following topics for this module's essay. To write this essay, you may use the readings you have done in this module as resources, along with your journal entries. Both essay assignments ask you to examine your own experience learning English as a second language in light of what you have read.

You will need to write at least two or three drafts for this essay, along with the final version. The drafts will be read, commented on, and evaluated by your instructor and your peers, using the evaluation forms and checklist provided in this section.

Alternative 1

Write an essay in which you describe your experiences learning to write in a second language. Since this topic is very broad, you will need to narrow it down. Make sure that you clearly present a thesis and that you provide sufficient evidence to support your thesis. Here are some sample theses. You may, of course, make up your own.

- Learning to write in a second language is not an easy task, but it can be done.
- Several factors (including good teachers, my parents' expectations, low anxiety classrooms, and my positive attitude) helped me learn to write fluently in English.
- Anxiety can be both beneficial and detrimental when writing in a second language.
- My English instructors did not adequately prepare me for university English writing. (For example, they did not assign appropriate reading, give adequate feedback, or make me write.)
- My English input was not adequate for the purposes of writing. (For example, I did not read, the reading was too easy or too difficult, and I learned only oral English from TV.)

Use your resources for ideas: your journal, the readings (Lopez, Hong Kingston, Scarcella and Perkins, Omaggio), your experience.

Alternative 2

Hong Kingston in "The Misery of Silence" discusses how her personality and development have been affected by her language learning experiences.

(She says that "a dumbness—a shame—still cracks my voice in two, even when I want to say 'hello' casually, or ask an easy question in front of the check-out counter, or ask directions of the bus driver." Even as an adult, she feels the effects of her childhood language learning experiences.) Consider your language learning experiences and discuss how they have affected *your* personality and development.

Before beginning to write your essay, read and discuss the composing process of two students who respond to these topics. The composing process for Essay Alternative 1 follows this paragraph. The composing process for Essay Alternative 2 begins on page 60.

Essay Alternative 1: The Composing Process

To help you see the changes that one student made when gathering ideas, revising, and editing, we have included one student's brainstorming activity, first and second drafts, and final version for this essay (see pages 54–60). This material is intended for discussion purposes and is not to be used as a model. In the following section, you will discuss questions pertaining to this student's composing process. Refer to the student's writing when indicated.

DISCUSSION QUESTIONS

Work in groups of three to discuss the following questions:

1. *Look at the brainstorming activity* (page 54).
   a. Discuss other factors the student might have included.
   b. Do you think the student has done sufficient brainstorming? Why or why not?

2. *Read the first draft* (pages 54–55).
   a. There are many grammatical errors in the first draft. Why doesn't the instructor correct them?
   b. The instructor comments that the thesis is clear. Underline the thesis.
   c. The writer of this essay followed a five-paragraph-essay formula. (This formula requires an introduction with a thesis, a body made up of three paragraphs each with a clear topic sentence, and a concluding paragraph which more or less repeats the thesis sentence and ties the essay together.) This type of essay is acceptable because it presents ideas clearly, but it is often uninspiring. The instruc-

tor's comments include ways to make this formulaic essay more in-teresting. What are those comments?

d. What are some ways that you would make the introduction more interesting?

e. What are some ways that you could make the conclusion more creative?

f. Often a first draft provides a basic "skeleton" for your ideas and needs expansion. The instructor comments include suggestions for expansion in many places in this essay. Why is this type of expansion important? How would you expand this essay?

g. Look at the peer review sheet on page 56. Do you agree with the peers' ratings on the content and organization of the first draft? What types of suggestions for improving the first draft do the peers make? Do you agree with these suggestions? What would you suggest?

3. *Read the second draft of this essay* (pages 57–58). (In this draft, the instructor has indicated the grammar mistakes.

a. Why does the instructor think the introduction is much better? Do you agree?

b. In the third paragraph, the instructor's comment is "better transition." Compare this paragraph with the one in the first draft. Why does the transition make the essay better?

c. The teacher comments that the conclusion is "better." Why is it better?

d. Before reading the final version, see if you can correct the grammar mistakes.

4. *Read the final version* (pages 58–60).

a. On a scale from 1 to 10, rate this final version for content and originality (with 10 indicating excellent content and a high degree of originality, and 1 indicating poor content and little originality).

b. On a scale from 1 to 10, rate this final version for organization (with 10 indicating excellent organization, and 1 indicating poor organization).

c. There is a saying that a composition is never finished . . . it is only abandoned. This means that a composition can continually be revised. The writer of this essay chose to stop after writing two drafts. If he wanted to continue revising, what might he work on?

BRAINSTORMING

GOOD TEACHERS
- Care about students
- Encourage students to study hard
- Give positive feedback
- Make class fun
- Guide students to learn the language
- Give interesting writing assignments
- Encourage students to participate

LOW ANXIETY CLASSROOMS
- Let students relax so they can enjoy the class
- Students feel comfortable speaking up and participating
- Non-stressful
- Don't force students to participate if they don't want to
- Friendly and informal atmosphere
- Don't put too much emphasis on grades

FACTORS HELPED ME LEARN TO WRITE

GOOD READING
- Makes us want to read even more
- Gives us new information
- Helps us learn what other people think
- Improves our vocabulary
- Helps us see how others express themselves in writing
- Helps us create our own writing styles
- We can imitate it in our writing

DRAFT 1

Experiences Learning to Write in English

This is okay as an introduction, but why not make it more interesting by leading up to your thesis? Get the readers involved!

The factors really helped me to learn to write fluently in English are good teachers, low anxiety classrooms and good readings. Good teachers encourage students to study hard and give positive feedback when necessary; low anxiety classrooms stimulate students' interest in learning to write while good reading provides students valuable resources to learn the language.

Clear thesis. Good.

Having a good teacher is very important when one start to learn English as a second language. A good teacher can guide students to successful language development. For example, when I first learned English, my teacher always encouraged me to write in English. At the beginning, I made copious grammar mistakes because I used my first language to do the brainstorm. Then I translated the meaning to English. When (she) read my essays, she did not emphasize in my grammar mistakes. All she told me to do was to write more in English. Gradually, my English writing improved. Thus, a good teacher can influence his or her students to learn how to write in English.

who?

Emphasize what made your teacher so good.

Lowing the anxiety of the classrooms helps in learning English. When the pressure is not that high, one can enjoy one's class and get into it. When I was in high school, my teacher assigned reading only once a week but she explained the meaning of the vocabulary and sentence structure in details. I had plenty of time to go over the essays. So whenever I had time, I would read the essays until I became very familiar with it. If I came across a good sentence structure, I would memorize it. So next time, when I want to express myself in similar situations, I could use it.

Give me more details so that I understand what you mean by a low-anxiety class.

In addition, good reading is very helpful in writing English since it provides genuine opportunity for students to get new information. From a good reading, I can discover new ideas concerning what other people think and the most important thing is that I can see the way people express themselves. Then I can compare them with my own essays. In this way, I can imitate other people's writing and then create my own way of writing.

Perhaps you can give details about types of reading.

Seeing the above, in order to write English well, I think to have a good teacher in class, lowing the anxiety of classrooms, and good reading are necessary. (H.C.)

This is weak as a conclusion. Try to be more creative and end on a final note without repeating all your ideas.

PEER REVIEW OF DRAFT 1

Reviewers __S.R._____ and __L.S._____
Paper which is being reviewed: __H.C._____

What do you believe the author's purpose was in writing this essay? (For example, the author wanted to show how . . . ; the author wanted to describe an event to entertain us . . . ; the author wanted to convince us that . . . ; the author wanted to explain . . .)

He wanted to tell us what factors helped him learn to write in English.

On a scale from 1 to 10, rate the essay for content (with 10 indicating excellent content and a high degree of originality and 1 indicating poor content and little originality).

Rating for content: __3__

Reasons for giving this rating: Not very original. Too general. Not enough information.

I don't think this writer is very interested in what he is writing.

What would you suggest? (Be specific. For instance, if a certain paragraph needs more detail, state which paragraph you are talking about.)

Needs better personal examples.
Needs to think about topic in more depth.

On a scale from 1 to 10, rate this essay for organization (with 10 indicating excellent organization, and 1 indicating poor organization).

Rating for organization: __5__

Reasons for giving this rating: Organization is not interesting; too much repetition; conclusion is boring. Very clear thesis; paragraphs are unified.

What would you suggest?

Make organization more original.
Rewrite introduction and conclusion.

DRAFT 2

Experiences Learning to Write in English

much better these lines get me curious.

Redundant; can you use a greater variety of words?

Omaggio (1987) asks why "the success record for acquiring skill in a second or foreign language is so poor for so many students." Learning how to write English is not as difficult as Omaggio may think. The key to success is to mix the right elements together. These elements are good teachers, low anxiety classrooms and good readings. Good teachers encourage students to study hard and give positive feedback when necessary; low anxiety classrooms stimulate students' interest in learning to write while good readings provide students with valuable resources to learn the language.

agreement

Having a good teacher is very important when one start to learn English as a second language. As suggested by Scarcella and Perkins (1989), a good teacher can guide students to successful language development. For example, when I first learned English, my teacher always encouraged me to write in English. In the beginning, I made copious grammar mistakes because I used my first

ing

language to do the brainstorm and then I translated the meaning to English. When the teacher read my essays, she did not emphasize my grammar mistakes which made me feel better. If I saw many

verb tense

red ink correction marks in my paper, I probably would be discouraged. All she told me to do was to write more in English. She even used her leisure time to teach me. Without her enthusiasm

verb form

and encouragement, I could not have been improved that fast. This makes me believe that a good teacher can motivate his or her students which in turn helps them to learn how to write in English.

On addition to V+ing this is a better transition!

omissing verb   er

In addition to a good teacher, lowing the anxiety of the classrooms helps students learn English. In low anxiety classrooms, we do not need to worry about tests. When the pressure is not that high, one can enjoy one's class and get into it. When I was in high school, my teacher assigned reading only once a week. During the weekdays, she explained the meaning of the vocabulary and sentence structure in details. She just wanted us to get all the "meat" out of every essay that she assigned. It ended up that I had plenty of time to go over the essays again and again until I became familiar with them. I didn't have to worry about quizzes and tests that much because she did not give us that many tests anyway. I found that I was studying for myself and I was eager to express myself in English.

Inappropriate transition

Furthermore, good reading is very helpful in writing English since it provides genuine opportunity for students to obtain new information. From a good reading, I can discover new ideas concerning what other people think and—most importantly—I can see the way people express themselves. For me, the best type of reading is the short essay that relates to my interests because it would encourage me to imitate other people's writing and create my own later.

Learning to write English was not as difficult for me as Omaggio might have predicted. However, I was fortunate to have good teachers, low anxiety classrooms and good readings. This combination helped me to become a writing success. (H.C.)

FINAL VERSION

Experiences Learning to Write in English

In Omaggio's (1987) seminal article, she asks why "the success record for acquiring skill in a second or foreign language is so poor for so many students." Learning how to write English is not as difficult as Omaggio may think. The key to success is mixing the right ingredients together. These ingredients are competent teachers, low anxiety classrooms and interesting readings. Effective teachers encourage students to study diligently and give positive feedback when necessary; low anxiety classrooms stimulate students' interest in writing while good readings provide students with valuable resources to learn the language.

Having an effective teacher is particularly important when just beginning to learn English as a second language. As suggested by Scarcella and Perkins (1989), a good teacher can guide students to successful language development. For example, when I first learned English, my teacher always encouraged me to write in English. In the beginning, I made copious grammar mistakes because I used my first language to do the brainstorming and then I translated the meanings of the words I used into English. When the teacher read my essays, she did not emphasize my grammar mistakes which made me feel better. If I had seen many red ink correction marks on my paper, I probably would have been discouraged. All she told me to do was to write more in English. She even used her leisure time to teach me. Without her enthusiasm and encouragement, I could not have improved that fast. This makes me believe that a dedicated teacher can motivate his or her students which in turn helps them to learn how to write in English.

In addition to having a good teacher, lowering the anxiety of the classroom helps students learn English. In low anxiety classrooms, we do not need to worry about tests. When the pressure is not that high, one can enjoy one's class and get into it. When I was in high school, my teacher assigned reading only once a week. During the week days, she explained the meaning of the vocabulary and sentence structure in detail. She just wanted us to get all the "meat" out of every essay that she assigned. It ended up that I had plenty of time to go over the essays again and again until I became familiar with them. I didn't have to worry about quizzes and tests that much because the teacher did not give us that many exams anyway. I found that I was studying for myself, and I was eager to express myself in English.

Interesting reading is also very helpful in writing English since it provides a genuine opportunity for students to obtain new information. From stimulating reading material, I can discover new ideas concerning what other people think and—most importantly—I can understand the way people express themselves. For me, the best type of reading is the short essay that relates to my interests because that kind of reading encourages me to imitate other people's writing and create my own later.

Learning to write English was not as difficult for me as Omaggio might have predicted. However, I was fortunate to have dedicated teachers, low anxiety classrooms and opportunities to read interesting material. This combination helped me to become a writing success. (H.C.)

Essay Alternative 2: The Composing Process

To help you see the changes that one student made when gathering ideas, revising, and editing, you can follow one student's brainstorming activity, first and second drafts, and final version for this essay topic (see pages 62–69). This material is intended for discussion purposes and is not to be used as a model. In the following section, you will discuss questions pertaining to this student's composing process. Refer to the student's writing when indicated.

DISCUSSION QUESTIONS

Work in groups of three to discuss the following questions.

1. *Look at the student's brainstorming activity* (page 62).
   a. Discuss how Hong Kingston's language learning is similar or dissimilar to the student's language learning experience.
   b. Do you think that the student has done sufficient brainstorming? Why or why not?

2. *Read the first draft* (pages 62–64).

    a.   Consider the instructor's comments on the first draft. The instructor comments on the content and organization but not the grammar. Why do you think the instructor does this?

    b.   Look at the instructor's comments on the introduction. What does the instructor mean by "choppy"? The instructor says there are "a lot of ideas jumping from one to another." What ideas?

    c.   In the first paragraph, the instructor suggests that the writer needs to clarify a single thesis. Reread the essay question and try to suggest one.

    d.   Why does the instructor point out one sentence in the body and say "this is the most important sentence in this essay"? Why is it so important?

    e.   Often a first draft provides a basic "skeleton" for your ideas and needs expansion. Why does the instructor suggest that the writer expand her ideas in the last paragraph?

    f.   Why does the instructor say that the writer needs to "balance" her description of Hong Kingston's experience with the writer's own?

    g.   Read the peer review sheet on pages 64–65. Do you agree with the peers' ratings on the content and organization of the first draft? What types of suggestions for improving the first draft do the peers make? Do you agree with these suggestions? What would you suggest?

3. *Read the second draft* (pages 65–67). (In this draft, the teacher has indicated the grammar errors.)

    a.   Compare the introduction in the second draft to the introduction in the first draft. How has the writer improved the introduction in the second version?

    b.   The writer expanded the last paragraph to include a narrative. How does this expansion improve her essay?

    c.   Compare the conclusion in the second draft to the end of the first draft. How has the writer improved the conclusion in the second version?

    d.   Before reading the final version, see if you can correct the grammar mistakes.

4. *Read the final version* (pages 67–69).

    a.   On a scale from 1 to 10, rate this final version for content and originality (with 10 indicating excellent content and a high degree of originality, and 1 indicating poor content and little originality).

    b.   On a scale from 1 to 10, rate this final version for organization (with 10 indicating excellent organization, and 1 indicating poor organization).

c. There is a saying that a composition is never finished . . . it is only abandoned. This means that a composition can continually be revised. The writer of this essay chose to stop after writing two drafts. If she wanted to continue revising, what might she work on?

BRAINSTORMING

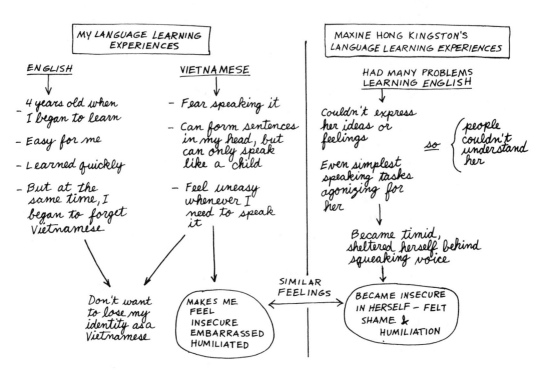

DRAFT 1

The "Misery of Silence" is a story of Kingston's struggle as child to adopt the English language. Her insecurity in herself and her inability to convey her ideas and feelings were the roots of her misery and sometimes a source of shame and humiliation. Due to her solitary nature, Hong Kingston was reluctant to undue the chains that impeded her ability to learn the English language. A probably attribute of many young Chinese girls, Hong Kingston turned extremely timid during situation that was unpleasant for her. Instead of confronting her dilemma, she shelters herself behind her "squeaking voice." Because of her lack of boldness, say-

This seems choppy. A lot of ideas—jumping from one to another. Perhaps omit the boxed part; you talk about it later anyway. Also you need

to clarify a single thesis.

ing a casual "hello" or remark often become a tedious and agonizing task.

Part of Hong Kingston's "misery of silence" was due people's incapacity to understand her. During her first three years, Hong Kingston constantly blanketed her drawings with a layer black shading, representing a stage curtain that was about to open. Her teacher, though, misinterpreted Hong Kingston's drawings as a learning disorder. Only Hong Kingston knew that under the layer of black film, there was a wonderful world of excitement and splendor, a world of "sunlight and mighty operas." Unable to understand the outside world, Hong Kingston lived behind "her curtain," a player, on stage made by her imagination. Here was where she retreated and played until she felt ready to venture out.

Good paragraph. Excellent description.

Soon though, Hong Kingston was able to open up. On an occasion, Hong Kingston drank out of a toy saucer, not out of habit, but to amuse the children watching her. In an obscure way, it was Hong Kingston's cry to be accepted. Hong Kingston's first acquaintances, outside from her own Chinese friends, were the Negro children, or "Black Ghosts." Their loud and outgoing nature was totally opposite to hers, but it was this sociable aspect of the Black children, which Hong Kingston lacked so much of, that she found comforting. To her, the Black children were as loud as she was quiet.

Good paragraph. I like the way you maintain cohesion by using transitions and pronouns.

When Hong Kingston first realizes that she needs to speak in order to pass kindergarten, her heart aches knowing that she is still mentally incapable of gathering enough strength to surmount her fears of speech. By this time, with pressures from her teachers and friends, Hong Kingston wants to talk, but finds herself still trapped behind her squeaky voice. It is this fear that she must finally overcome in order for her progress and eventually master her English learning abilities.

makes sense

This is the most important sentence in this essay. From this point on, you need to show how Maxine's experience parallels your own and how your personality has been affected.

In a way, there is an Hong Kingston in us all, causing fear and hesitation in the things we do. As a child, my fear was not so obvious, but was always present. _Expand. How has this fear shown?_ Being enrolled in school since four, I never considered myself different from any other of the children. Because I enrolled at such an early age, I began my education in English with almost the same proficiency level of English as my native English-speaking classmates. Eventually, I began to lose my Vietnamese identity. I lost touch with certain Vietnamese customs as well as the language. Like Hong Kingston feared to speak English, I now fear to speak my native tongue. Long sentences form in my head but when it comes from my mouth, it is only at the level of a Vietnamese child of the grade school level. My words stumble over my tongue one by one with a sense of humiliation and embarrassment. I now take courses to make up for what I lost, but like Hong Kingston, I must surmount my insecurity take on my task at hand. (T.B.) _I like the descriptions of Maxine's experiences. Now you need to balance that description by explaining how that relates to you and your own experience and personality development._

PEER REVIEW OF DRAFT 1

Reviewers __T.N._____ and __L.D.__

Paper which is being reviewed: __T.B.__

What do you believe the author's purpose was in writing this essay? (For example, the author wanted to show how . . . ; the author wanted to describe an event to entertain us . . . ; the author wanted to convince us that . . . ; the author wanted to explain . . .)

The author tried to relate Maxine's learning experience to her own experience.

On a scale from 1 to 10, rate the essay for content (with 10 indicating excellent content and a high degree of originality, and 1 indicating poor content and little originality).

Rating for content: __6__

Reasons for giving this rating: Gives good information

about Maxine's experience, but lacks details about the author's experience in learning a language.

What would you suggest? (Be specific. For instance, if a certain paragraph needs more detail, state which paragraph you are talking about.)

Tell more about your own experience rather than Maxine's.
Give more details about yourself.

On a scale from 1 to 10, rate this essay for organization (with 10 indicating excellent organization, and 1 indicating poor organization).

Rating for organization: ___4___

Reasons for giving this rating: *No clear thesis.*
Doesn't answer essay question adequately.

What would you suggest?
Needs a clear thesis.
Needs to answer essay question directly.

DRAFT 2

The "Misery of Silence" is a story of Hong Kingston's struggle *○missing article* as child to adopt the English language. Her insecurity in herself and her inability to convey her ideas and feelings were the roots

Good introduction! Very unified!

of her misery and sometimes a source of shame and humiliation. Unable to confront her dilemma, she shelters herself behind her "squeaky" voice. By the same token, my own insecurity has caused *incorrect verb form* an uneasiness in me every time I'm called upon to <u>expressed</u> myself in my native language. Unlike Hong Kingston, who struggled to overcome her barriers in learning a new language, I'm now facing the problems associated with learning a language that I have lost. My personality and development have been affected by my loss of Vietnamese, my first language.

Part of Hong Kingston's "misery of silence" was due to people's incapacity to understand her. During her first three years,

Hong Kingston constantly blanketed her drawings with a layer *[o] missing preposition* black shading, representing a stage curtain that was about to open. Her teacher, though, misinterpreted Hong Kingston's drawings as a sign of a learning disorder. Only Hong Kingston knew that under that layer of black film, there was a wonderful world of excitement and splendor, a world of "sunlight and mighty operas." Unable to understand the outside world Hong Kingston lived behind "her curtain," a player, on *[o] missing article* stage made by her imagination. Here was where she retreated and played until she felt ready to venture out. *wrong word* Oppositely, my stage was everything around me. Unlike Hong Kingston's curtain, my curtain was always open, letting in a constant flow of information. I was consistently eager to learn new words and phrases even though they were sometimes *non-count noun* slangs or profanity. I was like a vacuum, sucking in everything that sparked my curiousity.

When Hong Kingston first realizes that she needs to speak in order to pass kindergarten, her heart aches knowing that she is still mentally incapable of gathering enough strength to surmount her fears of speech. By this time, with pressures from her teachers and friends, Hong Kingston wants to talk, but finds herself still trapped behind her squeaky voice. It is this fear that she must finally overcome in order for her *[o] missing word* progress and eventually master English.

incorrect article In a way, there is an Hong Kingston in us all, causing fear and hesitation in the things we do. As a child, my fear was not so obvious, but as the years went by, it slowly began to materialize. I realized my early enrollment in school and immediate adoption of the English language also had a *one word* draw-back. My interactions with my English-speaking friends had progressively changed me. I was losing my Vietnamese identity.

The idea first struck me during a phone conversation with a Vietnamese lady, a friend of my mother's.

"Is your mother home?" she asked in Vietnamese.

"No," I replied, hoping that she would hang-up. [*two words*] Unfortunately, she continued on, trying to strike a conversation with me. ["to strike up a conversation"] After each question, I attempted to pick out a few words from her speech that I could comprehend, hoping that I would understand enough to be able to answer her. There were long empty moments after her questions while I tried to reply. My words stumbled over my tongue one by one with a sense of humiliation and shame. The intermissions after her questions became longer, causing a slow, agonizing build-up of tension in me. It was then that I exploded with frustration. As I slammed the telephone to the ground, in my mind, a cry of hopelessness raged, "Damn it! Why can't I understand her?"

It was then that I realized what was happening to me. All those times, avoiding conversations with my elders, I never knew that I was hiding a fear, a fear of being a disgrace, not only in my parents' eyes but my own. Just like Hong Kingston, I have my own "misery of silence," but through a willingness to try, I hope that I will finally surmount my insecurity to overcome that misery. (T.B.)

FINAL VERSION

The "Misery of Silence" is a story of Hong Kingston's struggle as a child to adopt the English language. Her insecurity in herself and her inability to convey her ideas and feelings were the roots of her misery and sometimes a source of shame and humilation. Unable to confront her dilemma, she shelters herself behind her "squeaky" voice. By the same token, my own insecurity has caused an uneasiness in me every time I'm called upon to express myself in my native language. Unlike Hong Kingston, who struggled to overcome her barriers in learning a new language, I'm now facing the problems associated with learning a language that I have lost.

My personality and development have been affected by my loss of Vietnamese, my first language.

Part of Hong Kingston's "misery of silence" was due to people's incapacity to understand her. During her first three years, Hong Kingston constantly blanketed her drawings with a layer of black shading, representing a stage curtain that was about to open. Her teacher, though, misinterpreted Hong Kingston's drawings as a sign of a learning disorder. Only Hong Kingston knew that under that layer of black film, there was a wonderful world of excitement and splendor, a world of "sunlight and mighty operas." Unable to understand the outside world, Hong Kingston lived behind "her curtain," a player on a stage made by her imagination. Here was where she retreated and played until she felt ready to venture out. On the other hand, my stage was everything around me. Unlike Hong Kingston's curtain, my curtain was always open, letting in a constant flow of information. I was consistently eager to learn new words and phrases even though they were sometimes slang or profanity. I was like a vacuum, sucking in everything that sparked my curiosity.

When Hong Kingston first realizes that she needs to speak in order to pass kindergarten, her heart aches knowing that she is still mentally incapable of gathering enough strength to surmount her fears of speech. By this time, with pressures from her teachers and friends, Hong Kingston wants to talk, but finds herself still trapped behind her squeaky voice. It is this fear that she must finally overcome in order for her to progress and eventually master English.

In a way, there is a Hong Kingston in us all, causing fear and hesitation in the things we do. As a child, my fear was not so obvious, but as the years went by, it slowly began to materialize. I realized my early enrollment in school and immediate adoption of the English language also had a drawback. My interactions with my English-speaking friends had progressively changed me. I was losing my identity as a Vietnamese.

The idea first struck me during a phone conversation with a Vietnamese lady, a friend of my mother's.

"Is your mother home?" she asked in Vietnamese.

"No," I replied, hoping that she would hang up. To my misfortune, she continued on, trying to strike up a conversation with me. After each question, I attempted to pick out a few words from her speech that I could understand enough to be able to answer her. There were long empty moments after her questions while I tried to reply. My words stumbled over my tongue one by one with a sense of humiliation and shame. The intermissions after her questions became longer, causing a slow, agonizing build-up of tension in me. It was then that I exploded with frustration. As I slammed the telephone to the ground, in my mind, a cry of hopelessness raged, "Damn it! Why can't I understand her?"

It was then that I realized what was happening to me. All those times, avoiding conversations with my elders, I never knew that I was hiding a fear, a fear of being a disgrace, not only in my parents' eyes but my own. Just like Hong Kingston, I have my own "misery of silence," but through a willingness to try, I will finally surmount my insecurity to overcome that misery. (T.B.)

Evaluating Introductions and Conclusions

Before writing your essay for this unit, do the exercise on introductions and conclusions on the following pages. These activities will help you develop criteria for writing and evaluating your own introductions and conclusions.

ACTIVITY 1: EVALUATING INTRODUCTIONS

The following introductions were written in answer to either the question "What factors have prevented you from being able to write well?" or "What factors have helped you to write well?" In groups of three, read the introductions. As a group, rank the introductions from best to worst.

Best   _____

_____

_____

_____

Worst   _____

1. *Writing in a second language is like running in a race. I long to win the race and yet at the same time, I keep tumbling down. Similarly, I want to know how to write a sufficiently well-written paper, but I just can't possibly do so because several factors impede my ability to write well. The most important of these factors are negative feelings toward myself, poor teachers, and insufficient practice in writing. (P.G.)*

2. *When I first came to this place, the United States, the only English words I knew were "thank you" and "you're welcome." Everything else I heard sounded like E.T. language to me. I told myself that I had to learn English as fast as I could so I could become part of their society. The following factors helped me to acquire English writing fluency. (A.L.)*

3. *Several factors which impede my ability to write in my second language are lack of reading, insufficient feedback, and a poor attitude. (M.T.)*

4. *Learning a second language takes a great deal of time and effort. Among all second language learners, when children and adults are compared, there is a great deal of difference. For example, children are not afraid or shy about speaking or writing the language they do not know well while adults are more cautious about their errors and reputation regarding second language usage. Some factors which impeded my ability to write English included overcrowded classrooms, poor teachers, and ineffective teaching materials. (Q.T.)*

5. *Have you ever tried to attain something that was out of your reach? Have you ever wanted something that*

*seemed impossible to obtain? I have. Good writing
seems to be that unattainable goal for me. In my
opinion, a number of factors have kept me from this
objective. (C.X.)*

Share your rankings with the class. Discuss what criteria you used to decide your rankings. (What made a good introduction? a bad introduction?)

ACTIVITY 2: EVALUATING INTRODUCTIONS AND CONCLUSIONS

Following are the introductions and conclusions written to answer the questions "What factors have prevented you from being able to write well?" or "What factors have helped you to write well?" Rank these introductions and conclusions (from best to worst) and discuss your rankings as a class. What criteria did you use to create your rankings? (In other words, what makes a good introduction and conclusion?)

In groups of three, rank the introductions and conclusions.

Best _____ _____ _____ Worst

1. *Writing in a second language is like running in a race. I long to win the race and yet at the same time, I keep tumbling down. Similarly, I want to know how to write a sufficiently well-written paper, but I just can't possibly do so because several factors impede my ability to write well. The most important of these factors are negative feelings toward myself, poor teachers, and insufficient practice in writing. . . .*

   Hence, winning the race is hard but nevertheless if I have a good coach, work hard on my physical condition, and always think positively, I can win the race. The same goes for writing. To write well, one needs to have a good teacher, practice writing regularly, and think positively. These factors are what I need during my journey to the "writing land." (P.G.)

2. *Several factors which impede my ability to write in my second language are lack of reading, insufficient feedback, and a poor attitude. . . .*

   In conclusion, from my experience in English writing, if I read more books, get lots of adequate feed-

back, and have a better attitude when learning to write, I shall be able to succeed in English. (T.T.L.)

3. *When I first came to this place, the United States, the only English words I knew were "thank you" and "you're welcome." Everything else I heard sounded like E.T. language to me. I told myself that I had to learn English as fast as I could so I could become part of their society. The following factors helped me to acquire English writing fluency. . . .*

   I have been using strategies to improve my writing skills but I still think I need to work harder in order to become a good writer in English. Everybody knows it is not easy to learn how to write in a second language but if I put my heart and effort into it, I think I'll soon become a good language learner. (L.N.)

Essay Writing Checklist

Before turning in your final essay, check the following points.

CONTENT AND ORGANIZATION

_____ 1. My thesis is clearly stated.

_____ 2. The body of my essay adequately supports my thesis.

_____ 3. My introduction captures the readers' attention.

_____ 4. My essay sufficiently answers the question or addresses the topic.

_____ 5. My essay contains original ideas.

_____ 6. I have provided sufficient information to adequately support my statements (for instance, statistics, quotes, examples).

_____ 7. My conclusion contributes to the overall coherence of my essay.

LANGUAGE

_____ 1. I have corrected grammar, punctuation, and spelling errors that were indicated by my teacher.

_____ 2. I have tried to use a variety of words and have avoided using the same words again and again.

_____ 3. I have chosen words that express my ideas precisely.

Additional Readings for Module 1

The following readings complement the first module. You may want to use some or all of them as resources.

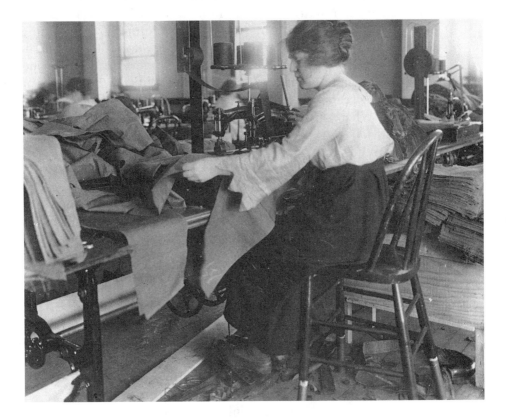

America and I

Anzia Yezierska

In her book *Children of Loneliness: Stories of Immigrant Life in America*, Anzia Yezierska describes her experiences as a new immigrant from Russia. During her first work experience in the new country, she was cheated out of her wages by a family who assumed that she should be happy just to live with an American family and take care of their children. As this excerpt begins, Anzia Yezierska is ready to begin a new job. What types of difficulties do you think she might encounter in this new job?

(1) From the outside my second job seemed worse than the first. It was in a sweatshop of a Delancey Street basement, kept up by an old, wrinkled woman that looked like a witch of greed. My work was sew-

ing on buttons. While the morning was still dark, I walked into a dark basement. And darkness met me when I turned out of the basement.

(2) Day after day, week after week, all the contact I got with America was handling dead buttons. The money I earned was hardly enough to pay for bread and rent. I didn't have a room to myself. I didn't even have a bed. I slept on a mattress on the floor in a rat hole of a room occupied by a dozen other immigrants. I was always hungry—oh, so hungry! The scant meals I could afford only sharpened my appetite for real food. But I felt myself better off then working in the "American" family, where I had three good meals a day and a bed to myself. With all the hunger and darkness of the sweatshop, I had at least the evening to myself. And all night was mine. When all were asleep, I used to creep up on the roof of the tenement and talk out my heart in silence to the stars in the sky.

(3) "Who am I? What am I? What do I want with my life? Where is America? Is there an America? What is this wilderness in which I'm lost?"

(4) I'd hurl my questions and then think and think. And I could not tear it out of me, the feeling that America must be somewhere, somehow—only I couldn't find it—*my America*, where I would work for love and not for a living. I was like a thing following blindly after something far off in the dark!

(5) "Oi weh!"[1] I'd stretch out my hand up in the air. "My head is so lost in America! What's the use of all my working if I'm not in it? Dead buttons is not me."

(6) Then the busy season started in the shop. The mounds of buttons grew and grew. The long day stretched out longer. I had to begin with the buttons earlier and stay with them till later in the night. The old witch turned into a huge greedy maw for wanting more and more buttons.

(7) For a glass of tea, for a slice of herring over black bread, she would buy us up to stay another and another hour, till there seemed no end to her demands.

(8) One day, the light of self-assertion broke into my cellar darkness.

(9) "I don't want the tea. I don't want your herring," I said with terrible boldness. "I only want to go home. I only want the evening to myself!"

(10) "You fresh mouth, you!" cried the old witch. "You learned already too much in America. I want no clock-watchers in my shop. Out you go!"

(11) I was driven out to cold and hunger. I could no longer pay for my mattress on the floor. I no longer could buy the bite in the mouth. I walked the streets. I knew what it is to be alone in a strange city, among strangers.

[1]Oi weh!: (Yiddish) an expression of exasperation or frustration like "Oh my goodness!"

(12) But I laughed through my tears. So I learned too much already in America because I wanted the whole evening to myself? Well America has yet to teach me still more: how to get not only the whole evening to myself, but a whole day a week, like the American workers.

(13) That sweatshop was a bitter memory but a good school. It fitted[2] me for a regular factory. I could walk in boldly and say I could work at something, even if it was only sewing on buttons.

(14) Gradually, I became a trained worker. I worked in a light, airy factory, only eight hours a day. My boss was no longer a sweater[3] and a blood-squeezer. The first freshness of the morning was mine. And the whole evening was mine. All day Sunday was mine.

(15) Now I had better food to eat. I slept on a better bed. Now I even looked dressed up like the American-born. But inside of me I knew that I was not yet an American. I choked with longing when I met an American-born and I could say nothing.

(16) Something cried dumb in me. I couldn't help it. I didn't know what it was I wanted. I only knew I wanted. I wanted. Like the hunger in the heart that never gets food.

(17) An English class for foreigners started in our factory. The teacher had such a good, friendly face; her eyes looked so understanding, as if she could see right into my heart. So I went to her one day for an advice:[4]

(18) "I don't know what is with me the matter," I began. "I have no rest in me. I never yet done what I want."[5]

(19) "What is it you want to do, child?" she asked me.

(20) "I want to do something with my head, my feelings. All day long, only with my hands I work."[6]

(21) "First you must learn English." She patted me as if I was not yet grown up. "Put your mind on that, and then we'll see."

(22) So for a time I learned the language. I could almost begin to think with English words in my head. But in my heart, the emptiness still hurt.

[2]"Fit" is the more correct form of the past tense of "to fit."

[3]Yezierska means "someone who makes you sweat or work hard." However, "sweater" is not used in this sense in English. An informal word for this type of boss might be "backbreaker" or "blood-squeezer."

[4]"Advice" is a noncountable noun; therefore, Yezierska should have said "I went to her for advice."

[5]In correct English, this would read "I don't know what is the matter with me. I never feel content. I haven't yet done what I want."

[6]In correct English, this would read, "I work only with my hands."

Vocabulary Gloss

The definitions given next are intended to aid your comprehension. Numbers in parentheses refer to the paragraphs in which the words appear. (Since you are not expected to understand each word in the reading passage, not all the words you do not know are glossed. You will need to guess the meaning of other words you do not understand.)

sweatshop	(1)	(n.)	a factory or workroom where workers produce goods under poor working conditions for long hours and for little money
basement	(1)	(n.)	a room or rooms in a building that are below street level
greed	(1)	(n.)	strong desire to obtain a lot or more than what is fair, especially of food, money, or power
scant	(2)	(adj.)	hardly enough
tenement	(2)	(n.)	a large building divided into apartments, especially in the poorer area of a city
wilderness	(3)	(n.)	an unchanging stretch of land, water, etc., with no sign of human presence
to hurl	(4)	(v.)	to throw with great force
self-assertion	(8)	(n.)	the action of pushing forward one's own claims or abilities over those of others
fresh	(10)	(adj.)	bold; impertinent
longing	(15)	(n.)	a feeling of wanting something; a strong wish
dumb	(16)	(adj.)	unable to speak; silent

Cultural Patterns and Rhetoric

Dale Johnson

Johnson is an undergraduate student at the University of California at Irvine. She wrote this essay as part of an assignment in a linguistics course. She believes that a person's culture affects his or her writing. Do you agree with her?

(1) Just because ESL students are capable of writing good essays in their native languages, they will not necessarily be able to write good essays in English. Students who know all the grammatical patterns of English will not necessarily know English rhetorical patterns.

(2) Kaplan, a North American applied linguist, says that English paragraph development can be contrasted with paragraph development in other cultures. According to Kaplan, the English paragraph is never digressive.
He takes the view that English paragraphs are linear; that is, they get straight to the point. In his words,

> There is nothing in the paragraph that does not belong here; nothing that does not contribute significantly to the central idea. The flow of ideas occurs in a straight line from the opening sentence to the last sentence.[7]

[7]Kaplan, Robert, 1966. Cultural thought patterns in intercultural education. *Language Learning* 16:1–20.

(3) To examine whether other cultures value paragraph development that differs from that valued in the United States, Kaplan analyzed approximately six hundred ESL university student compositions.

(4) Kaplan's study suggests that some "Asian" paragraph writing is marked by what he called an "approach by indirection." His Asian writers were Chinese and Korean. Kaplan states:

> In this kind of writing, the development of the paragraph may be said to be "turning and turning in a widening gyre." The circles or gyres turn around the subject and show it from a variety of tangential views, but the subject is never looked at directly. Things are developed in terms of what they are not, rather than in terms of what they are.[8]

As Kaplan points out, such development in a modern English paragraph would strike the English reader as awkward and unnecessarily indirect.

(5) Kaplan further suggests that like Asian writing style, Romance language writing style also differs from English. This is because speakers of Romance languages tolerate many more digressions than do speakers of English. What is "off topic" to an English speaker is not "off topic" to a Spanish speaker.

(6) Russian paragraph writing style, for Kaplan, is similar to Romance paragraph writing style. He remarks that Russian writers can even digress from digressions.

(7) Kaplan represents the development of various paragraphs in the following manner.[9]

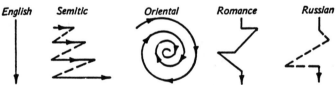

He, of course, cautions that more detailed and accurate descriptions are required before any meaningful contrastive system can be discussed.

(8) Kaplan argues that each language and each culture has a paragraph development unique to itself, and that mastering this part of the learning of a particular language is important. His discussion is not intended to offer any criticism of other existing paragraph developments; rather it is intended only to demonstrate that paragraph developments other than those normally written in English do exist. His study demonstrates that writers often write paragraphs which are consistent with the typical paragraph structures appreciated in their own cultures.

[8]Ibid.
[9]Ibid.

Vocabulary Gloss

The definitions given next are intended to aid your comprehension. Numbers in parentheses refer to the paragraphs in which the words appear. (Since you are not expected to understand each word in the preceding reading passage, not all the words you do not know are glossed. You will need to guess the meaning of other words you do not understand.)

rhetorical	(1)	(adj.)	organizational
applied linguist	(2)	(n.)	a person who studies the science of language and language learning and puts the study to practical use
to contrast	(2)	(v.)	to compare so that differences are made clear
to digress	(2)	(v.)	to turn aside or wander away from the subject
indirection	(4)	(n.)	roundabout (not straight) act or procedure
tangential	(4)	(adj.)	moving or going out in different directions
awkward	(4)	(adj.)	clumsy; having little skill or grace
to tolerate	(5)	(v.)	to put up with, allow, without protest
to caution	(7)	(v.)	to warn
unique	(8)	(adj.)	one of a kind; being the only one of its sort
consistent	(8)	(adj.)	continually keeping to the same principles; having a regular pattern

Contrastive Rhetoric: An American Writing Teacher in China

Carolyn Matalene
University of South Carolina

Matalene was an English teacher when she wrote this article about her experiences teaching English composition skills in a university in China. What types of teaching situations do you think she encountered in China?

(1) Rhetoric, in writing, is shaped by culture. Examining the rhetorical practices of a culture other than our own can provide us with a clearer understanding of the culture we study and can make us more aware of our own.

(2) North American rhetorical values emphasize originality and individuality. North Americans encourage self-expression and stylistic innovation. They subscribe to Aristotle's dictum, "State your case and prove it," and they expect to see inductive or deductive reasoning. They call this a "logical" argument. They strongly favor Pound's dictum, "Make it new," and they insist that their students use words in unique ways. They believe that original writing involves a chaotic discovery process but requires that finished texts be cohesive, coherent, and explicitly unified. They expect rhetoric to help them achieve control and to be a force for change.

(3) This essay attempts to identify and suggest some of the differences between Chinese and Western rhetoric that confront an American writing teacher in China. Certainly, I did not understand these different cultural assumptions while I was experiencing them during my semester at Shanxi Daxue, a provincial university of about four thousand students

in Taiyuan, the capital of Shanxi Province. Here I taught composition to fifty senior English majors for a semester. Only in retrospect and after study and discussion did I begin to understand the linguistic and rhetorical agendas that were influencing my students' writing in English. Had I known then what I have come to know now, I am sure that my classroom teaching might well have been more effective.

(4) Over my head as I stood at the yellow lectern with the red star were the thoughts of Chairman Mao in eight large characters: Be united, Be alert, Be earnest, Be lively. That "being united" meant "don't be different" did not occur to me when I suggested to my students that they keep journals, the favorite self-expressive mode of Western writing teachers. Not surprisingly, only some students were comfortable with this kind of writing, and as the semester progressed, "the leaders" seemed to be more and more uncomfortable with it. The number of journals turned in gradually and silently diminished.

(5) Chinese speakers—literate or not—also absorb a vast number of proverbs, maxims, and pieces of folklore. There is an "old Chinese saying" for every situation: "When a girl marries it is like water sprinkled on the ground," "Fallen leaves fly to the trunk," "Under the sun all crows are black," and from Confucius himself, "By reviewing old knowledge one can acquire new." Chinese speakers and writers depend heavily upon such sayings. Thus, one of my students lamented, "The difference between composing in Chinese and composing in English is that in Chinese there are many proverbs, and in order to make my composition more vivid and beautiful, I can use many proverbs in composing in Chinese; but in English, because of the limit of our non-native speakers' vocabulary, it's very hard to write a real beautiful and vivid essay."

(6) A profound respect for traditional forms is fundamental to Chinese culture. The Chinese arts are in fact all based on mastering the established forms and recreating them to perfection. For example, students of *tai ji quan*, boxing, learn the eighty-five forms and practice them for the rest of their lives. Students of Chinese painting learn the traditional styles of painting, the rules of composition, the techniques of painting particular objects, such as the three different stages of painting bamboo (in the eye, in the mind, in the hand) and then forever try to transfer the compositions in their minds to the paper.

(7) The examination system made memorizing the classics and composing poems and essays according to the traditional form prerequisites for membership in the governing elite. Through centuries, the examinations required candidates to compose poems and essays in a variety of elaborately rule-governed forms. As early as the Tang dynasty a number of poetic forms were standardized, and composing in these complex forms became part of the examination procedure.

(8) To be indirect in both spoken and written discourse, to expect the audience to infer meanings rather than to have them spelled out is a defining characteristic of Chinese rhetoric. The linguistic and social tendencies toward indirection are naturally reflected in the ways Chinese writers deal with topics and present their ideas. Many of my students, in responding to questions about composing in Chinese and in English, commented on the need to be direct and explicit in English. "My greatest difficulty is to keep direct connection to the topic. When I wrote indirectly about the topic, you would think it was out of order." "It seems that we need a conclusion in English, but we often leave it out to let people think when we write in Chinese." "We must explain things more clearly and exactly for Americans." They must have wondered about the stupidity of the teacher who had to have everything spelled out. As one student notes with typical, polite indirection, "When an American teacher puts a ? by what I like best, it seems to pour a basin of cold water on me."

(9) Another teacher in China, Joan Gregg, found the Chinese practice of not citing references a major problem for her graduate students as she tried to teach them to write English expository compositions. Citing references, as Gregg notes, is a cultural practice based on individualism; Western readers want the information that enables them to continue their own inquiries. And Western writers want careful credit for their own ideas, for their own unique inventions. For the Chinese writer who has memorized and mastered a fund of set phrases, conventional forms, and accepted messages, invention not surprisingly means imitation. Every Chinese schoolchild memorizes the lines of the great Du Fu: "If you read ten thousand books until they are well worn, you will be inspired in your writing." When Yang De You explained these lines to me, he wanted me to understand that the important phrase was *well worn*, not *ten thousand*; it's better, he said, to read one book one hundred times than one hundred books once. Surely such study is intended to yield writing that imitates the original. What Chinese students consider perfectly acceptable imitation, however, is often defined by Western teachers as stealing.

(10) The most acute disagreement and misunderstanding that occurred between me and my wonderfully quick and highly motivated Chinese students was over this issue. Closely imitating a model was to them the obvious way to compose. Our confrontation came after I asked them to read a brief essay, "My Turkish Grandmother," from Anais Nin's diary, and then write about an experience of their own in meeting a person from a different social or cultural background. Student after student retold Nin's story, changing only the details to make them Chinese. When I expressed my displeasure at their fabricating, one student asked with unusual directness, "Why should what we write be true?" Why indeed?

(11) Not surprisingly, there is an old Chinese saying which affirms such practices. "Keep reading the three hundred Tang poems until you are familiar with them and you'll be able to fabricate, if not compose." Chinese writers and artisans in general can imitate with consummate skill. They also, of course, innovate and create, but usually within existing formal traditions. Variations from a norm are valued; radical departures are not.

(12) The art of rhetoric in China, then, emphasizes repeating set phrases and maxims, following patterns, and imitating texts; it requires remembering and remembering. These rhetorical practices can be seen as consistent with a language that requires memorizing characters and phrases and with a culture that values the harmony of the group over the desires of the individual.

Vocabulary Gloss

The definitions given here are intended to aid your comprehension. Numbers in parentheses refer to the paragraphs in which the words appear. (Since you are not expected to understand each word in the preceding reading passage, not all the words you do not know are glossed. You will need to guess the meaning of other words you do not understand.)

rhetoric	(1)	(n.)	the art of speaking or writing effectively
innovation	(2)	(n.)	the introduction of something new
to subscribe to	(2)	(v.)	to agree with; to approve of
dictum	(2)	(n.)	wise saying
inductive reasoning	(2)	(n.)	a way of reasoning or thinking using known facts to produce general rules
deductive reasoning	(2)	(n.)	a way of reasoning from a general idea or set of facts to a particular idea or facts
chaotic	(2)	(adj.)	in a state of complete disorder and confusion; confused
cohesive	(2)	(adj.)	tending to stick together tightly
coherent	(2)	(adj.)	being naturally or reasonably connected; easily understood
assumption	(3)	(n.)	something that is taken as a fact or true without proof
retrospect	(3)	(n.)	the act of looking back towards the past

agenda	(3)	(n.)	fixed ideas concerning how to do something
lectern	(4)	(n.)	a sloping table for holding a book, often used by instructors when lecturing
diminish	(4)	(v.)	to become smaller
proverb	(5)	(n.)	a short, well-known saying; "A cat has nine lives" is a proverb
maxim	(5)	(n.)	rule for good behavior; especially when expressed in a short, well-known saying
to lament	(5)	(v.)	to feel or express grief or sorrow
profound	(6)	(adj.)	deep, complete; very strongly felt
bamboo	(6)	(n.)	a tall plant of the grass family, found especially in tropical areas, with hard, hollow jointed stems, and of which some parts can be eaten when young
prerequisite	(7)	(n.)	something that is necessary before something else can happen or be done
elite	(7)	(adj.)	the best or most important people in a social group
discourse	(8)	(n.)	a speech or piece of writing
to infer	(8)	(v.)	to draw a conclusion from something
indirection	(8)	(n.)	an act or procedure that is roundabout (not straight or direct)
to cite	(9)	(v.)	to mention a passage written or spoken by someone else or the person who wrote such a passage
inquiry	(9)	(n.)	the act of asking for information
to yield	(9)	(v.)	to give; to produce; to bear
acute	(10)	(adj.)	severe; strong; deep
to fabricate	(10)	(v.)	to make or invent in order to deceive

consummate	(11)	(adj.)	perfect; complete
to innovate	(11)	(v.)	to make changes
radical	(11)	(adj.)	extreme
harmony	(12)	(n.)	a state of agreement (in feelings, ideas etc.); peacefulness

Module 2:

□ *Education*

CONTENTS

How does one generation pass on knowledge to the next one? Different societies have come up with different answers to this question. In this module, you will be reading others' ideas about what education is and what education should or shouldn't be. In addition, you will be examining your own educational experiences and exploring your personal opinions about education. Some of the questions you will consider in this module include:

- What is education?
- What are the positive and negative effects of the American educational system?
- What are the positive and negative effects of a different culture's educational system?
- What should a formal educational system look like?

In this module, your final task will be to write an essay with multiple drafts on one aspect of your educational experience. Specific assignments are on page 158. All the readings and activities in this module are designed to prepare you for this final task by providing you with appropriate ideas and language.

KEEPING A JOURNAL

There are many different types of writing and many different reasons to write. One type of writing is journal writing. This writing is for the writer, not for an audience (although the journals of many people have been published). You will be asked to keep a journal while you use this book. Keep the following guidelines in mind when writing your journal:

1. Write at least one page a day.
2. Do not write a list of events. Your journal will be more meaningful if you see it as a place to put your thoughts, your reactions. Rather than writing everything that happened in a day, perhaps you might write about one thought that really struck you, or about something you read or saw.
3. Your journal is for you. Do not be overly concerned with grammar or style. Your goal should be to get your ideas down. Your journal will not be checked for grammar.
4. In your journal, approximately half of your entries will be "free," that is, on the topic of your choice. The other half will be in response to questions in this book or additional questions that your teacher gives you.

Enjoy writing in your journal. Enjoy the conversation with yourself. (Refer to Appendix A to read reflections by two famous authors on their own journals.)

JOURNAL TOPICS

The general topic for this module is education. Here are some suggested journal topics. (As part of this module's journal writing assignments, choose three of the following questions to discuss in your journal each week.)

GENERAL QUESTIONS ABOUT EDUCATION

1. What teacher is most memorable to you? Why?
2. What experiences stand out when you think back to your public school days?
3. What experiences stand out when you think about your high school days?
4. In what classes did you learn the most? Why?
5. How is schooling different in the U.S. as compared to a different country? What are the strengths and weaknesses of each system?

SPECIFIC QUESTIONS ABOUT COLLEGE

6. What is the one thing at college that puts the most pressure on you? Why? How do you handle it? How could you handle it better?
7. Imagine you are forty-years-old and looking back on your college days. What things do you think will most remain in your memory twenty years from now? Why?
8. Many people probably gave you advice about college before you came here. What advice proved to be helpful? What advice proved to be useless?
9. How did your preconceptions about college compare with what you found? (That is, before you came to college, you probably had some expectations about what you would find. How did these expectations compare to the reality?)
10. Would you prefer to go to college in a different country (if you could and if political and economic factors were not a consideration) or in the U.S.? Why?

Reading Unit 2A

College Pressures

William Zinsser

In this essay, Zinsser discusses four types of pressures that affect college students. What types of pressures affect the college students you know? Who is responsible for these pressures?

(1)   Dear Carlos: I desperately need a dean's excuse for my chem midterm which will begin in about one hour. All I can say is that I totally blew it this week. I've fallen incredibly, inconceivably behind.

Carlos: Help! I'm anxious to hear from you. I'll be in my room and won't leave it until I hear from you. Tomorrow is the last day for . . .

Carlos: I left town because I started bugging out again. I stayed up all night to finish a take home make-up exam and am typing it to hand in on the 10th. It was due on the 5th. P.S. I'm going to the dentist. Pain is pretty bad.

Carlos: Here follows a tale of woe. I went home this weekend, had to help my Mom, and caught a fever so didn't have much time to study. My professor . . .

(2) Who are these wretched supplicants, scribbling notes so laden with anxiety, seeking such miracles of postponement? They are men and women who belong to Branford College, one of the twelve residential colleges at Yale University, and the messages are just a few of the hundreds that they left for their dean, Carlos Hortas—often slipped under his door at 4 A.M.— last year.

(3) But students like the ones who wrote those notes can also be found on campuses from coast to coast—especially in New England and at many other private colleges across the country that have high academic standards and highly motivated students. Nobody could doubt that the notes are real. In their urgency and their gallows humor they are authentic voices of a generation that is panicky to succeed.

(4) My own connection with the message writers is that I am master of Branford College. I live in its Gothic quadrangle and know the students well. (We have 485 of them.) I am privy to their hopes and fears—and also to their stereo music and their piercing cries in the dead of night ("Does anybody ca-a-are?"). If they went to Carlos to ask how to get through tomorrow, they come to me to ask how to get through the rest of their lives.

(5) Mainly I try to remind them that the road ahead is a long one and that it will have more unexpected turns than they think. There will be plenty of time to change jobs, change careers, change whole attitudes and approaches. They don't want to hear such liberating news. They want a map— right now—that they can follow unswervingly to career security, financial security, Social Security and, presumably, a prepaid grave.

(6) What I wish for all students is some release from the clammy grip of the future. I wish them a chance to savor each segment of their education as an experience in itself and not as a grim preparation for the next step. I wish them the right to experiment, to trip and fall, to learn that defeat is as instructive as victory and is not the end of the world.

(7) My wish, of course, is naive. One of the few rights that America does not proclaim is the right to fail. Achievement is the national god, venerated in our media—the million-dollar athlete, the wealthy executive— and glorified in our praise of possessions. In the presence of such a potent state religion, the young are growing up old.

(8) I see four kinds of pressure working on college students today: economic pressure, parental pressure, peer pressure, and self-induced pressure. It is easy to look around for villains—to blame the colleges for charging too much money, the professors for assigning too much work, the parents for pushing their children too far, the students for driving themselves too hard. But there are no villains; only victims.

(9) "In the late 1960s," one dean told me, "the typical question that I got from students was 'Why is there so much suffering in the world?' or 'How can I make a contribution?' Today it's 'Do you think it would look better for getting into law school if I did a double major in history and political science, or just majored in one of them?' " Many other deans confirmed this pattern. One said: "They're trying to find an edge—the intangible something that will look better on paper if two students are about equal."

(10) Note the emphasis on looking better. The transcript has become a sacred document, the passport to security. How one appears on paper is more important than how one appears in person. A is for Admirable and B is for Borderline, even though, in Yale's official system of grading, A means "excellent" and B means "very good." Today, looking good is no longer good enough, especially for students who hope to go on to law school or medical school. They know that entrance into the better schools will be an entrance into the better law firms and better medical practices where they will make a lot of money. They also know that the odds are harsh; Yale Law School, for instance, matriculates 170 students from an application pool of 3,700; Harvard enrolls 550 from a pool of 7,000.

(11) It's all very well for those of us who write letters of recommendation for our students to stress the qualities of humanity that will make them good lawyers or doctors. And it's nice to think that admission officers are really reading our letters and looking for the extra dimension of commitment or concern. Still, it would be hard for a student not to visualize these officers shuffling so many transcripts studded with A's that they regard a B as positively shameful.

(12) The pressure is almost as heavy on students who just want to graduate and get a job. Long gone are the days of the "gentleman's C," when students journeyed through college with a certain relaxation, sampling a wide variety of courses—music, art, philosophy, classics, anthropology, poetry, religion—that would send them out as liberally educated men and women. If I were an employer I would rather employ graduates who have this range and curiosity than those who narrowly pursued safe subjects and high grades. I know countless students whose inquiring minds exhilarate me. I like to hear the play of their ideas. I don't know if they are getting A's or C's, and I don't care. I also like them as people. The country needs them, and they will find satisfying jobs. I tell them to relax. They can't.

(13) Nor can I blame them. They live in a <u>brutal</u> economy. Tuition, room, and board at most private colleges now comes to at least $7,000, not counting books and fees. This might seem to suggest that the colleges are getting rich. But they are equally battered by inflation. Tuition covers only 60% of what it costs to educate a student, and ordinarily the remainder comes from what colleges receive in endowments, grants, and gifts. Now the remainder keeps being swallowed by the cruel costs—higher every year—of just opening the doors. Heating oil is up. Insurance is up. Postage is up. Health premium costs are up. Everything is up. Deficits are up. We are witnessing in America the creation of a brotherhood of <u>paupers</u>—colleges, parents, and students, joined by the common bond of <u>debt</u>.

(14) Along with economic pressure goes parental pressure. Inevitably, the two are deeply <u>intertwined</u>.

(15) I see many students taking pre-medical courses with joyless tenacity. They go off to their labs as if they were going to the dentist. It saddens me because I know them in other corners of their life as cheerful people.

(16) "Do you want to go to medical school?" I ask them.

(17) "I guess so," they say, without <u>conviction</u>, or "Not really."

(18) "Then why are you going?"

(19) "Well, my parents want me to be a doctor. They're paying all this money and . . . "

(20) Poor students, poor parents. They are caught in one of the oldest webs of love and duty and guilt. The parents mean well; they are trying to steer their sons and daughters toward a secure future. But the sons and daughters want to major in history or classics or philosophy—subjects with no "practical" value. Where's the payoff on the humanities? It's not easy to persuade such loving parents that the humanities do indeed pay off. The intellectual faculties developed by studying subjects like history and classics—an ability to synthesize and relate, to weigh cause and effect, to see events in perspective—are just the faculties that make creative leaders in business or almost any general field. Still, many fathers would rather put their money on courses that point toward a specific profession—courses that are pre-law, pre-medical, pre-business, or, as I sometimes hear it put, "pre-rich."

(21) But the pressure on students is severe. They are truly torn. One part of them feels obligated to fulfill their parents' expectations; after all, their parents are older and presumably wiser. Another part tells them that the expectations that are right for their parents are not right for them.

(22) I know a student who wants to be an artist. She is very obviously an artist and will be a good one—she has already had several modest local exhibits. Meanwhile, she is growing as a <u>well-rounded</u> person and taking humanistic subjects that will enrich the inner resources out of which her

art will grow. But her father is strongly opposed. He thinks that an artist is a "dumb" thing to be. The student vacillates and tries to please everyone. She keeps up with her art somewhat furtively and takes some of the "dumb" courses her father wants her to take—at least they are dumb courses for her. She is a free spirit on a campus of tense students—no small achievement in itself—and she deserves to follow her muse.

(23) Peer pressure and self-induced pressure are also intertwined, and they begin almost at the beginning of the freshman year.

(24) "I had a freshman student I'll call Linda," one dean told me, "who came in and said she was under terrible pressure because her roommate, Barbara, was much brighter and studied all the time. I couldn't tell her that Barbara had come in two hours earlier to say the same thing about Linda."

(25) The story is almost funny—except that it's not. It's symptomatic of all the pressures put together. When every student thinks every other student is working harder and doing better, the only solution is to study harder still. I see students going off to the library every night after dinner and coming back when it closes at midnight. I wish they would sometimes forget about their peers and go to a movie. I hear the clacking of typewriters in the hours before dawn. I see the tension in their eyes when exams are approaching and papers are due: "Will I get everything done?"

(26) Probably they won't. They will get sick. They will get "blocked." They will sleep. They will oversleep. They will bug out. Hey Carlos, help!

(27) Part of the problem is that they do more than they are expected to do. A professor will assign five-page papers. Several students will start writing ten-page papers to impress him. Then more students will write ten-page papers, and a few will raise the ante to fifteen. Pity the poor student who is still just doing the assignment.

(28) "Once you have twenty or thirty percent of the student population deliberately overexerting," one dean points out, "it's bad for everybody. When a teacher gets more and more effort from his class, the student who is doing normal work can be perceived as not doing well. The tactic works, psychologically."

(29) Why can't the professor just cut back and not accept longer papers? He can, and he probably will. But by then the term will be half over and the damage done. Grade fever is highly contagious and not easily reversed. Besides, the professor's main concern is with his course. He knows his students only in relation to the course and doesn't know that they are also overexerting in their other courses. Nor is it really his business. He didn't sign up for dealing with the student as a whole person and with all the emotional baggage the student brought along from home. That's what deans, masters, chaplains, and psychiatrists are for.

(30) Ultimately it will be the students' own business to break the

circles in which they are trapped. They are too young to be prisoners of their parents' dreams and their classmates' fears. They must be jolted into believing in themselves as unique men and women who have the power to shape their own future.

(31) "Violence is being done to the undergraduate experience," says Carlos Hortas. "College should be open-ended: at the end, it should open many, many roads. Instead, students are choosing their goal in advance, and their choices narrow as they go along. It's almost as if they think that the country has been codified in the type of jobs that exist—that they've got to fit into certain slots. Therefore, fit into the best-paying slot.

(32) "They ought to take chances. Not taking chances will lead to a life of colorless mediocrity. They'll be comfortable. But something in the spirit will be missing."

(33) I have painted too drab a portrait of today's students, making them seem a solemn lot. That is only half of the story; if they were so dreary, I wouldn't so thoroughly enjoy their company. The other half is that they are easy to like. They are quick to laugh and to offer friendship. They are not introverts. They are unusually kind and are more considerate of one another than any student generation I have known. . . .

(34) I tell students that there is no one "right" way to get ahead—that each of them is a different person, starting from a different point and bound for a different destination. I tell them that change is a tonic and that all the slots are not codified nor the frontiers closed. One of my ways of telling them is to invite men and women who have achieved success outside the academic world to come and talk informally with my students during the year. They are heads of companies or ad agencies, editors of magazines, politicians, public officials, television magnates, labor leaders, business executives, Broadway producers, artists, writers, economists, photographers, scientists, historians—a mixed bag of achievers.

(35) I ask them to say a few words about how they got started. The students assume that they started in their present profession and knew all along that it was what they wanted to do. Luckily for me, most of them got into their field by a circuitous route, to their surprise, after many detours. The students are startled. They can hardly conceive of a career that was not pre-planned. They can hardly imagine allowing the hand of God or chance to nudge them down some unforeseen trail.

Vocabulary Gloss

The definitions given here are intended to aid your comprehension. Numbers in parentheses refer to the paragraphs in which the words appear. (Since you are not expected to understand each word in the preceding reading passage, not all the words you do not know are glossed. You will need to guess the meaning of other words you do not understand.)

wretched	(2)	(adj.)	miserable
supplicant	(2)	(n.)	one who asks for something humbly and sincerely
miracle	(2)	(n.)	an extremely unusual and outstanding, almost unbelievable, event or accomplishment
postponement	(2)	(n.)	a delay, something that has been rescheduled to a later time
urgency	(3)	(n.)	the quality or state of requiring immediate attention
gallows humor	(3)	(n.)	humor that makes fun of a very serious situation
authentic	(3)	(adj.)	real, not fake
generation	(3)	(n.)	a group of individuals living in the same time period, of approximately the same age
panicky	(3)	(adj.)	with sudden fright
to be privy to something	(4)	(v.)	to have the opportunity to hear someone's secret
unswervingly	(5)	(adv.)	not turning aside, steadily moving in one direction
grip	(6)	(n.)	a strong grasp
to savor	(6)	(v.)	to enjoy or delight in an experience
grim	(6)	(adj.)	very sad, depressing
naive	(7)	(adj.)	lacking informed judgment; the quality of being innnocent about the world
to proclaim	(7)	(v.)	to state or declare in front of the public
to venerate	(7)	(v.)	to regard with respect or admiration
peer pressure	(8)	(n.)	stress coming from those in one's own age group
self-induced	(8)	(adj.)	caused by oneself
villain	(8)	(n.)	enemy; an evil person
to drive oneself	(8)	(v.)	to motivate oneself
sacred	(10)	(adj.)	worthy of religious respect; holy
odds	(10)	(n.)	the possibility of something occurring

to exhilarate	(12)	(v.)	to enliven or excite
brutal	(13)	(adj.)	cruel
pauper	(13)	(n.)	extremely poor person, beggar
debt	(13)	(n.)	something which is owed
intertwined	(14)	(adj.)	mutually involved; interconnected
conviction	(17)	(n.)	a strong belief
well-rounded	(22)	(adj.)	knowledgeable of many diverse subjects
to vacillate	(22)	(v.)	to sway in mind or feelings; to hesitate when deciding among one's choices
furtively	(22)	(adv.)	done in secret
tense	(22)	(adj.)	nervous; worried
to overexert	(28)	(v.)	to try too hard; to put too much effort into something
mediocrity	(32)	(n.)	state of being average
drab	(33)	(adj.)	plain or dull
solemn	(33)	(adj.)	serious
dreary	(33)	(adj.)	sad or gloomy
introvert	(33)	(n.)	person who is primarily concerned with his or her own ideas and who does not like to spend a lot of time socializing with others
circuitous route	(35)	(n.)	a route which goes in circles before reaching the correct destination
detour	(35)	(n.)	a change from the direct course
startled	(35)	(adj.)	surprised
to nudge	(35)	(v.)	to push against gently
unforeseen	(35)	(adj.)	not known in advance; not seen beforehand

Comprehension Check

Fill in the blanks with a "T" if the statement is true or an "F" if the statement is false. Write the number of a paragraph (¶) which includes information to support your answer.

1. _____ Zinsser was a college student when he wrote this essay.   (¶ ___)

2. _____ Carlos, the recipient of the notes on the first page of the article, is a college student. (¶ ___)

3. _____ When Zinsser brings successful people to talk, students are surprised that these people took a winding "road" to get to their goals, not a direct path. (¶ ___)

For the following statements, fill in the blanks with a "T" if the statement is true or an "F" if the statement is false *according to Zinsser.*

4. _____ Students should have a clear path to follow toward security. (¶ ___)

5. _____ Students should always aim for success. (¶ ___)

6. _____ Young people are worrying and feeling pressure at too early an age. (¶ ___)

7. _____ Economic pressure and parental pressure are the two most powerful obstacles facing college students. (¶ ___)

8. _____ Parents, colleges, peers, and students should be *blamed* for the pressure of college life. (¶ ___)

9. _____ The transcript has become more important than it should be. (¶ ___)

10. _____ Emphasizing high grades and focusing on a narrow range of courses produces less interesting students. (¶ ___)

11. _____ The expense of education is a key pressure. (¶ ___)

12. _____ Students cause a cycle of problems when they write longer papers than their professors assign. (¶ ___)

13. _____ The primary way to break the cycle of pressure is for the parents to stop pressuring their children. (¶ ___)

14. _____ Students should take risks. (¶ ___)

15. _____ Students today are a dull group. (¶ ___)

Interaction Activity

Work in groups of three to answer the following questions. Try to reach a consensus; that is, discuss your different opinions and see if you can reach an agreement.

1. The four sample letters in ¶ 1 are part of the introduction to this essay. Why is this an effective introduction?

2. Paragraph 4 is also part of the introduction to this essay. Why is this an important part of the introduction?
3. Zinsser says that "the young are growing up old" (¶ 7). What does he mean by that?
4. Zinsser says that "violence is being done to the undergraduate experience" (¶ 31). What does he mean?
5. This article was written in 1979. Are the ideas mentioned in the article still relevant? Why or why not?

Vocabulary Acquisition

One way to learn vocabulary is to make a commitment to yourself to learn a certain number of words per week. In this chapter, you will use a certain form to learn words of your own choosing.

Your page will be divided into four columns. In the first column, you will list the word you want to learn. In the second column, you will copy the context (or sentence) in which you found the word. In the third column, you will copy a short dictionary definition of the word. In the fourth column, you will use the word in your own sentence.

Choose ten words that you would like to learn from "College Pressures."

EXAMPLE

WORD	CONTEXT	DEFINITION	OWN SENTENCE
authentic	. . . they are authentic voices of a generation that is panicky to succeed.	genuine, real	That is an authentic Picasso.

SHORT WRITING: RESPONDING TO IDEAS IN AN ARTICLE

In a paragraph or two, react to one of the ideas mentioned in Zinsser's article. (For example, you might start by saying "Zinsser believes that 'one of the few rights that America does not proclaim is the right to fail' (¶ 7). I agree with him because . . .") Discuss this idea in relation to your own experiences. Before writing your reaction, read the peer writing samples and do the peer editing exercises that follow.

Peer Writing Samples

Read the following student writing samples and discuss whether your own views match the writers' views.

1. *According to Zinsser, students "ought to take chances." I agree. Taking chances can be rewarding. Why? Because you are exposed to diverse life experiences. Risk-taking enables you to be somebody you have always dreamed of, experience aspects of life never experienced before, and see for yourself what you have not seen previously. This suggests that students should start by taking many detours and travel many unknown routes. Eventually, they will find their way. (T.T.)*

2. *Zinsser says he wishes the students had "the right to experiment, to trip and fall, to learn that defeat is as instructive as victory and is not the end of the world." It is hard to accept failure, especially if one is used to success. I remember once my peer advisor told me to fail at least one of my classes during my four years of college. At that time, I didn't understand her advice. However, as I have thought about it more, I have realized that I am here to be educated and not here to learn how to be perfect. Education, after all, is supposed to prepare a person to live in the outside world; it is supposed to teach us more than how to survive in school.*

    What if one day when I become a doctor (as I hope to be), I fail to cure my patient? What if I accidentally kill my patient by mistake? If I have never failed, I may not be able to deal with this "failure"; I may choose to leave the medical profession. However, if I have experienced failure in life, I may realize that "perfection" is impossible and that everyone sometimes fails. Should I carry the depression of one failure throughout my life, when failure is inevitable?

    Therefore, education about failure is as important as education about success. Maybe I shouldn't feel too depressed about having bad grades once in a while; rather, I should learn to cope with my imperfections. (H.T.)

3. *According to Zinsser, "along with economic pressure goes parental pressure." Most parents are pushing their children too far. Some do not even care what their children are interested in. My parents always say that they have lived longer than I have so they know what*

is best for me. I know they are pushing me for a good reason—success in life—but they don't understand what real success is.

How can you spend all your life doing something that you don't like? If I get dizzy when I see blood, how can my parents expect me to go to Med School? If my cousin wants to be an artist, how can my uncle force him to be a lawyer? To me, real success is doing what you enjoy—whether you get paid well or not. (E.C.)

4. *According to Zinsser, peer pressure and self-induced pressure are intertwined and they begin almost at the beginning of the freshman year. When I read about Linda in Zinsser's essay, I had to grin to myself because Linda seemed just like me. Pressure from peers is my heaviest burden and my greatest fear. When I go to bed at one o'clock in the morning after finishing all of my work, the silent pressure from my peers who still are studying seems to say, "I got you! Because you are studying less, you will be behind me." (S.L.)*

5. *Zinsser says that "not taking chances will lead to a life of colorless mediocrity." I like this idea. What is important in our lives is the process, not the goal. We could make our lives safe by not taking chances, studying hard, and getting good grades. By doing these things, we could guarantee ourselves "nice" jobs after graduating and then spend all of our lives in "nice" companies. Taking this safe route, however, will not get us a more colorful life; it will just bring us monotony. We only live once, and we deserve to live well and experience many things. (P.N.)*

Peer Editing

1. The following writing sample contains five verb form errors involving modal auxiliaries. Read the sample and correct the errors.

   According to Zinsser, a student should enjoys life and not study all the time. In his words, "the student needs to take a chance." I disagree. As a student, my most important goal must be learning. A student must to prepare for her classes well. To get good grades, she must works hard. If she risks wasting her time playing around and relaxing, she will to fail her courses. The chance of failure is very high. If a student doesn't want to study and learn, there is no reason for her to come to class. School is a place where training should is given. After graduating from school, a student will be well-educated. Then, there will be plenty of time to waste in search of pleasure. (A.V.L.)

2. The following paragraph contains a lot of redundancy. Instead of switching between pronouns and nouns, as the U.S. American reader expects, the writer uses nouns where pronouns are expected. Revise the paragraph by replacing nouns with pronouns where appropriate so that the paragraph becomes more coherent.

Zinsser says he sees four kinds of pressure working on college students today: economic pressure, parental pressure, peer pressure, and self-induced pressure. According to Zinsser, there are no villains, only victims. Zinsser believes that the students are the victims since college ruins their lives. I strongly agree with Zinsser. Nowadays, college students do not have much choice about running their own lives. Students' lives run them. Students have to overexert themselves just to obtain good grades. For instance, I know one biology major who is under considerable economic pressure and self-induced pressure. The biology major wants to be a doctor. The biology major cares about grades very much. The biology major told me that she has no time to cook. The biology major needs all her time to study. Even on the weekends, the biology major studies and does not enjoy her time off. The goals of the biology major actually run her life. (E.B.)

ADDITIONAL JOURNAL TOPICS

Your journal will continue on the topic of education; however, you may want to go into greater depth and focus specifically on issues raised in the readings in this module. Following are suggested journal topics for "College Pressures."

1. Zinsser names four pressures that affect college students: economic pressure, peer pressure, parental pressure, and self-induced pressure. Rank these four pressures in your life from heaviest pressure to least pressure and discuss why you ranked them the way you did.

2. Of the four types of pressures affecting college students, which one of these weighs most heavily on you? What can you do to reduce this pressure?

Reading Unit 2B

Fresh Start

Evelyn Herald

In this narrative essay, Herald shares a key lesson that she learned during her first few weeks in college. In order to learn this lesson, she had to make mistakes and learn from the experience. Think about mistakes that you made when entering a new environment—a new school, a new neighborhood, a new country. Did you ever feel embarrassed? What lessons did you learn from your experiences?

(1) I first began to wonder what I was doing on a college campus anyway when my parents drove off, leaving me standing pitifully in a parking lot, wanting nothing more than to find my way safely to my dorm room. The fact was that no matter how <u>mature</u> I liked to consider myself, I was feeling just a bit first-gradish. Adding to my <u>distress</u> was the distinct im-

pression that everyone on campus was watching me. My plan was to keep my ears open and my mouth shut and hope no one would notice I was a freshman.

(2) With that thought in mind, I raised my head, squared my shoulders, and set off in the direction of my dorm, glancing twice (and then ever so discreetly) at the campus map clutched in my hand. It took everything I had not to stare when I caught my first glimpse of a real live college football player. What confidence, what reserve, what muscles! I only hoped his attention was drawn to my air of assurance rather than to my shaking knees. I spent the afternoon seeking out each of my classrooms so that I could make a perfectly timed entrance before each lecture without having to ask dumb questions about its whereabouts.

(3) The next morning, I found my first class and marched in. Once I was in the room, however, another problem awaited me. Where to sit? Freshman manuals advised sitting near the front, showing the professor an intelligent and energetic demeanor. After much deliberation, I chose a seat in the first row and to the side. I was in the foreground (as advised), but out of the professor's direct line of vision.

(4) I cracked my anthology of American literature and scribbled the date at the top of a crisp ruled page. "Welcome to Biology 101," the professor began. A cold sweat broke out on the back of my neck. I groped for my schedule and checked the room number. I *was* in the right room. Just the wrong building.

(5) So now what? Get up and leave in the middle of the lecture? Wouldn't the professor be angry? I knew everyone would stare. Forget it. I settled into my chair and tried to assume the scientific pose of a biology major, bending slightly forward, tensing my arms in preparation for furious notetaking, and cursing under my breath. The bottled snakes along the wall should have tipped me off.

(6) After class I decided my stomach (as well as my ego) needed a little nourishment, and I hurried to the cafeteria. I piled my tray with sandwich goodies and was heading for the salad bar when I accidentally stepped in a large puddle of ketchup. Keeping myself upright and getting out of the mess was not going to be easy, and this flailing of feet was doing no good. Just as I decided to try another maneuver, my food tray tipped and I lost my balance. As my rear end met the floor, I saw my entire life pass before my eyes; it ended with my first day of college classes.

(7) In the seconds after my fall, I thought how nice it would be if no one had noticed. But as all the students in the cafeteria came to their feet, table by table, cheering and clapping, I knew they had not only noticed, they were determined that I would never forget it. Slowly I kicked off my ketchup-soaked sandals and jumped clear of the toppled tray and spilled food. A cleanup brigade came charging out of the kitchen, mops in hands.

I sneaked out of the cafeteria as the cheers died down behind me.

(8) For three days I dined alone on nothing more than humiliation, shame, and an assortment of junk food from a machine strategically placed outside my room. On the fourth day I couldn't take another crunchy-chewy-salty-sweet bite. I needed some real food. Perhaps three days was long enough for the campus population to have forgotten me. So off to the cafeteria I went.

(9) I made my way through the food line and tiptoed to a table, where I collapsed in relief. Suddenly, I heard a crash that sounded vaguely familiar. I looked up to see that another poor soul had met the fate I'd thought was reserved only for me. I was even more surprised when I saw who the poor soul was: the very composed, very upperclass football player I'd seen just days before (though he didn't look quite so composed wearing spaghetti on the front of his shirt). My heart went out to him as people began to cheer and clap as they had for me. He got up, hands held high above his head in a victory clasp, grinning from ear to ear. I expected him to slink out of the cafeteria as I had, but instead he turned around and began preparing another tray. And that's when I realized I had been taking myself far too seriously.

(10) What I had interpreted as a malicious attempt to embarrass a naive freshman had been merely a moment of college fun. Probably everyone in the cafeteria had done something equally dumb when he or she was a freshman—and had lived to tell about it.

(11) Who cared whether I dropped a tray, where I sat in class, or even whether I showed up in the wrong lecture? Nobody. This wasn't like high school. Popularity was not so important; running with the crowd was no longer a law of survival. In college, it didn't matter. This was my big chance to do my own thing, be my own woman—if I could get past my preoccupation with doing everything perfectly.

(12) Once I recognized that I had no one's expectations to live up to but my own, I relaxed. The shackles of self-consciousness fell away, and I began to view college as a wonderful experiment. I tried on new experiences like articles of clothing, checking their fit and judging their worth. I broke a few rules to test my conscience. I dressed a little differently until I found the Real Me. I discovered a taste for jazz, and I decided I liked going barefoot.

(13) I gave up trying to act my way through college (this wasn't drama school) and began not acting at all. College, I decided, was probably the only time I would be completely forgiven for massive mistakes (including stepping in puddles of ketchup and dropping food trays). So I used the opportunity to make all the ones I thought I'd ever make.

(14) Three years after graduation, I'm still making mistakes. And I'm even being forgiven for a few.

Vocabulary Gloss

The definitions given here are intended to aid your comprehension. Numbers in parentheses refer to the paragraphs in which the words appear. (Since you are not expected to understand each word in the preceding reading passage, not all the words you do not know are glossed. You will need to guess the meaning of other words you do not understand.)

mature	(1)	(adj.)	having adult judgment
distress	(1)	(n.)	trouble
discreetly	(2)	(adv.)	done carefully so as not to be seen doing it
confidence	(2)	(n.)	assurance; feeling of trust in one's abilities
reserve	(2)	(n.)	self-control
assurance	(2)	(n.)	self-confidence
demeanor	(3)	(n.)	outward manner or behavior toward others
deliberation	(3)	(n.)	a consideration of the reasons for and against something
anthology	(4)	(n.)	a collection of written work
to tip someone off	(5)	(v.)	to give someone an item of information (often secret information)
ego	(6)	(n.)	self-identity
humiliation	(8)	(n.)	extreme embarrassment
composed	(9)	(adj.)	calm; self-possessed
my heart went out to him	(9)	(idiom)	I felt sorry for him
victory clasp	(9)	(n.)	a sign indicating success, formed by holding one's hands together above one's head
to grin	(9)	(v.)	to smile broadly
malicious	(10)	(adj.)	evil
naive	(10)	(adj.)	lacking informed judgment; the quality of being innocent about the world
preoccupation	(11)	(n.)	worry
self-consciousness	(12)	(n.)	the state of being aware of one's behavior and appearance (often to an extreme)
conscience	(12)	(n.)	sensitivity to fairness or justice

Comprehension Check

Fill in the blanks with a "T" if the statement is true or an "F" if the statement is false. Write the number of a paragraph (¶) which includes information to support your answer if the answer is explicitly found in this story.

1. _____ At first, Herald tried to act assured even though she wasn't. (¶ ___)

2. _____ At first, Herald was afraid to appear uninformed. (Inference)

3. _____ Herald stayed in the wrong classroom primarily because she did not want to offend the teacher. (Inference)

4. _____ Herald learned her lesson right after she slipped in the cafeteria. (¶ ___)

5. _____ Herald primarily felt angry when the students clapped after her fall. (¶ ___)

6. _____ Herald admired other students' assurance. (¶ ___)

7. _____ The students in the cafeteria were really clapping about something else; their applause had nothing to do with Herald's fall. (¶ ___)

8. _____ When Herald saw the football player fall, she expected him to feel humiliated. (¶ ___)

9. _____ The football player was just a little less ashamed than Herald had been. (¶ ___)

10. _____ Right after she fell, Herald thought that the students had clapped because they were mean. (¶ ___)

11. _____ One lesson Herald learned was to always have a confident demeanor, even if she was not feeling confident. (¶ ___)

12. _____ Another lesson Herald learned was that it is important to make mistakes in college in order to explore the world and oneself. (¶ ___)

13. _____ Herald stopped trying to live up to others' expectations after the football player's fall. (¶ ___)

14. _____ Herald thinks college is a place where one is completely forgiven for mistakes. (¶ ___)

15. _____ The lessons Herald learned from this experience affected her even after her graduation. (¶ ___)

Interaction Activity

Work in small groups to discuss the following questions.

1. What does the title "Fresh Start" refer to?
2. Where are the main points of this essay stated—toward the beginning or the end? Why do you think Herald chose to do this?
3. Can you empathize with Herald's story? When you began a new school, did you make any similar "mistakes"? If so, what did you learn from those experiences?
4. Herald says that college is "probably the only time I would be completely forgiven for massive mistakes" (¶13). What do you think? Is college a time when one is completely forgiven for massive mistakes?
5. When Herald stopped trying to live up to others' expectations, she "began to view college as a wonderful experiment" (¶12). Have you had experiences in your life that you consider "wonderful experiments"? Describe those experiences to your group.

Vocabulary Acquisition

One way to learn vocabulary is to make a commitment to yourself to learn a certain number of words per week. In this chapter, you will use a certain form to learn words of your own choosing.

Your page will be divided into four columns. In the first column, you will list the word you want to learn. In the second column, you will copy the context (or sentence) in which you found the word. In the third column, you will copy a short dictionary definition of the word. In the fourth column, you will use the word in your own sentence.

Choose ten words that you would like to learn from "Fresh Start."

EXAMPLE

WORD	CONTEXT	DEFINITION	OWN SENTENCE
mature	The fact was that no matter how <u>mature</u> I liked to consider myself, I was feeling just a bit first-gradish.	fully grown or developed	Yesterday, she acted like a child; today, she seems so <u>mature</u>.

SHORT WRITING: VARYING A POINT OF VIEW

The narrator of this story is clearly Evelyn Herald. She is speaking from the point of view of an adult looking back at her experiences. Write about this event from someone else's point of view. (For example, how would the football player see the same events? Evelyn's roommate? a stranger who observed both falls?) Before writing, read the peer writing samples and do the peer editing exercises which follow.

Peer Writing Samples

Read the following student writing samples and determine whose point of view is being expressed.

1. *Summer is finally over. I got back to school a week earlier than most juniors because my football coach wanted me to warm up before the season began. As I was walking down to the field wearing my football uniform, I saw a girl look at me with an expression of awe. I figured that she was a freshman because most freshmen look at me like that.*

   After the football practice, I was so hungry that I went straight to the cafeteria to buy myself some food. That night they were serving the chicken special so I got myself five pieces of fried chicken and sat down at a big round table to enjoy my meal. As I was eating, I suddenly heard a crash, and I saw people beside me start to clap. Turning my head to see why everyone was clapping, I saw the same girl I had seen staring at me earlier on the floor with her food on the ground. She quickly stood up and looked around to see if anyone saw the incident. When she realized that she was the center of attention, she started to run toward the door. I tried to go over to her to tell her that those kinds of things happen to me all the time and that the incident was nothing to feel bad about. However, she was running so fast that I couldn't catch up with her. My head told me to follow her and talk to her but my stomach was telling me to go back to finish my delicious fried chicken. As usual, my stomach won. I wonder how she is doing now. (W.C.)

2. *As I started toward my dorm, my heart started to pound. I was afraid that I would not fit in. I was afraid that my roommate would hate me or we wouldn't get along.*

I walked into my dorm with my head held up high, not showing how frightened I was. My roommate was not as bad as I feared. She was quiet but we were both shy. We only exchanged a few words.

Later that day, looking for my classes, I spotted my roommate trying to find her classes, too. What I remember most was how she was staring at the football player. I agree that he was good-looking but she was eying him in a weird way. She looked a bit scared.

The next day finally came and I was relieved to be sitting in class and not looking dumb. I again saw my roommate. It seemed strange; I knew that she was not enrolled in my class. I figured that she had walked into the wrong class. I tried to call her name but the teacher started the lecture. I couldn't believe that she didn't walk out. I felt sorry for her. I never told her that I saw her in my class. I didn't want to embarrass her.

I decided to get a quick bite to eat in the cafeteria. Suddenly, I heard someone scream and then I heard a loud crash. I turned around and saw my roommate on the floor. Everybody was clapping and cheering while she got up and ran out the door.

She spent the next three days hiding in our dorm. Finally, on the fourth day, she went back to the cafeteria. When that football player (the very same one my roommate had stared at) slipped and fell, once again everyone laughed and clapped. However, the football player just got up to get another tray of food. I looked at my roommate to see her reaction; when she first saw the fall, she appeared embarrassed but when she saw the football player grin and make a victory sign, she began to smile broadly.

From that day on, she looked different, more confident. I have learned from her; I, too, am not afraid of making mistakes. I have become more open and now do things that I never thought I would do. (L.M.)

Peer Editing

1. In the following student writing sample, there are five word form errors. (For example, an adjective is used when it would be correct to use an adverb.) Read the sample and try to correct the errors.

> *I observed Evelyn fall in the cafeteria. I understand how she felt when she fell in front of others, especial, on the first day of college. She was sad because she lost her pride. For the next few days, she felt ashamed and refused to go to the cafeteria because she feared someone might recognize her. I tried to make her feel better but she wouldn't listen.*
>
> *After she saw what the football player did, she had more confidence and began to experience more of college life. She became more independence. Though she made mistakes, she learned from them.*
>
> *From this experience, she learned to be self-confidence. She became a very success person. She is now very pride of her success. (B.W.)*

2. In the following student sample, there are nine verb tense errors. (These are underlined.) Read the sample and try to correct the errors.

> *On the first day of school, I saw a woman slip on the cafeteria floor and drop a tray of food all over. We were all clapping and cheering because she <u>puts</u> on a great show. Looking embarrassed, she then <u>run</u> away through the back door.*
>
> *I saw the same woman in my Biology 101 class. She seemed to be confused.*
>
> *I later <u>find</u> out that this girl was my new roommate. After we got to know each other, she told me the whole story, how she <u>feel</u> afraid to walk out of the Biology class after it started. She also told me that she slipped in the cafeteria.*

I pretend that I had not seen her fall.

For three days, I saw her eat junk food from vending machines. I wanted to help her regain her confidence. I then ask a football player, a close friend of mine, to fake a fall in the cafeteria. My friend do a superior job of acting. When Evelyn saw him, she regains her confidence. I haven't told her yet that I planned the whole thing but I intended to do so. (D.C.)

SHORT WRITING: RESPONDING TO A CHARACTER

Can you empathize with Evelyn Herald's story? How do you feel about the conclusions she has drawn? Write a response to Herald describing your reaction to her experiences and her lessons. Before writing your response, read the peer writing samples and do the peer editing exercises which follow.

Peer Writing Samples

Read the following letters in response to Herald's story. Which writers had the most embarrassing experiences, in your opinion—Herald, T.H, or P.D.?

1. Dear Evelyn,

I'm a freshman in college and I know how it feels on the first day in a new school. On my first day of college, I felt overwhelmed by the vastness of the campus—it was ten times larger than my high school. Everything was so strange and I was scared. However, like you, I kept my head high and tried to look confident (and I prayed that I would not make a stupid mistake which would cause me embarrassment). Luckily, I didn't make any really serious blunders; I only got lost on campus a few times.

After a few days, I, too, realized that no one cared what anybody else did. I saw people do strange things like singing and making fun of themselves. Nobody cared! I also noticed that I didn't even care. I just laughed at them and then forgot about them the next minute. In that way, I began to tell myself that I didn't have to worry so much about acting perfectly. I started to be myself.

After reading your story, I feel even more self-confident. I'm inspired and encouraged to make mistakes and enjoy myself in college. I now feel that there is nothing wrong with making mistakes as long as you learn from the experience.

Sincerely,

T.H.

2. Dear Evelyn,

After reading your article, I have realized that you were not the only one making mistakes on your first day in college. I understand the reason why you felt embarrassed about being a freshman. It's funny, but I experienced similar events. To make you feel better, I'm going to tell you about my first day in college.

On the first day when I had just moved into my dorm, I locked myself out. I left my key inside the room and, to make matters worse, my roommate was not there. I was too embarrassed to go to the housing officers to ask them for the master key. Can you imagine what they would have thought about this? I also didn't want anybody from my suite to find out about my problem. I wouldn't have been able to handle the laughter and the remarks they would make. So I just went outside and sat on the grass under the shade of a gigantic tree and waited for my roommate to show up.

But that wasn't the only embarrassing moment I had during my first day of college. Another bad experience happened when I left my meal card on the food tray and it ended up in the trash can. I didn't drop the food tray as you did, but I had to turn the trash can upside down and rummage through it for my meal card. I squished all kinds of food and smelled all kinds of odors. The manager of the cafeteria gave me a strange look and that made my face turn red and my entire body shake. Eventually, I grabbed my meal card. I wanted to rush out of the cafeteria but before I could leave, I asked the manager for water to wash my hands. He just started laughing. Seeing him laugh, I realized how funny my situation was. I smiled back at him weakly and left without being embarrassed anymore.

Like you, I survived many of these unexpected experiences (and I still expect to go through many more). I also learned that these "mistakes" can teach us valuable lessons and that college is a perfect place to make them.

Sincerely,

P.D.

Peer Editing

1. The following student letter contains eight adjective errors (e.g. *fascinated* versus *fascinating, interesting* versus *interested*). Read the letter and try to correct these errors.

   Dear Evelyn,

   When I was reading your college life story, I remembered myself when I was in a similar situation. During my first few weeks of college, I was exciting but I was also confuse and frighten. Every time I made a mistake, I felt embarrass and guilty. I had many embarrass moments during my first year in college. Like you, I made a big deal of them.

   Now, I really do not feel bad or embarrass about the mistakes I made. Instead, I learn from them. Evelyn, I agree with you. It is better to accept our mistakes and learn from them. If we try to avoid making mistakes, life will be bored. Taking risks and sometimes failing and sometimes succeeding makes life more interested. (D.V.)

2. The following student letter contains twelve article errors. Read the letter and try to correct the errors.

   Dear Evelyn,

   Your story reminded me of mistake that I made when I was freshman. When I was freshman, I didn't know anyone at my school. Only one I knew was my cousin. He tried to help me learn about college life. The first mistake that I made was going to wrong class. I thought it was my class but it wasn't mine. It was upper-division class. In that class, I was only freshman. I was listening to professor's lecture and I didn't understand single word he said. I thought that this class was too much for me. After that class, I walked to library with some seniors. They asked me a lot of questions about how I got that class. They thought I was really smart because I was taking upper-division class.

Fortunately, they didn't know that I was in wrong class. (S.H.Y.)

ADDITIONAL JOURNAL TOPIC

Your journal will continue on the topic of education. However, you may want to go into greater depth and focus specifically on issues raised in the readings in this module. Following is the suggested journal topic for "Fresh Start."

Write about an event from your school years that taught you an important lesson.

Reading Unit 2C

What Is College For?

Careers, say students; learning, argues a
major new study

Ezra Bowen

**In this magazine article, Bowen summarizes a report about the U.S. college
experience. One key point of the report is that people—parents, students,
teachers, administrators—all have different expectations about the college
experience. In your opinion, what is college for? Does your view match your
parents' view?**

(1) "I want to go to college to become a doctor," the high school pupil
told the researchers. Why? "Basically so I can make some money and take
it easy." A college student described her <u>priority</u> as "having a job when
you get out." As for broad scholarship that might expand one's <u>vision</u> or
<u>values</u>, another student declared: "I'm not interested in hearing about the
professor's Ph.D. dissertation."

(2) According to a major new study, conducted by the Carnegie Foundation for the Advancement of Teaching and released this week, such
careerist replies reflect the views of 90% of U.S. high school students and

88% of parents on the <u>prime</u> purpose of a college education. Only 28% of parents and 27% of high school students see college as a place to become a more thoughtful citizen. . . .

(3) The 242 page study, titled *College: The Undergraduate Experience in America*, draws on surveys of 5,000 college faculty, 4,500 undergraduates and 1,300 presidents and other administrators, as well as 1,200 high school students. The author, Carnegie president Ernest L. Boyer, points to the realities beneath such <u>vocationalism</u>: . . . the University of Illinois reports that only 19% of its humanities students have guaranteed jobs upon graduation <u>versus</u> 90% for business majors. Small wonder that according to U.S. government statistics, bachelor's degrees in business have doubled from 114,865 in 1971 to 230,031 in 1984, while B.A.s in English and literature have plunged from 57,026 to 26,419. In the competition for enrollments, some schools have dropped B.A.s in subjects such as geology and music education to emphasize business specialties like restaurant management. Says one college president: "It's all right to talk about <u>liberal arts</u> goals, but we have to face up to what students want today."

(4) Since it <u>yields</u> in these ways to societal pressures, the report argues, the baccalaureate is a "troubled institution. Driven by careerism and professional education, the nation's colleges . . . are more successful in <u>credentialing</u> [for future jobs] than in providing a quality education." The document singles out several "deep divisions" in the typical undergraduate experience in the U.S. Among them:

- a <u>mismatch</u> . . . between faculty expectations and the academic preparation of entering students. Said a math professor: "The biggest problem I have with my students is getting them to read and write."
- a "<u>disjointed</u>" <u>curriculum</u> whose "<u>disciplines</u> have <u>fragmented</u> into smaller and smaller pieces, unrelated to an educational whole."
- a <u>cleft</u> between undergraduates who expect to be taught and faculty for whom "promotion and tenure hang on research and publication."
- a divorce between an undergraduate's major and general education requirements, which students often see as something "to get out of the way." Many schools permit such narrow focus on the major that what Boyer calls the "great commonalities of learning" are lost.
- disagreements and confusion over goals. The student-body president at one public university told Carnegie interviewers: "If there are any goals around here, they haven't been expressed to me."

(5) The Carnegie report is far from the only alarm being raised about the baccalaureate. . . . During the past two years, similar criticisms of

undergraduate curricula and values have come from such authoritative sources as the National Institute of Education and the Association of American Colleges.

(6) As for what can be done, Boyer argues that colleges should upgrade language proficiency by, first, requiring a written essay of incoming freshmen. Freshmen ought then to take a yearlong English course with emphasis on writing that should extend to other courses through all four years. The heart of those four years, he declares, should be a required core curriculum that embraces language, the arts, history, social and governmental institutions and the natural sciences. Thus everyone, regardless of individual goals, gets a base of essential common knowledge. Moreover, the major subject must be enriched with related requirements on the history of the field, its socioeconomic implications and the ethical issues it raises. If, writes Boyer, a major cannot be discussed in these terms, "it belongs in a trade school."

(7) The status of teachers, he continues, must be raised through higher salaries and departmental standing, as well as cash prizes for top instructors and grants to develop improved teaching methods.... "If I were to open a college tomorrow," Boyer sums up, "I'd tell the students, 'You're not going to come away from this place without experiencing the common agenda that I call the core of the learning experience'—so they'd have a set of values to encase their competence."

Vocabulary Gloss

The definitions given below are intended to aid your comprehension. Numbers in parentheses refer to the paragraphs in which the words appear. (Since you are not expected to understand each word in the preceding reading passage, not all the words you do not know are glossed. You will need to guess the meaning of other words you do not understand.)

priority	(1)	(n.)	superiority in position
vision	(1)	(n.)	idea gained through imagination
values	(1)	(n.)	beliefs concerning right and wrong
prime	(2)	(adj.)	the most important
vocationalism	(3)	(n.)	emphasis on preparation for a particular occupation
versus	(3)	(prep.)	in contrast to

liberal arts	(3)	(n.)	college studies (including history, philosophy, languages, and literature) intended to increase the students' general knowledge.
to yield	(4)	(v.)	to give up; to hand over possession to
to credential	(4)	(v.)	to give a diploma or certificate to
mismatch	(4)	(n.)	lack of similarity between two items
disjointed	(4)	(adj.)	lacking order or logical connections; not fitting together smoothly
curriculum	(4)	(n.)	set of courses offered by an institution
disciplines	(4)	(n.)	academic fields (such as literature, biology, and philosophy)
to fragment	(4)	(v.)	to break into pieces
cleft	(4)	(n.)	a hole made by a split
to upgrade	(6)	(v.)	to improve in quality
proficiency	(6)	(n.)	competence; abilities
regardless of	(6)	(prep.)	in spite of
implications	(6)	(n.)	something suggested but not stated explicitly
ethical	(6)	(adj.)	related to a system of moral principles or values
trade school	(6)	(n.)	a school which teaches manual or mechanical skills
status	(7)	(n.)	position or rank
core	(7)	(n.)	center; foundation
competence	(7)	(n.)	proficiency or ability

Comprehension Check

Fill in the blanks with a "T" if the statement is true or an "F" if the statement is false. Write the number of a paragraph (¶) which includes information to support your answer.

1. _____ The article reports on a study about education around the world. (Inference)

2. _____ The study says that the great majority of U.S. high school students and parents see broad scholarship as the key purpose of a college education. (¶ ___)

3. _____ The name of the study is the Carnegie Foundation for the Advancement of Teaching. (¶ ___)

4. _____ The study only surveyed faculty, administrators, and students on college campuses. (¶ ___)

5. _____ The survey showed that most high school students consider job preparation as the key role of college. (¶ ___)

6. _____ The study says that some colleges have adapted to meet the more career-focused demands of students. (¶ ___)

7. _____ The study says that students' skills are falling short of (not meeting the level of) faculty expectations. (¶ ___)

8. _____ The study says that the college curriculum is encouraging a broad understanding rather than a narrow view of the field. (¶ ___)

9. _____ One problem that the study mentions is that students expect good teaching but faculty don't know how to teach well. (¶ ___)

10. _____ The study is the first one that has questioned and criticized the college experience. (¶ ___)

11. _____ The author of the study thinks that writing should be emphasized regardless of the discipline. (¶ ___)

12. _____ The author of the study believes that students should be exposed to a broad range of courses outside of their major. (¶ ___)

13. _____ The author of the study believes that universities should not have job preparation as their prime emphasis. (¶ ___)

14. _____ The author of the study believes that all subjects in the university should be discussed from a historical and ethical perspective. (¶ ___)

15. _____ The author of the study believes that teachers should be better rewarded for good teaching. (¶ ___)

Interaction Activity

Work in groups of three and fill out the following chart showing Boyer's point of view and your group's view.

	BOYER'S VIEW	YOUR GROUP'S VIEW
Suggestions regarding the role of language at a university		
Suggestions regarding curriculum and what should be in it		
Suggestions regarding teachers' roles in a university		
Purpose of a university		

Vocabulary Acquisition

One way to learn vocabulary is to make a commitment to yourself to learn a certain number of words per week. In this chapter, you will use a certain form to learn words of your own choosing.

Your page will be divided into four columns. In the first column, you will list the word you want to learn. In the second column, you will copy the context (or sentence) in which you found the word. In the third column, you will copy a short dictionary definition of the word. In the fourth column, you will use the word in your own sentence.

Choose ten words that you would like to learn from "What Is College For?"

EXAMPLE

WORD	CONTEXT	DEFINITION	OWN SENTENCE
prime	Such careerist replies reflect the views of 90% of U.S. high school students and 88% of parents on the prime purpose of a college education.	main, key	My prime interest is sociology.

SHORT WRITING: RESPONDING TO IDEAS IN AN ARTICLE

Write a response to Boyer's suggestions for improving the undergraduate experience. Before writing your response, read the peer writing samples and do the peer editing exercises which follow.

Peer Writing Samples

Read the following student writing samples and discuss whether your own views match the writer's views.

1. *I totally agree with Boyer's suggestion for improving the undergraduate experience. As a peer counselor last year, I encountered a very interesting situation. A friend of mine, who was on the Decathlon Team and an honors student, didn't want to go to college.*

He said that in a month, after he graduated from high school, he would be making $40,000 a year. This amount would be the same, he said, if he went to a university and got a job afterwards. He said, "why go through four or five years of hard and demoralizing work and get the same amount of money as I can make now?" The college counselor and I talked to him and made him analyze his goals. Both the college counselor and I told him that he shouldn't go to a university just because of the monetary result at the end but primarily because of the learning experience that he would have. A college experience broadens your views on how you see the world. After several weeks of talking to both of us, he finally decided to go to college. Therefore, I believe that Boyer's suggestions are essential: a university should emphasize the ethical and moral insights about the world around us and should not just be a job-training center. (M.A.)

2. I agree with Boyer's suggestion of raising teacher's salaries. If salaries are increased, more qualified people will remain in the academic world, instead of going into the business world. However, I do not like the idea of cash prizes for top instructors. How can one choose top instructors? If these instructors are chosen on the basis of student evaluations, then teachers may focus more on entertaining students rather than teaching them. If these instructors are chosen on the basis of student test scores, then teachers may focus more on the test instead of general knowledge. Rewarding individual teachers may be important but not as important as raising the status and salary of the profession as a whole. (K.O.)

Peer Editing

1. The following student sample has problems with pronoun reference and agreement. Read the sample and correct the errors.

I like Boyer's suggestions for improving the undergraduate experience. Boyer suggests that colleges should upgrade language proficiency by instituting a year long

English course, and require a core curriculum that embrace language, arts, history, social and government institutions, etc.

Upgrading language proficiency help undergraduates to write and think better. This would give him confidence in himself and his ability to write and think. A year long English course also give the students time to practice writing and as the saying go, "practice make perfect."

Requiring a core curriculum make students a better, more interesting person. He knows more about his surroundings. In addition, he can express his opinions or thoughts more easily because he has broad knowledge. (K.K.)

2. The following student sample contains five errors with verb phrases having the form "be + adj. + preposition" (e.g., be involved with something, be concerned about something, be interested in something, be aware of something, be satisfied with something, be afraid of something, be tired of something, be ashamed of something, be fascinated with something). Read the sample and correct the errors.

Boyer concerns about the vocationalism on college campuses and thinks that college should provide a broader education. He suggests that incoming college students should be required to take a core curriculum which would include language, the arts, history, social and governmental institutions, etc. I personally feel that the suggestion not only provides the students with the opportunity to come into contact with a broad range of courses but it also allows individuals to get a base of essential common knowledge.

More and more students interest in learning how to earn high salaries instead of expanding their knowledge. They don't concern the history, language, writing, and ethical issues because these subjects, in their minds, do not teach them how to become rich and famous. However, it is important to aware these subjects. We should be able to appreciate the beauty of the arts and be able to enjoy their attractions and charms. We ought to aware our own background and history because this knowledge helps us understand ourselves and our human nature. We ought to stress the importance of writing because it is needed at all times and all places. Writing allows us to express our uniqueness. We should also have information about our society and our government because we are part of a group and our environment affects us in many ways. (P.R.)

ADDITIONAL JOURNAL TOPICS

Your journal entries will continue on the topic of education. However, you may want to go into greater depth and focus specifically on issues raised in the readings in this module. Following are the suggested topics for "What Is College For?"

1. *There are two views discussed in this article: college as an institution that prepares people for careers versus college as an institution that broadens people's knowledge. Discuss how these two views relate to you and your own situation.*
2. *How would you organize a university if you were given the opportunity to open and develop one? (Consider the purpose of the university education, environment, curriculum, teacher-student interaction, among other things.)*

Reading Unit 2D

Schools Are Bad Places for Kids

John Holt

Holt, a noted author and educator, has been a vocal critic of the traditional U.S. schooling system. In this abridged article, he discusses his reasons for saying that "schools are bad places for kids." Before reading, you might consider whether school was ever "bad" for you. Did school have negative effects on you?

(1) Almost every child, on the first day he sets foot in a school building, is smarter, more <u>curious</u>, less afraid of what he doesn't know, better at finding and figuring things out, more <u>confident</u>, <u>resourceful</u>, <u>persistent</u>, and independent, than he will ever again be in his schooling or, unless he is very unusual and lucky, for the rest of his life. Already, by paying close attention to and <u>interacting</u> with the world and people around him,

and without any schooltype formal instruction, he has done a <u>task</u> far more difficult, complicated, and abstract than anything he will be asked to do in school or than any of his teachers has done for years. He has solved the mystery of language. He has discovered it—babies don't even know that language exists—and he has found out how it works and learned to use it. He has done it, as I described in my book *How Children Learn*, by exploring, by experimenting, by developing his own model of the grammar of language, by trying it out and seeing whether it works, by gradually changing it and refining it until it does work. And while he has been doing this, he has been learning a great many other things as well, including a great many of the "<u>concepts</u>" that the schools think only they can teach him, and many that are more complicated than the ones they do try to teach him.

(2) In he comes, this curious, patient, <u>determined</u>, energetic, skillful learner. We sit him down at a desk, and what do we teach him? Many things. First, that learning is separate from living. "You come to school to learn," we say, as if the child hadn't been learning before, as if living were out there and learning were in here and there were no connections between the two. Secondly, that he cannot be trusted to learn and is no good at it. Everything we do about reading, a task far simpler than what the child has already <u>mastered</u>, says to him, "If we don't make you read, you won't, and if you don't do it exactly the way we tell you, you can't." In short, he comes to feel that learning is a <u>passive</u> process, something that someone else does *to* you, instead of something you do *for* yourself.

(3) In a great many other ways he learns that he is worthless, <u>untrustworthy</u>, fit only to take other people's orders, a blank sheet for other people to write on. Oh, we make a lot of nice noises in school about respect for the child and individual differences and the like. But our acts, as opposed to our talk, say to the child, "Your experience, your concerns, your curiosities, your needs, what you know, what you want, what you wonder about, what you hope for, what you fear, what you like and dislike, what you are good at or not so good at—all this is of not the slightest importance, it counts for nothing. What counts here, and the only thing that counts, is what we know, what we think is important, what we want you to do, think, and be." The child soon learns not to ask questions: the teacher isn't there to satisfy his curiosity. Having learned to hide his curiosity, he later learns to be ashamed of it. Given no chance to find out who he is, and to develop that person, whoever it is, he soon comes to accept the adults' evaluation of him. Like some highly advantaged eighth graders I once talked with in a high-powered private school, he thinks of himself, "I am nothing, or if something, something bad; I have no interests or concerns except trivial ones, nothing that I like is any good, for me or anyone else; any choices or decisions I make will be stupid; my only hope of surviving

in this world is to cling to some authority and do what he says."

(4) He learns many other things. He learns that to be wrong, uncertain, confused, is a crime. Right answers are what the school wants, and he learns, as I described in *How Children Fail*, countless strategies for prying these answers out of the teacher, for conning her into thinking he knows what he doesn't know. He learns to dodge, bluff, fake, cheat. He learns to be lazy. Before he came to school, he would work for hours on end, on his own, with no thought of reward, at the business of making sense of the world and gaining competence in it. In school, he learns, like every buck private or conscript laborer, to goldbrick, how not to work when the boss isn't looking, how to make him think you are working when you know he is looking. He learns that in real life you don't do anything unless you are bribed, bullied, or conned into it, that nothing is worth doing for its own sake, or that if it is, you can't do it in school. He learns to be bored, to work with a small part of his mind, to escape from the reality around him into daydreams and fantasies—but not fantasies like those of his preschool years in which he played a very active part.

(5) There is much fine talk in schools about Teaching Democratic Values. What the children really learn is Practical Slavery. How to suck up to the boss. How to keep out of trouble, and get other people in. "Teacher, Billy is . . . " Set into mean-spirited competition against other children, he learns that every man is the natural enemy of every other man. Life, as the strategists say, is a zero-sum game: what one wins, another must lose, for every winner there must be a loser. (Actually, our educators, above all our so-called and self-styled prestige universities, have turned education into a game in which for every winner there are about twenty losers.) He may be allowed to work on "committees" with other children, but always for some trivial purpose. When important work is being done— important to the school—then to help anyone else, or get help, is called "cheating."

(6) He learns, not only to be hostile, but to be indifferent—like the 38 people who, over a half-hour period, saw Kitty Genovese attacked and murdered without offering help or even calling for help. He comes to school curious about other people, particularly other children. The most interesting thing in the classroom—often the only interesting thing in it—is the other children. But he has to act as if these other children, all about him, only a few feet away, were not really there. He cannot interact with them, talk with them, smile at them, often even look at them. In many schools, he can't talk to other children in the halls between classes; in more than a few, and some of these in stylish suburbs, he can't even talk to them at lunch. Splendid training for a world in which, when you're not studying the other person to figure out how to do him in, you pay no attention to him.

(7) In fact, he learns how to live without paying attention to anything going on around him. You might say that school is a long lesson in How To Turn Yourself Off, which may be one reason why so many young people, seeking the awareness of the world and responsiveness to it they had when they were little, think they can only find it in drugs. Aside from being boring, the school is almost always ugly, cold, and inhuman, even the most stylish, glass-windowed, $20-a-square-foot schools. I have by now been in a good many school buildings—hundreds, many of them very new, but I can count on the fingers on two hands those in which the halls were made more alive and human by art or decoration, of the children or any-one else—pictures, murals, sculpture. Usually, the only thing that may be legitimately put up on the walls is a sign saying "Beat Jonesville" or "Go You Vampires" or the like.

(8) Sit still! Be quiet! These are the great watchwords of school. If an enemy spy from outer space were planning to take over earth, and if his strategy were to prepare mankind for this takeover by making men's children as stupid as possible, he could find no better way to do it than to require them, for many hours a day, to be still and quiet. It is absolutely guaranteed to work. Children live all of a piece. Their bodies, their muscles, their voices, and their brains all are hooked together. Turn off a part of them, and you turn them off altogether.

Vocabulary Gloss

The definitions given here are intended to aid your comprehension. Numbers in parentheses refer to the paragraphs in which the words appear. (Since you are not expected to understand each word in the preced-ing reading passage, not all the words you do not know are glossed. You will need to guess the meaning of other words you do not understand.)

curious	(1)	(adj.)	marked by the desire to know; inquisitive
confident	(1)	(adj.)	self-reliant; characterized by assurance
resourceful	(1)	(adj.)	capable of acting effectively or imaginatively, especially in difficult situations
persistent	(1)	(adj.)	continuing one's efforts even when encountering problems
to interact	(1)	(v.)	to communicate with others
task	(1)	(n.)	assignment; duty; work
concept	(1)	(n.)	idea

determined	(2)	(adj.)	firm in one's desire to reach a goal; resolved
to master	(2)	(v.)	to become skilled or proficient at doing something (speaking a foreign language, riding a bike, driving, etc.)
passive	(2)	(adj.)	not active
untrustworthy	(3)	(adj.)	not being a person others can rely or count on
to cling	(3)	(v.)	to hold together strongly as if glued
authority	(3)	(n.)	person with power
to pry	(4)	(v.)	to pull out with difficulty
to con	(4)	(v.)	to fool or trick
to dodge	(4)	(v.)	to avoid responsibility for duties, usually by tricking others
to bluff	(4)	(v.)	to pretend to know an answer when you really do not
competence	(4)	(n.)	ability or proficiency
to bribe	(4)	(v.)	to offer money or a favor in return for some service
to bully	(4)	(v.)	to treat others poorly or abusively (when one has more power than others)
to do something for its own sake	(4)	(v.)	to do something for the fun of doing it
democratic values	(5)	(n.)	values of freedom and equality for all
slavery	(5)	(n.)	the practice of owning slaves (individuals with no freedom)
trivial	(5)	(adj.)	unimportant
hostile	(6)	(adj.)	very unfriendly
indifferent	(6)	(adj.)	marked by a lack of interest or concern

Comprehension Check

Fill in the blanks with a "T" if the statement is true or an "F" if the statement is false *according to Holt*. Write the number of a paragraph (¶) which includes information to support your answer if the answer is explicitly found in this essay.

1. _____ Schools harm people's intelligence.   (¶ ___)

2. _____ Learning a first language is easier than learning to read.   (¶ ___)

3. _____ Learning and living are separate events.   (¶ ___)

4. _____ Schools give children confidence in their abilities.   (¶ ___)

5. _____ Schools respect the child and individual differences.   (¶ ___)

6. _____ Schools don't really encourage students to ask questions.   (¶ ___)

7. _____ Schools encourage students to make important decisions.   (¶ ___)

8. _____ Students cheat because they are lazy.   (¶ ___)

9. _____ Schools teach democratic values.   (¶ ___)

10. _____ Schools encourage friendly competition.   (¶ ___)

11. _____ Schools should encourage students to interact more with each other.   (¶ ___)

12. _____ Students take drugs because they are immature.   (¶ ___)

13. _____ Many schools are attractive.   (¶ ___)

14. _____ Schools should have art in the halls. (Inference)

15. _____ Forcing children to sit still and be quiet for long periods of time makes them less intelligent.   (¶ ___)

Interaction Activity

Work in groups of three to do the following activity. First, write down ten reasons why Holt believes that schools are bad places for children. Then, discuss each reason in your group and decide whether you believe his reason is valid based on your own experiences. Jot down notes from your discussion so that you can share your ideas with the rest of the class.

HOLT'S REASONS WHY SCHOOL IS A BAD PLACE FOR KIDS	OUR GROUP'S REACTION TO THIS REASON BASED ON OUR OWN EXPERIENCES
1.	
2.	
3.	
4.	
5.	
6.	
7.	
8.	
9.	
10.	

Vocabulary Acquisition

One way to learn vocabulary is to make a commitment to yourself to learn a certain number of words per week. In this chapter, you will use a certain form to learn words of your own choosing.

Your page will be divided into four columns. In the first column, you will list the word you want to learn. In the second column, you will copy the context (or sentence) in which you found the word. In the third column, you will copy a short dictionary definition of the word. In the fourth column, you will use the word in your own sentence.

Choose ten words that you would like to learn from "Schools are Bad Places for Kids."

EXAMPLE

WORD	CONTEXT	DEFINITION	OWN SENTENCE
curious	Almost every child, on the first day he sets foot in a school building, is smarter, more curious... than he will ever again be in his schooling...	wanting to know or learn more	What a curious child; she always asks questions.

SHORT WRITING: RESPONDING TO IDEAS IN AN ARTICLE

Holt's article is considered by some to be too negative and exaggerated. Others consider his ideas to be true to a great degree. Choose one of Holt's comments and write a reaction to it based on your own thoughts and experiences. Before writing your reaction, read the peer writing samples and do the peer editing exercises which follow.

Peer Writing Samples

Read the following student writing samples and discuss whether your own views match the writers' views.

1. *Holt's article is somewhat negative; however, I have to admit that he told us a lot of truths and said something that I have wanted to say but could not say as well. First, he wrote that "the child soon learns not to ask questions; the teacher isn't there to satisfy his curiosity." This is exactly what I experienced in my schooling, especially in my elementary school. Teachers in elementary school have almost absolute authority; they also have a much more important position in the minds of their students. Students respect them too much to ask questions. If students ask simple questions, the teacher might think they are stupid. If students ask hard questions that the teacher cannot answer, he might think that they are trouble-makers and that they are not complying with the order in the class. As a result, most students in my elementary school in China were quiet all the time in classes.*

Holt also said that most schools are ugly, cold, and inhuman. I have to agree with him again. For instance, the high school that I attended was pretty small and was composed of buildings with no style. There was little landscaping (no grass, few trees and flowers) and little artwork (no pictures, murals, or sculptures). It was like a prison in some ways. Teachers forced students to digest the material that they thought was important.

Finally, Holt mentioned that students are required to "sit still" and "be quiet." I, too, experienced countless hours of sitting motionless in the classroom obeying the "no talking" rule. That is what I really disliked. How can a smart, energetic student do that? Holt is right; that is the best way to suppress someone's intelligence, not increase it. (V.C.)

2. *After reading Holt's "Schools Are Bad Places For Kids," I strongly felt that Holt downgraded every aspect of the schooling system and I disagree with his ideas. According to Holt, "what children really learn is Practical Slavery" and "their [children's] only hope of survival is to cling to some authority and do what he says." However, this is only looking at the negative side; there is a reason why the schooling system requires submission to authority. Schools, especially elementary schools, must be places for children to learn how to exist in the society around them. They have to learn to obey the rules and laws of the society and they have to learn to respect others. In order to learn these things, children must restrain themselves and not submit to their own desires.*

There may be better ways to socialize children but at this point we have only one way that works. Traditional schooling is the way. (M.I.)

Peer Editing

1. In the following student sample, there are five errors involving uncountable nouns. Read the sample and try to correct the errors.

I agree with Holt. As a college student, I see that the school system creates many competitions among students. As a result, students develop a low evaluation of themselves which creates a loss of self-confidence. School is supposed

*to be an enjoyable place to develop interests and gather
knowledges, but the pressures at school make students lose
their enthusiasms. Students just start doing the works that
they are told to do and only learn the informations that they
are told to learn. (T.B.)*

2. In the following student sample there are four singular/plural errors.
   Read the sample and correct the errors.

   *According to Holt, schools only encourage students to
   make trivial decisions. I disagree. One of the good thing
   about schools is that they teach kids how to make important
   decision. Schools actually help student to make important
   decision such as what career to pursue, whether to go to
   college, etc. (H.P.)*

3. The following student sample contains four subject/verb agreement
   errors. Read the sample and correct the errors.

   *Holt think that the competition in schools are bad; I think
   it is good. Schools are places for students to experience
   interacting with strangers. Schools also teach students how
   to survive among competitors. Everybody are competing in
   this world; thus, it is not immoral to do one's best to defeat
   one another. There is always losers and winners. Losers
   should work harder to get to the top; otherwise, they will
   never succeed. (X.L.)*

4. It is often helpful to use quotes when writing. However, there are
   certain conventions that need to be considered when using quotes. The
   following student samples contain errors in using quotes. Before correcting the samples, note the two examples below. (See Appendix B for
   further explanation and exercises on using quotes.)

Using Brackets to Add Needed Information to Quotes

   Example: "He learns many other things. He learns that to
   be wrong, uncertain, confused is a crime." I support Holt's
   statement because schools encourage right answers and

success on tests. Schools do not accept the idea that people learn from mistakes.

In the preceding quote, who does "he" refer to? It may not be clear to the reader. Therefore, a good writer will insert words enclosed in brackets to clarify this point.

> "He [a child] learns many other things. He learns that to be wrong..."

Using Introductory Clauses

> Example: According to Holt, "forcing children to sit still and be quiet for long periods of time makes children less intelligent."

Phrases such as "according to Holt" or "as suggested by Holt" are not part of the main sentence; they are participial phrases. They are followed by a comma and a complete sentence.

Correct the following student samples.

a. *"Right answers are what the school wants, and he learns countless strategies for prying these answers out of the teacher, for conning her into thinking he knows what he doesn't know." This is one of the biggest problems in our school system. (A.L.)*

b. *According to Holt believes "what children really learn in school is Practical Slavery." (U.G.)*

c. *One of Holt's ideas, "right answers are what the school wants." I agree with this point. (R.A.)*

d. *As suggested by Holt teachers usually believe that "if we don't make you read, you won't and if you don't do it the way we tell you, you can't." (T.P.)*

 *ADDITIONAL JOURNAL TOPIC*

Your journal will continue on the topic of education. However, you may want to go into greater depth and focus specifically on issues raised in the readings in this module. Following is the suggested journal topic for "Schools Are Bad Places for Kids."

> *Holt discusses the negative psychological effects that he believes that schools have on children. What negative psychological effects has your schooling had on you? Why? What positive psychological effects has your schooling had on you? Why?*

Reading Unit 2E

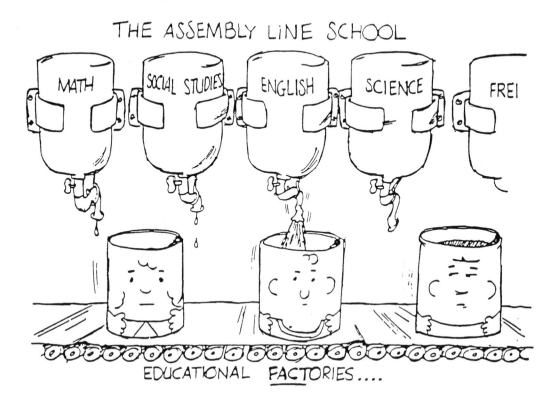

THE ASSEMBLY LINE SCHOOL

MATH · SOCIAL STUDIES · ENGLISH · SCIENCE · FREI

EDUCATIONAL <u>FACTORIES</u>....

Expelled

John Cheever

The following excerpts are from a story written by John Cheever, an American novelist, when he was a teenager. This particular story is set at a college preparatory school, a type of private school whose main purpose is to help its students get into the best colleges. In his descriptions of this school and the people who came and went through that school, Cheever is trying to communicate his ideas about the real meaning of education. Prior to reading, consider what a "real education" means to you. Is it book learning? Is it another kind of learning? What kind? Can you think of people who have given you a "real education"? What did they do?

(1) It didn't come all at once. It took a very long time. First I had a <u>skirmish</u> with the English department and then all the other departments. Pretty soon something had to be done. The first signs were <u>cordialities</u>

on the part of the headmaster. He was never nice to anybody unless he was a football star, or hadn't paid his tuition, or was going to be expelled. That's how I knew.

(2) He called me down to his office with the carved chairs arranged in a semicircle and the brocade curtains resting against the vacant windows. All about him were pictures of people who had got scholarships at Harvard. He asked me to sit down.

(3) "Well, Charles," he said, "some of the teachers say you aren't getting very good marks."

(4) "Yes," I said, "that's true." I didn't care about the marks.

(5) "But Charles," he said, "you know the scholastic standard of this school is very high and we have to drop people when their work becomes unsatisfactory." I told him I knew that also. Then he said a lot of things about the traditions, and the elms, and the magnificent military heritage from our West Point founder.

(6) It was very nice outside of his room. He had his window pushed open halfway and one could see the lawns pulling down to the road behind the trees and the bushes. The gravy-colored curtains were too heavy to move about in the wind, but some papers shifted around on his desk. In a little while, I got up and walked out. He turned and started to work again. I went back to my next class.

(7) The next day was very brilliant and the peach branches were full against the dry sky. I could hear people talking and a phonograph playing. The sounds came through the peach blossoms and crossed the room. I lay in bed and thought about a great many things. My dreams had been thick. I remembered two converging hills, some dry apple trees, and a broken blue egg cup. That is all I could remember.

(8) I put on knickers and a soft sweater and headed toward school. My hands shook on the wheel. I was like that all over.

(9) Through the cloudy trees I could see the protrusion of the new tower. It was going to be a beautiful new tower and it was going to cost a great deal of money. Some thought of buying new books for the library instead of putting up a tower, but no one would see the books. People would be able to see the tower five miles off when the leaves were off the trees. It would be done by fall.

(10) When I went into the building the headmaster's secretary was standing in the corridor. She was a nice sort of a person. She smiled. I guess she must have known.

THE COLONEL

(11) Every morning we went up into the black chapel. The brisk headmaster was there. Sometimes he had a member of the faculty with him. Sometimes it was a stranger.

(12) He introduced the stranger, whose speech was always the same. In the spring life is like a baseball game. In the fall it is like football. That is what the speaker always said.

(13) The hall is damp and ugly with skylights that rattle in the rain. The seats are hard and you have to hold a <u>hymnbook</u> in your lap. The hymnbook often slips off and that is embarrassing.

(14) On Memorial Day they have the best speaker. They have a mayor or a governor. Sometimes they have a governor's second. There is very little preference.

(15) The governor will tell us what a magnificent country we have. He will tell us to beware of the Red menace. He will want to tell us that the goddam foreigners should have gone home a hell of a long time ago. That they should have stayed in their own goddam countries if they didn't like ours. He will not <u>dare</u> say this though.[1]

(16) If they have a mayor the speech will be longer. He will tell us that our country is beautiful and young and strong. That the War is over, but that if there is another war we must fight. He will tell us that war is a <u>masculine</u> <u>trait</u> that has brought present civilization to its fine condition. Then he will leave us and help stout women place lilacs on <u>graves</u>. He will tell them the same thing.

(17) One Memorial Day they could not get a governor or a mayor. There was a <u>colonel</u> in the same village who had been to war and who had a chest thick with <u>medals</u>. They asked him to speak. Of course he said he would like to speak.

(18) He was a thin colonel with a soft nose that rested quietly on his face. He was nervous and pushed his wedding ring about his thin finger. When he was introduced he looked at the audience sitting in the uncomfortable chairs. There was silence and the dropping of hymnbooks like the water spouts in the aftermath of a heavy rain.

(19) He spoke softly and quickly. He spoke of war and what he had seen. Then he had to stop. He stopped and looked at the boys. They were staring at their boots. He thought of the empty rooms in the other buildings. He thought of the rectangles of empty desks. He thought of the curtains on the stage and the four Windsor chairs behind him. Then he started to speak again.

(20) He spoke as quickly as he could. He said war was bad. He said that there would never be another war. That he himself should stop it if

---

[1]Cheever is trying to give the impression that the governor is a person who thinks in terms of good or evil (with no middle ground), who sees Communism as an evil that is trying to take over the world ("the Red menace"), who believes that it is unacceptable to criticize his country, and who doesn't like "foreigners." Cheever sees this as propaganda to make people support one's country unquestioningly in a war against Communism.

he could. He swore. He looked at the young faces. They were all very clean. The boys' knees were crossed and their soft pants hung loosely. He thought of the empty desks and began to whimper.

(21) The people sat very still. Some of them felt tight as though they wanted to giggle. Everybody looked serious as the clock struck. It was time for another class.

(22) People began to talk about the colonel after lunch. They looked behind them. They were afraid he might hear them.

(23) It took the school several weeks to get over all this. Nobody said anything, but the colonel was never asked again. If they could not get a governor or a mayor they could get someone besides a colonel. They made sure of that.

LAURA DRISCOLL

(24) History classes are always dead. This follows quite logically, for history is a dead subject. It has not the death of dead fruit or dead textiles or dead light. It has a different death. There is not the timeless quality of death about it. It is dead like scenery in the opera. It is on cracked canvas and the paint has faded and peeled and the lights are too bright. It is dead like old water in a zinc bathtub.

(25) "We are going to study ancient history this year," the teacher will tell the pupils. "Yes, ancient history will be our field."

(26) "Now of course, this class is not a class of children any longer. I expect the discipline to be the discipline of well bred young people. We shall not have to waste any time on the scolding of younger children. No. We shall just be able to spend all our time on ancient history."

(27) "Now about questions. I shall answer questions if they are important. If I do not think them important I shall not answer them, for the year is short, and we must cover a lot of ground in a short time. That is, if we all cooperate and behave and not ask too many questions we shall cover the subject and have enough time at the end of the year for review."

(28) "You may be interested in the fact that a large percentage of this class was certified last year. I should like to have a large number this year. Just think, boys: wouldn't it be fine if a very large number—a number larger than last year—was certified? Wouldn't that be fine? Well, there's no reason why we can't do it if we all cooperate and behave and don't ask too many questions."

(29) "You must remember that I have twelve people to worry about and that you have only one. If each person will take care of his own work and pass in his notebook on time it will save me a lot of trouble. Time and trouble mean whether you get into college or not, and I want you all to get into college."

(30) "If you will take care of your own little duties, doing what is assigned to you and doing it well, we shall all get along fine. You are a brilliant-looking group of young people and I want to have you all certified. I want to get you into college with as little trouble as possible."

(31) "Now about the books..."

(32) I do not know how long history classes have been like this. One time or another I suppose history was alive. That was before it died its horrible unquivering death.

(33) Everyone seems to know that history is dead. No one is <u>alarmed</u>. The pupils and the teachers love dead history. They do not like it when it is alive. When Laura Driscoll dragged history into the classroom, <u>squirming</u> and smelling of something <u>bitter</u>, they fired Laura and <u>strangled</u> the history. It was too <u>tumultuous</u>. Too <u>turbulent</u>.

(34) In history one's <u>intellect</u> is used for mechanical speculation on a century or background. One's memory is applied to a list of dead dates and names. When one begins to apply one's intellect to the mental scope of the period, to the emotional development of its inhabitants, one becomes dangerous. Laura Driscoll was terribly dangerous. That's why Laura was never a good history teacher.

(35) She was not the first history teacher I had ever had. She is not the last I will have. But she is the only teacher I have ever had who could feel history with an emotional <u>vibrance</u>. She was five feet four inches tall, brown-haired, and bent-legged from horseback riding. All the boys thought Laura Driscoll was a swell teacher.

(36) She was the only history teacher I have ever seen who was often <u>ecstatic</u>. She would stand by the boards and shout out her discoveries on the Egyptian cultures. She made the gargoylic churnings of Chartres[2] in a heavy rain present an applicable meaning. She taught history as an interminable flood of events viewed through the <u>distortion</u> of our own <u>immediacy</u>. She taught history as a <u>hypothesis</u> from which we could <u>extract</u> the <u>evaluation</u> of our own lives.

(37) She was the only teacher who realized that, coming from the West, she had little business to be teaching these children of New England.

(38) "I do not know what your reaction to the sea is," she would say. "For I have come from a land where there is no sea. My elements are the fields, the sun, the plastic cadence of the clouds and the cloudlessness. You have been brought up by the sea. You have been coached in the cadence of the breakers and the strength of the wind."

---

[2]Chartres Cathedral is a church in France, known for the great amount of detail and sculpture (including gargoyles, frightening imaginary animals) that make up the building itself.

(39) "My emotional viewpoints will differ from yours. Do not let me impose my perceptions upon you."

(40) However, the college-board people didn't care about Chartres as long as you knew the date. They didn't care whether history was looked at from the mountains or the sea. Laura spent too much time on such trivia and all of her pupils didn't get into Harvard. In fact, very few of her pupils got into Harvard and this didn't speak well for her.

(41) However, the consummation did not occur until late in February. It was cold and clear and the snow was deep. Outside the windows there was the enormous roaring of broken ice. It was late in February that Laura Driscoll said Sacco and Vanzetti[3] were undeserving of their treatment.

(42) This got everyone all up in the air. Even the headmaster was disconcerted.

(43) The faculty met.

(44) The parents wrote letters.

(45) Laura Driscoll was fired.

(46) "Miss Driscoll," said the headmaster during her last chapel at the school, "has found it necessary to return to the West. In the few months that we have had her with us, she has been a staunch friend of the academy, a woman whom we all admire and love and who, we are sure, loves and admires the academy and its elms as we do. We are all sorry Miss Driscoll is leaving us . . ."

(47) Then Laura got up, called him a damned liar, swore down the length of the platform and walked out of the building.

(48) No one ever saw Laura Driscoll again. By the way everyone talked, no one wanted to. That was all late in February. By March, the school was quiet again. The new history teacher taught dates. Everyone carefully forgot about Laura Driscoll.

(49) "She was a nice girl," said the headmaster, "but she really wasn't made for teaching history. . . . No, she really wasn't a born history teacher."

FIVE MONTHS LATER

(50) The spring of five months ago was the most beautiful spring I have ever lived in. The year before I had not known all about the trees and the heavy peach blossoms and the tea-colored brooks that shook down over the brown rocks. Five months ago it was spring and I was in school.

---

[3]Nicola Sacco and Bartolomeo Vanzetti were Italian immigrants who were sentenced to death by the American government in 1927 for robbery and murder. However, there were people at that time who believed that they were innocent and that they were found guilty only because of their leftist political beliefs. This was a big controversy.

(51) In school the white limbs beyond the study hall shook out a greenness, and the tennis courts became white and scalding. The air was empty and hard, and the vacant wind dragged shadows over the road. I knew all this only from the classrooms.

(52) I knew about the trees from the window frames. I knew the rain only from the sounds on the roof. I was tired of seeing spring with walls and awnings to intercept the sweet sun and the hard fruit. I wanted to go outdoors and see the spring. I wanted to feel and taste the air and be among the shadows. That is perhaps why I left school.

(53) In the spring I was glad to leave school. Everything outside was elegant and savage and fleshy. Everything inside was slow and cool and vacant. It seemed a shame to stay inside.

(54) But in a little while the spring went. I was left outside and there was no spring. I did not want to go in again. I would not have gone in again for anything. I was sorry, but I was not sorry over the fact that I had gone out. I was sorry that the outside and the inside could not have been open to one another. I was sorry that there were roofs on the classrooms and trousers on the legs of the instructors to insulate their contacts. I was not sorry that I had left school. I was sorry that I had left for the reasons that I did.

(55) If I had left because I had to go to work or because I was sick it would not have been so bad. Leaving because you are angry and frustrated is different. It is not a good thing to do. It is bad for everyone.

(56) Of course it was not the fault of the school. The headmaster and faculty were doing what they were supposed to do. It was just a preparatory school trying to please the colleges. A school that was doing everything the colleges asked it to do.

(57) It was not the fault of the school at all. It was the fault of the system—the noneducational system, the college-preparatory system. That was what made the school so useless.

(58) As a college-preparatory school it was a fine school. In five years they could make raw material look like college material. They could clothe it and breed it and make it say the right things when the colleges asked it to talk. That was its duty.

(59) They weren't prepared to educate anybody. They were members of a college-preparatory system. No one around there wanted to be educated.

(60) They presented the subjects the colleges required. They had math, English, history, languages, and music. They once had had an art department but it had been dropped. "We have enough to do," said the headmaster, "just to get all these people into college without trying to teach them art. Yes sir, we have quite enough to do as it is."

(61) Of course there were literary appreciation and art appreciation and musical appreciation, but they didn't count for much. If you are young, there is very little in Thackeray[4] that is parallel to your own world. Van Dyke's[5] "Abbe Scaglia" and the fretwork of Mozart[6] quartets are not for the focus of your ears and eyes. All the literature and art that holds a similarity to your life is forgotten. Some of it is even forbidden.

(62) Our country is the best country in the world. We are swimming in prosperity and our President is the best president in the world. We have larger apples and better cotton and faster and more beautiful machines. This makes us the greatest country in the world. Unemployment is a myth. Dissatisfaction is a fable. In preparatory school America is beautiful. It is the gem of the ocean and it is too bad. It is bad because people believe it all. Because they have become indifferent. Because they marry and reproduce and vote and they know nothing.

(63) But I will not say anymore. I do not stand in a place where I can talk.

(64) And now it is August. The orchards are stinking ripe. The tea-colored brooks run beneath the rocks. There is sediment on the stone and no wind in the willows. Everyone is preparing to go back to school. I have no school to go back to.

(65) I am not sorry. I am not at all glad.

(66) It is strange to be so very young and to have no place to report to at nine o'clock. That is what education has always been. It has been laced curtseys and perfumed punctualities.

(67) But now it is nothing. It is symmetric with my life. I am lost in it. That is why I am not standing in a place where I can talk.

(68) The school windows are being washed. The floors are thick with fresh oil.

(69) Soon it will be time for the snow and the symphonies. It will be time for Brahms[7] and the great dry winds.

---

[4]William Thackeray—nineteenth-century English author
[5]Sir Anthony Van Dyke—seventeenth-century Flemish-born painter who lived in England
[6]Wolfgang Mozart—eighteenth-century Austrian composer
[7]Johannes Brahms—nineteenth-century German pianist and composer

Vocabulary Gloss

The definitions given here are intended to aid your comprehension. Numbers in parentheses refer to the paragraphs in which the words appear. (Since you are not expected to understand each word in the preceding reading passage, not all the words you do not know are glossed. You will need to guess the meaning of other words you do not understand.)

skirmish	(1)	(n.)	minor fight
cordialities	(1)	(n.)	words or deeds expressing politeness or courtesy
to be expelled	(1)	(v.)	to be cut off from membership in a group
tradition	(5)	(n.)	pattern of thought and action, passed on over time; custom
heritage	(5)	(n.)	traditions passed from a parent or predecessor
chapel	(11)	(n.)	a place to worship and pray
hymnbook	(13)	(n.)	a book of religious song
to dare	(15)	(v.)	to risk performing an action
masculine	(16)	(adj.)	relating to males
trait	(16)	(n.)	characteristic; feature
grave	(16)	(n.)	place where a dead body is buried
colonel	(17)	(n.)	a high-ranking military officer
medal	(17)	(n.)	metal decoration awarded for exceptional behavior or duty
to whimper	(20)	(v.)	to make a low crying noise as if in pain
to giggle	(21)	(v.)	to laugh in a silly manner
discipline	(26)	(n.)	controlled behavior
well bred	(26)	(adj.)	having or displaying good behavior
to be certified	(28)	(v.)	to receive a diploma or certificate
to be alarmed	(33)	(v.)	to be surprised and frightened
to squirm	(33)	(v.)	to twist about like a worm
bitter	(33)	(adj.)	having a taste that is sharp and unpleasant
to strangle	(33)	(v.)	to choke; to kill something by cutting off its air supply
tumultuous	(33)	(adj.)	marked by violence or a disorderly disturbance
turbulent	(33)	(adj.)	tumultuous

intellect	(34)	(n.)	ability to think or reason
vibrance	(35)	(n.)	the quality of being energetic and full of life
ecstatic	(36)	(adj.)	extremely excited
distortion	(36)	(n.)	the act of changing the true meaning of something
immediacy	(36)	(n.)	the quality or state of being immediate; related to the present moment
hypothesis	(36)	(n.)	a tentative assumption; an unproven theory
to extract	(36)	(v.)	to take out
evaluation	(36)	(n.)	test
to impose	(39)	(v.)	to force
perception	(39)	(n.)	observation; belief
trivia	(40)	(n.)	unimportant matters
consummation	(41)	(n.)	an ultimate end or goal
to get people up in the air	(42)	(idiom)	to upset people
disconcerted	(42)	(adj.)	upset
to intercept	(52)	(v.)	to interrupt progress
vacant	(53)	(adj.)	empty
to insulate	(54)	(v.)	to prevent the passage of heat or electricity or sound into or out of
contacts	(54)	(n.)	associations or relationships
frustrated	(55)	(adj.)	feeling discouraged
duty	(58)	(n.)	work; responsibility
forbidden	(61)	(adj.)	not permitted; prohibited
prosperity	(62)	(n.)	wealth
myth	(62)	(n.)	traditional story which tells about a people's beliefs; legend; saga
dissatisfaction	(62)	(n.)	unhappiness
fable	(62)	(n.)	story; fictitious narrative
gem	(62)	(n.)	jewel
indifferent	(62)	(adj.)	marked by a lack of interest
symmetric	(67)	(adj.)	having a relationship of equivalence or correspondence

Comprehension Check

Fill in the blanks on the left with a "T" if the statement is true or an "F" if the statement is false. Write the number of a paragraph (¶) which includes information to support your answer if the answer is explicitly found in this story.

1. _____ In the first section of the story, Charles (the narrator) is talking to the headmaster about his chances for a scholarship at Harvard. (¶ ___)

2. _____ It was generally easy to predict what the speeches in the chapel would be like. (¶ ___)

3. _____ On Memorial Day, the school didn't care who they got as long as they got a good speaker. (¶ ___)

4. _____ Because they couldn't get a governor or mayor on one Memorial Day, they invited a colonel. (¶ ___)

5. _____ The colonel gave the same kind of speech as the governor or mayor would have given. (¶ ___)

6. _____ Usually the speaker on Memorial Day talked about how important war is and about men's and boys' responsibility during war. (¶ ___)

7. _____ The colonel started to cry because of the tragedy of wars. (¶ ___)

8. _____ The school officials will not invite any colonel to speak again. (¶ ___)

9. _____ The narrator thinks that Laura Driscoll's classes were like other history classes. (¶ ___)

10. _____ The narrator thinks that typical history classes are dead because they do not deal with the meaning of history for present-day living. (Inference)

11. _____ The narrator thinks that typical history teachers are only concerned about teaching the required material, not about students' curiosity. (Inference)

12. _____ Laura Driscoll was bored with teaching history. (¶ ___)

13. _____ Laura Driscoll respected the students' viewpoints. (¶ ___)

14. _____ Laura Driscoll was fired because she said that Sacco and Vanzetti were being mistreated. (¶ ___)

15. _____ The headmaster pretended to the school that Laura Driscoll was leaving the school of her own free will. (¶ ___)

16. _____ The headmaster believed that Laura Driscoll was not a good history teacher.   (¶ ___)

17. _____ Charles (the narrator) left school because he had to go to work.   (¶ ___)

18. _____ Charles (the narrator) blames the college-preparatory system for his leaving.   (¶ ___)

19. _____ Charles (the narrator) believes that schools should be insulated from the outside world.   (¶ ___)

20. _____ Charles (the narrator) feels lost, not being in school.   (¶ ___)

Interaction Activity

Work in groups of three to answer the following questions. Try to reach a consensus; that is, discuss your different opinions and see if you can reach an agreement about your answer.

1. What is Cheever trying to say about the school's priorities in ¶9?

2. Do you think that the narrator liked the traditional speakers or the colonel better (¶11 to ¶23)? Why? Why do you think the school chose to "forget" the colonel soon after he spoke and return to using mayors or governors? What view is Cheever trying to express about college-preparatory education in his story of the colonel?

3. Why does Cheever say that "the pupils and the teachers love dead history. They do not like it when it is alive" (¶33)? Do you prefer "dead" or "alive" history? Why?

4. "When Laura Driscoll dragged history into the classroom, squirming and smelling of something bitter, they fired Laura and strangled the history" (¶33). What does Cheever mean by this line? What image is Cheever using to help the reader visualize Laura Driscoll's teaching of history?

5. Why does Cheever say that Laura Driscoll was "terribly dangerous" (¶34)? In the same paragraph, Cheever says that "she was not a good history teacher." According to whose standards of "good"?

6. What quality is Cheever emphasizing about Laura Driscoll in ¶37 to ¶39?

7. Why does Cheever end Laura's story with the headmaster's words (¶49)? Do you think Cheever agrees with the headmaster? Do you?

8. Why does Cheever say that "no one around there [the college-preparatory school] wanted to be educated" (¶59)?

9. In ¶63 and ¶67, the narrator says "I do not stand in a place where I can talk." Why?

Vocabulary Acquisition

One way to learn vocabulary is to make a commitment to yourself to learn a certain number of words per week. In this chapter, you will use a certain form to learn words of your own choosing.

Your page will be divided into four columns. In the first column, you will list the word you want to learn. In the second column, you will copy the context (or sentence) in which you found the word. In the third column, you will copy a short dictionary definition of the word. In the fourth column, you will use the word in your own sentence.

Choose ten words that you would like to learn from "Expelled."

EXAMPLE

WORD	CONTEXT	DEFINITION	OWN SENTENCE
skirmish	I had a <u>skirmish</u> with the English department.	a small fight	I had a <u>skirmish</u> with my best friend regarding our holiday plans.

SHORT WRITING: VARYING THE POINT OF VIEW

The narrator of this story is Charles, a teenager. How would the headmaster have seen the same events? the colonel? Laura Driscoll? Charles' roommate? Write about this event in the "voice" of someone other than Charles. Before writing, read the peer writing samples and do the peer editing exercises which follow.

Peer Writing Samples

Read the following student writing samples and determine whose point of view is discussed.

> *1. After walking out of the building, I felt so good about telling the headmaster what a liar he was. How*

could he have told the students that I left of my own free will? I had never thought of leaving the school because the students seemed to appreciate my teaching. Although I understood that my methods of teaching were different from those approved by the headmaster, I believe these methods are what students need.

I remember one very interesting student, Charles, who seemed to participate actively in my history class discussions. He was not one of those students who restricted himself to events and dates but rather, he liked to "dig out" the facts and reasons behind the events. I was surprised to find out that he wasn't doing well in his other classes; perhaps students like Charles need to be in a freer learning environment in order to show their ability and intelligence.

As I look back now, I feel that Charles and I shared sentiments. Neither one of us fit into the college preparatory school system. (A.Q.P.N.)

2. Charles was one of the most interesting guys I had ever met. On the outside, he was an average person, a teenager who did not like school and went his own way. (Then again, can you show me any teenagers who like school?) However, inside, Charles was a unique individual. He liked to do things others might consider unusual. He liked things that were intangible: ideas, motivations, emotions. He liked subjects that other students hated to think about. He was always frustrated when the classes had no connection to real life. This is what caused his grades to go down.

Charles' uniqueness often got him into trouble. He was called into the headmaster's office once or twice; eventually, he just left school.

I wonder how he is doing now. I wonder if he is happy with the decisions he made. (J.C.)

3. My job is getting tougher and tougher these days. The kids today just aren't like the ones back in my time when students did what they were supposed to and most importantly, what they were told to do. Now, the kids have their own opinions. They are ready to question things that you tell them to do. Take that Charles kid, for example, the one who just left school. That kid had no concern about his school work and grades. I remember talking to him five months ago about the important traditions of this school and the image that its students had to maintain. I hoped that our talk would straighten him out. I am sorry that it didn't work. (W.C.)

Peer Editing

1. In the following student sample, there are two run-on sentences and three sentence fragments. Before correcting the sample, practice correcting run-on and fragment errors by doing the exercise below.

    Run-on Sentences—Rewrite the following run-on sentences so that they are grammatical by using appropriate transitions or punctuation, or by dividing them into two sentences.

    a. I like the way you wrote your paper, it is very good.
    b. From my point of view, students should wear uniforms, it would help them be more serious about learning.
    c. There is a full moon tonight, it would be a good time for an evening walk.

    Sentence Fragments—Make complete sentences out of the sentence fragments that follow.

    a. The house that I live in. My house has an usual design.
    b. Although I enjoy swimming. I rarely go to the beach.
    c. The school will be closed on Tuesday. So I will go shopping.

    The other day when I was walking home. I saw my old friend, Charles. In my opinion, Charles is confused, I really don't know why he is doing so poorly in school. When we were in junior high school. He frequently helped me with my homework. I don't know what is on his mind anymore but he recently told me that he might quit high school. I was shocked. He told me that his high school teachers only care about getting students into the best colleges, he says that there is more to education than that. He wants to leave school in the spring. So he can be free and find out about the outside world. I told him that the school is only trying to help so he can have a brighter future. He didn't listen to me. (T.T.)

2. In the following student writing sample, there are ten verb form errors. Read the sample and try to correct the errors.

    I knew that this would happened to me sooner or later, but it did happened today. What a day it was! I just got fired by the headmaster of the school. I was very upset when I first heared the news, but I don't know how I feel anymore. I'm concerned about the students at that school. If the school keeps firing those instructors who teach what the students should really learned, then the students will not learn about life at all. Education is connect to the outside world. That's how everyone should learned in school. We have to look at the connection between education and life. The school just wants these poor students to learn history straight from the text without consider how it relates to their own lives. We should discussed and debate current history instead of just learning what is in the books without have a discussion of the subject matter. The school only cares about the number of students who get into Harvard rather than the number of students who have learn about life in general. They don't value each student's view. They don't care whether history relates to everyday life. History is not only the past but rather a part of our life. I hope that the school will understand my point of view someday so that the students can have a better education. (T.N.)

SHORT WRITING: RESPONDING TO A CHARACTER

What do you think of Charles' attitude? What do you think about his leaving school? What advice would you give Charles? Write a letter to Charles, letting him know what you think. Before writing your letter, read the peer writing samples and do the peer editing exercises which follow.

Peer Writing Samples

Read the following student letters and discuss the advice given. Would you give the same advice?

Dear Charles,

I think you are a very brave person because you did something that most people dare not to do. You are also a fairly smart person since you sensed what was happening to you and to your school, something that many other people were not aware of. You shouldn't be sorry about leaving school. Being sorry won't help you a bit. Entering college is a good thing, but it is not the only thing we can do in our lives. The most important thing is to be yourself, to become what you can be and to live your life with awareness. As you said, spring is beautiful outside the school. Spring is still beautiful. There are lots of roads in front of you. Stand up and choose one. Stop feeling sorry for yourself.

Sincerely,

V.C.

Dear Charles,

After I read your story, I felt really sad. I have some advice for you. First, I would like to say that you are very young. This is just one experience in life. I think you can get someting from this experience that will help you in your life later.

From your behavior, I can tell that you are a very bold man. You like to ask "why" about everything. If you ask "why" too frequently, you will have a lot of trouble in life because when you ask "why", your "why" will affect someone else's power. People don't want you to criticize them. They are afraid of losing their power and benefits. They don't want your comments. Because you didn't like the school system, you didn't study. You didn't get good grades. You won't get into a good school later. This is your loss. Nobody else cares about your deeds. You complained about the system; no one wanted to hear that.

The best thing to do is keep quiet. If you have suggestions, keep them in your mind. One day, if you have enough power, you can make changes. If you had been smarter, you would have kept quiet and gotten good grades and gone to a good college. Later, perhaps you would have become a college president. Then, you could have put your ideas into the real world.

Sincerely,

P.L.

Dear Charles,

I think I know what you feel and why you left school, but leaving school wasn't a very wise idea. You just ran away from the situation. I have to tell you that it won't make anything better; it will only make your life worse. Do you leave your family if you disagree with your family members and they do not think or behave as you think they should?

I know this whole thing is not simple, and I can't tell you what you should have done because I don't know either. I just want you to try your best. You are too young to give up easily. It is not too late to go back to school. Perhaps you should do that. Good luck!

Sincerely,

M.I.

Peer Editing

1. In the following student letter, there are four relative clause errors. Before correcting the sample, practice correcting relative clause errors by doing the exercise that follows.

Relative Clauses Correct the following sentences.

a. I read that book which you told me about it.
b. Anybody sees that movie will be frightened.
c. There is a person in your class has an interesting background.

Dear Charles,

I read your story and understood what you felt about the situation which you went through it. I understood you were angry and frustrated about the college preparatory system. However, I think you made a mistake about leaving school.

Every person lives in America should try to go to college. I also dislike what the system does but who do I blame for it? I am not the only one has to do it and neither are you. How are you going to feel when other people start to graduate from college? You will probably feel lost. You will feel alone. I don't want that to happen to you. Return to school. Although you don't like the college preparatory system, you should try to get through it. The college preparatory system will not change just because you quit school. One day, if there are many people argue about the system and give good reasons to change the system, there might be some changes, but you can't do it by yourself. I'm sorry to say that to you but it is true.

Please rethink your decision. Right now, you may not feel good but later, you will definitely thank me for this advice.

(J.H.K.L.)

2. In the following student letter, there are four parallelism errors. Before correcting the letter, practice correcting parallelism errors by doing these exercises.

Parallelism   Correct the following sentences.

   a.   School is the place where we explore new things and to experience many different paths.
   b.   I would like to take a class which is interesting as well as enjoyment.
   c.   Uniforms should not be required in schools because students should have a right to choose their own clothes and expresses their individuality.

Dear Charles,

   I read your story which described what college preparatory schools are like. I agree that schools should be a place where students can learn to think and applying their ideas to everyday life. School should be a place where students can learn from their own and others' mistakes. I am glad that someone really knows what schools should teach. Schools seem to want their students to grow up with the ability to memorize things and doing well on tests; they do not want to give their students the ability to think by themselves and giving their own opinions. I just hope that the school system changes before students turn into robots with no thoughts and opinions of their own. I know that you will find something to do in life that has more meaning and enjoyable. You're not lost because you're not alone. (C.N.)

ADDITIONAL JOURNAL TOPICS

Your journal will continue on the topic of education. However, you may want to go into greater depth and focus specifically on issues raised in the readings in this module. Following are the suggested journal topics for "Expelled."

1. Write about a teacher or school administrator whom you respect. What did they do to gain your respect? How did they differ from other teachers or school administrators?

2. Charles, the narrator, does not blame the college-preparatory school. He says it taught him what he needed to do in order to get into college. However, he feels that it did not give him a real education. Is school teaching you everything that you want to learn? If not, what do you wish it would teach you?

ESSAY WRITING: TOPICS

Select one of the following topics for this module's essay. To write this essay, you may use the readings in this module as resources, along with your journal entries. You will need to write at least two or three drafts for this essay, along with the final version. The drafts will be read, commented on, and evaluated by your instructor and your peers, using the evaluation forms and checklist provided in this section.

Alternative 1

Each of the readings in this module has, in some way, dealt with the negative and positive psychological effects of the educational system in the U.S. Discuss the negative and positive psychological effects that your own schooling has had on you. Use examples and ideas from your own experience as well as from the readings to support your points.

Alternative 2

Herald and Cheever each describe events in their education that left major impressions on them. Describe an event in your education that taught you a major life lesson. Use details, dialogue, etc., so that this event comes to life.

Before beginning to write your essay, read and discuss the composing process of two students who responded to these topics. The composing process for Essay Alternative 1 follows this paragraph. The composing process for Essay Alternative 2 begins on page 167.

Essay Alternative 1: The Composing Process

To help you see the changes that one student made when gathering ideas, revising, and editing, we have included one student's brainstorming activity, first and second drafts, and final version for this essay topic (see pages 160–166). This material is intended for discussion purposes and is not to be used as a model. In the following section, you will discuss questions pertaining to this student's composing process. Refer to the student's writing when indicated.

DISCUSSION QUESTIONS

Work in groups of three to discuss the following questions.

1. *Look at the brainstorming activity* (page 160).
   a. Discuss other factors the student might have included.
   b. Do you think the student has done sufficient brainstorming? Why or why not?

2. *Read the first draft* (pages 161–162).
   a. There are grammatical errors in the first draft. Why doesn't the instructor correct them?
   b. The instructor comments that the beginning of the essay is "very general" and that it might be better to lead up to the thesis in a more interesting way to arouse the reader's interests. Do you have any ideas about how the author might introduce this topic in a more interesting way?
   c. This essay contains a number of instructor comments indicating that something is off-topic. Examine the off-topic sections and try to figure out why they are off-topic.
   d. Often a first draft provides a basic "skeleton" for your ideas and needs expansion. The instructor comments in ¶2 that the author should "say more." Why is this expansion a good idea? How would you expand this paragraph?
   e. The instructor indicates that the student is not quite focusing on the essay question in ¶3. In what way is the student not directly answering the question?
   f. Look at the peer review sheet on page 163. Do you agree with the peers' ratings on the content and organization of the first draft? What types of suggestions for improving the first draft do the peers make? Do you agree with these suggestions? What would you suggest?

3. *Read the second draft of this essay* (pages 164–165). (In this draft, the instructor has indicated the grammar mistakes.)

   a. Why does the instructor think the introduction is much better? Do you agree?

   b. The student added transitions between the first three paragraphs. Does this improve the essay? Why or why not?

   c. Before reading the final version, see if you can correct the grammar mistakes.

4. *Read the final version* (pages 165–166).

   a. On a scale from 1 to 10, rate this final version for content and originality (with 10 indicating excellent content and a high degree of originality, and 1 indicating poor content and little originality).

   b. On a scale from 1 to 10, rate this final version for organization (with 10 indicating excellent organization, and 1 indicating poor organization).

   c. There is a saying that a composition is never finished . . . it is only abandoned. This means that a composition can continually be revised. The writer of this essay chose to stop after writing two drafts. If she wanted to continue revising, what might she work on?

BRAINSTORMING

SCHOOL

NEGATIVE
intimidating
stressful
ugly
frustrating
boring
purposeless
powerless

POSITIVE
empowering

free from distractions
learned some useful
   information
reading   writing   math
made friends

could help me get a
good job doing.... Art?!

Now I can share my
knowledge with others.

DRAFT 1

Through the years I have seen the United States' educational system has affected students in good and bad ways. In my own experience in public schools, I have found that the educational system affects me psychologically both negatively and positively. On the negative side, I found school is intimidating and stressful; however, on the positive side, I found it is empowering, since it increased my opportunities for success in life.

This introduction is very general. Perhaps you could lead up to your thesis in a more interesting way.

Good description. Say more.

I went to several different schools and I found every single one were oppressive. I was surrounded by plainness. I mean the school's architecture had no artwork which might serve to enliven students. I guess it was because school administrators think artwork is distracting. The coldness intimidated me.

I am confused here. Do you want to address public schools (kindergarten through the twelfth grade) or college education? The topic is schooling in general not just college.

The school system I encountered was very pressuring. I constantly struggled with economic, parental, and peer pressure and I soon burned out. My existence here at the University is through financial aid. If I don't do well in my studies, I will not receive financial help in the future years. My parents can't afford to pay for my studies so I need to get financial helps. My parents want me to have a degree so they are pushing me to study harder. All the classes are very demanding. It is not easy to meet the expectations of everyone and doing well academically at the same time. The only ones who survive college are the ones who have strong wills and the desire to succeed in life. By the way, I personally have a lot of desire to succeed and make it.

off-topic

Good transition

Despite these negatives, school is not a bad place for it helps you prepare for life. School has empowered me. It has given me choices and rewarding. Even though school does prohibit me from doing many things, it has given me many lessons in life. For instance, it taught me that I can't do what I want all the time. I have found going to school very helpful. I have learned to read, write, and do arithmetic. These are the most useful thing one must learn to be able to survive in our society. Learning to do these things have helped me to become a stronger individual. This will be important when I'm applying for a job and I can show my employer my abilities. I have also found that education increases life choices. I attended the Los Angeles County High School for the Arts, a school for students who have potential in the arts. Being able to attend school is the best reward one can give oneself. It provided me with a chance for a career in my field of preference and helped me earn a decent salary. Everything you learn in life is valuable and I find it more so when I share it with others. This is the one way that it is rewarding. You can teach your knowledge to others. You will be able to stand on your own and not depending on others.

The educational system has not affected me as much as I have thought. There are many things I do not agree with, but I have learned to cope with these things. While I have found school intimidating and stressful, I have also seen that school is a place that empowers people. It increases people's options in life and is a rewarding experience. No matter how negatively school affects us psychologically, it teaches us to be strong so that we are able to overcome any of life's obstacles. This is the key to achieving success. (Y.C.)

[Handwritten margin notes: "you've been talking about yourself. Why switch to 'oneself' here? 'oneself' It's very general."]

[Handwritten margin notes: "Off-topic. Link this to previous discussion or delete."]

[Handwritten margin notes: "Contradictory Off-topic"]

PEER REVIEW OF DRAFT 1

Reviewers ___H.B._____ and ___T.S._____
Paper which is being reviewed: ___Y.C._____

What do you believe the author's purpose was in writing this essay? (For example, the author wanted to show how ...; the author wanted to describe an event to entertain us...; the author wanted to convince us that...; the author wanted to explain that...)

We are not sure what the author's purpose is. We do not think that the author knows.

On a scale from 1 to 10, rate the essay for content (with 10 indicating excellent content and a high degree of originality, and 1 indicating poor content and little originality).

Rating for content: ___6___

Reasons for giving this rating: We like some of the examples the author gives—e.g., L.A. County High School, but we think the essay could be more informative. Also, the author wanders a lot.

What would you suggest? (Be specific. For instance, if a certain paragraph needs more detail, state which paragraph you are talking about.)

The author includes a lot of information that doesn't "fit". For example, in the first paragraph, the author talks about public schools and then, in the second paragraph discusses university life. We'd take out the part about the university.

On a scale from 1 to 10, rate this essay for organization (with 10 indicating excellent organization, and 1 indicating poor organization).

Rating for organization: ___7___

Reasons for giving this rating: Something seems wrong here, but we couldn't figure out what it is. Maybe the author wanders too much. We think that he needs a stronger thesis statement.

What would you suggest? Add a stronger thesis. Stick to this thesis and delete any discussion which is not related to it.

DRAFT 2

Better! I have a very clear idea of your thesis.

John Holt, a noted educator, argues that "schools are bad places for kids." Herald, a recent college graduate and author of "Fresh Start," argues that a major benefit of her college education was the freedom to make mistakes and not be blamed for them. If you ask a hundred people whether school has had positive or negative effects on them, you would probably receive a hundred different replies. For me, there have been both positives and negatives. (In my own experience) in public schools, (I found) public school intimidating and stressful; however, on the positive side, I found it is empowering since it increased my opportunities for success in life.

Redundant

to find something + adjective

The school buildings, themselves, had a negative affect on me. I went to several different schools and I found every single one oppressive. I was surrounded by plainness. The white concrete walls and windowless classrooms imprisoned me. I mean the school's architecture had no artwork which might serve to enliven students. Perhaps it was because school administrators think artwork is distracting. The coldness intimidated me.

slang

The physical oppression paralleled the mental oppression I sometimes felt. I felt a great deal of pressure because I constantly must struggle with economic, parental, and peer pressure and I soon burned out. I never had the resources I needed to excel. While other students had a quiet place to study at home, the cramped living quarters that I shared with my five siblings and parents made me hard to study. I lacked money for books and paper and could not even join sports teams as I couldn't afford to buy the require uniforms. My parents always pressured me to obtain good grades and I always feared letting them down. Even my peers at school pressured me. They wanted me to go different places with them, and I rarely had time for them.

verb tense

to make something hard for someone

It is hard for someone to + verb

wrong word form

adjective

Despite these negatives, school is not a completely bad place

Do you want to be general or personal?

for it helps (you) prepare for life. School has empowered me. It has
parallel structure problem.
given me choices and rewarding. There, I learned to read, write,
plural form needed
and do arithmetic. These are the basic which are needed to survive
agreement
in our society. Learning these things have helped me to become a
stronger individual. This knowledge which I obtained in school has
also increased my options. For example, I attended the Los Angeles
County High School for the Arts, a school for students who have
potential in the arts. The school provided me with the opportunity
to earn a living working in the field of my choice.

While I have found school intimidating and stressful, I have
also seen that school empowers me. It increases my options in life
and is a rewarding experience. No matter how negatively school
affects me psychologically, it also provides me with knowledge that
enables me to overcome any of life's obstacles. This is the key to
achieving success. (Y.C.)

FINAL VERSION

John Holt, a noted educator, argues that "schools are bad
places for kids." Herald, a recent college graduate and author of
"Fresh Start," argues that a major benefit of her college education
was the freedom to make mistakes and not be blamed for them. If
you ask a hundred people whether school has had positive or negative effects on them, you would probably receive a hundred different
replies. For me, there have been both positives and negatives. In
my own experience in public schools, I found public school
intimidating and stressful; however, on the positive side, I found
it empowering, since it increased my opportunities for success in
life.

The school buildings, themselves, had a negative effect on me.
I went to several different schools and I found every single one
oppressive. I was surrounded by plainness. The white concrete walls
and windowless classrooms imprisoned me. The school's archi-

tecture had no artwork which might serve to enliven students. The coldness intimidated me.

The physical oppression paralleled the mental oppression I sometimes felt. I constantly had to struggle with economic, parental, and peer pressure. I never had the resources I needed to excel. While other students had a quiet place to study at home, the cramped living quarters that I shared with my five siblings and parents made it hard for me to study. I lacked money for books and paper and could not even join sports teams as I couldn't afford to buy the required uniforms. My parents always pressured me to obtain good grades and I always feared letting them down. Even my peers at school pressured me. They wanted me to go different places with them, and I rarely had time for them.

Despite these negatives, school is not a completely bad place for it prepares me for life, and thus, empowers me. There, I learned to read, write, and do arithmetic. These are the basics which are needed to survive in our society. Other knowledge which I obtained in school has further increased my options. For instance, I attended the Los Angeles County High School for the Arts, a school for students who have potential in the arts. The school provided me with the opportunity to earn a living working in the field of my choice.

While I have found school intimidating and stressful, I have also seen that it has empowered me. It has increased my options in life and has been a rewarding experience. No matter how negatively school affects me psychologically, it gives me knowledge that enables me to overcome any of life's obstacles. This is the key to achieving success. (Y.C.)

Essay Alternative 2: The Composing Process

To help you see the changes that one student made when gathering ideas, revising, and editing, you can follow one student's brainstorming activity, first and second drafts, and final version for this essay topic (see pages 168–173). This material is intended for discussion purposes and is not to be used as a model. In the following section, you will discuss questions pertaining to this student's composing process. Refer to the student's writing when indicated.

DISCUSSION QUESTIONS

Work in groups of three to discuss the following questions.

1. *Look at the student's brainstorming activity* (page 168).
   a. Do you think the student has done sufficient brainstorming? Why or why not?
2. *Read the first draft* (pages 169–170).
   a. Consider the instructor's comments on the first draft. The instructor comments on the content and organization but not the grammar. Why do you think the instructor does this?
   b. Look at the instructor's comment on the first paragraph. How could the author "connect [his] introduction to the essay question so that the reader can more easily see the relation between [the] response and the question"?
   c. The instructor broke the third paragraph down into three shorter paragraphs. She did this "so that important stages in [the] narrative are emphasized more." How do these shorter paragraphs emphasize important stages? What are the important stages of the author's narrative?
   d. Often a first draft provides a basic "skeleton" for your ideas and needs expansion. Why does the instructor suggest that the writer expand his ideas in the last paragraph?
   e. Read the peer review sheet on page 170. Do you agree with the peers' ratings on the content and organization of the first draft? What types of suggestions for improving the first draft do the peers make? Do you agree with these suggestions? What would you suggest?
3. *Read the second draft* (pages 171–172). (In this draft, the teacher has indicated the grammar errors.)
   a. Compare the introduction in the second draft to the introduction in the first draft. How has the author improved the introduction in the second draft?

b. How has the student expanded the last paragraph? Does the essay now answer the essay question more completely?

c. Before reading the final version, see if you can correct the grammar mistakes.

4. *Read the final version* (pages 172–173).

a. The author expanded the last paragraph further. What information did he add? Does this improve the essay, in your opinion? How?

b. On a scale from 1 to 10, rate this final version for content and originality (with 10 indicating excellent content and a high degree of originality, and 1 indicating poor content and little originality).

c. On a scale from 1 to 10, rate this final version for organization (with 10 indicating excellent organization, and 1 indicating poor organization).

d. There is a saying that a composition is never finished . . . it is only abandoned. This means that a composition can continually be revised. The writer of this essay chose to stop after writing two drafts. If he wanted to continue revising, what might he work on?

BRAINSTORMING

Events in the Life of a Third Grader

I didn't do homework

I didn't want to go to school

I went to school anyway

Teacher called on me to read essay

I pretended to read essay =
I faked it!

Teacher caught me

Humiliation

DRAFT 1

Try to correct your introduction to the essay question so that the reader can more easily see the relation between your response and the question

The incident was caused by a little boy's innocent thought of not disappointing one who trusted in him; however, it turned out wrong.

I was in the third grade and I was one of the few boys who was not sick of school yet. I obeyed teachers and did exactly what I was told to do in the school and because of that, the teachers liked and trusted me a lot. I was the right example of what they thought students should be and they always pointed me out as <u>an excellent</u> *a model student?* standard for the student. I really liked the situation and I wanted to keep it that way and I was successful until one bright Monday morning of late March.

I've broken this long paragraph into shorter ones so that important stages in your narrative are empha- sized more

As the sun shined on my shoulder where my backpack was, I felt that the backpack was even heavier than usual. Unlike other days, I did not want to go to school that day because I have not done my homework, writing an essay. Somehow, I arrived at school and went to the class. In the class, I was so nervous. I was afraid of the moment when she would ask me to read my essay out loud and I dreaded that moment. I wished that the teacher would not call ¶ *New paragraph* my name that day, but it happened. She pointed me out and I stood up with my blank piece of paper in my hands. I did not write any- thing, yet I could not be honest with the teacher because I did not want to disappoint her. I started to make up the essay off the top of my head and because of my strange behavior, the teacher ¶ noticed that I was making the essay up on the spot. "How could

What went through your mind as you stood against the wall? Please explain. This is the key part of your

you do that? How could you try to trick me?" she yelled at me. She told me to stand against the wall for the rest of the class. She told the class about my behavior. I was so embarrassed and I hated myself for trying not to disappoint the teacher as well as try to be the perfect student by the teacher's standard.

Looking back, I have been so passive in the school ever since

essay. Expand it to empha- size the lessons you learned.

then. I have not participated with <u>the teachers</u> and I even rebelled against them without reason at times. I think that the pressures from teachers affected me as much as peer and parental pressure can. (S.N.)

PEER REVIEW OF DRAFT 1

Reviewers __L.L._____ and __P.T._____

Paper which is being reviewed: __S.N._____

What do you believe the author's purpose was in writing this essay? (For example, the author wanted to show how ...; the author wanted to describe an event to entertain us ...; the author wanted to convince us that ...; the author wanted to explain that ...)

We think that the author wants to show the reader how much difference one teacher can make in a students life.

On a scale from 1 to 10, rate the essay for content (with 10 indicating excellent content and a high degree of originality, and 1 indicating poor content and little originality).

Rating for content: __8__

Reasons for giving this rating: This essay was interesting because the writer gives a good description of his feelings in elementary school. We felt like we were in the classroom watching him!

What would you suggest? (Be specific. For instance, if a certain paragraph needs more detail, state which paragraph you are talking about.)

We did <u>not</u> expect the conclusion. The writer should try to make it more connected to the rest of his essay. The content seems indirectly related.

On a scale from 1 to 10, rate this essay for organization (with 10 indicating excellent organization, and 1 indicating poor organization).

Rating for organization: _____8_____

Reasons for giving this rating: The body of the essay is excellent! We are not sure about the introduction and conclusion. They are a bit weak.

What would you suggest?

Write a better introduction and conclusion. Give us a better idea of where the essay is going!

DRAFT 2

I like this introduction much better. It connects your essay to the question and also makes me curious to read on.

The particular incident which left a major impression on me

verb form error

was cause by a little boy's innocent thought of not disappointing one who trusted in him; however, it turned out wrong and changed his life.

I was in the third grade and I was one of the few boys who was not sick of school yet. I obeyed teachers and did exactly what I was told to do in the school and because of that, the teachers liked and trusted me a lot. I was the perfect example of what they thought students should be and they always pointed me out as a model for other students. I really liked the situation and I wanted to keep it that way.

One bright Monday morning in March, I started to get tired

incorrect verb form

of school, however. As the sun shined on my shoulder where my backpack was, I felt that the backpack was even heavier than usual. Unlike other days, I did not want to go to school that day because

Wrong verb tense

I have not done my homework, writing an essay. Somehow, I arrived at school and went to the class. In the class, I was so nervous that I could not sit still. I dreaded the moment when my teacher would ask me to read my essay out loud. I wished that she would not call my name that day, but it happened.

She pointed me out and I stood up with my blank piece of paper in my hands. I did not write anything, yet I could not be honest with the teacher because I did not want to disappoint her. I started to make up the essay off the top of my head and because

Education **171**

of my strange behavior, the teacher noticed that I was making the essay up on the spot. I saw her face become angry.

"How could you do that? How could you try to trick me?" she yelled at me. She told me to stand against the wall for the rest of the class. She told the class about my behavior. I was so embarrassed and I hated myself for trying not to disappoint the

parallel structure problem

teacher as well as <u>try</u> to be the perfect student by the teacher's standard.

Due to this embarrassing experience, I have been so passive in the school ever since then. I have not participated in class and

verb tense problem

I even <u>rebelled</u> against teachers without reason at times. I think that the pressures from teachers affected me as much as peer and

wrong word

parental pressure <u>can</u>. Because I disappointed my teacher as a youth, it affected the way I acted and did academically. I do not worry as much about making my teacher happy, but just do what is asked of me and never forget my experience when I was young.

(S.N.)

FINAL VERSION

The particular incident which left a major impression on me was caused by a little boy's innocent thought of not disappointing one who trusted in him; however, events did not work out and had a negative impact on the boy's life.

I was in the third grade and I was one of the few boys who was not sick of school yet. I obeyed teachers and did exactly what I was told to do in school and because of that, the teachers liked and trusted me a lot. I was the perfect example of what they thought students should be and they always pointed me out as a model for other students. I really liked the situation and I wanted to keep it that way.

However, one bright Monday morning in March, I started to get tired of school. As the sun shone on my shoulder where my backpack was, I felt that the backpack was even heavier than usual. Unlike other days, I did not want to go to school that day because I had not done my homework, writing an essay. Somehow, I arrived at school and went to the class. In the class, I was so nervous that I could not sit still. I dreaded the moment when my teacher would ask me to read my essay out loud. I wished that she would not call my name that day, but it happened.

She pointed me out and I stood up with my blank piece of paper in my hands. I did not write anything, yet I could not be honest with the teacher because I did not want to disappoint her. I started to make up the essay off the top of my head and because of my strange behavior, the teacher noticed that I was making the essay up on the spot. I saw her face become angry.

''How could you do that? How could you try to trick me?'' she yelled at me. She told me to stand against the wall for the rest of the class. She told the class about my behavior. I was so embarrassed and I hated myself for trying not to disappoint the teacher as well as trying to be the perfect student by the teacher's standard.

Due to this embarrassing experience, I have been unusually passive in school. Although I had driven myself to the limit in order to meet the teacher's standard, I was not able to be perfect all the time and that fact disappointed the teacher as well as me; ever since then, I have not participated in classes and I have even rebelled against teachers without reason at times. I think the pressures from teachers have affected me as much as pressures from peers and parents. My experience of disappointing my teacher as a youth has affected the way I act and perform academically. I do not worry as much about making my teacher happy, but just do what is asked of me. I will never forget that experience of my youth. (S.N.)

Evaluating Paragraphs for Unity

Before writing your essay for this unit, do these exercises to fine-tune your ability to "stay on track." In the following student samples, cross out information that is off-topic.

1. Last year, I was panicked. I didn't know how to fill out my college applications and financial aid package. I felt confused and helpless. At first, nobody offered me any help. The high school counselor just turned me away saying, "I'm not sure how to complete those forms. I'll ask around and get back to you later." If I asked him a question, he just wrinkled his eyebrows and looked the other way. Fortunately, my English teacher offered to help. She was a great teacher who made fun of herself during school award assemblies. She spent the entire time going over the college application forms and answering our questions about college. She even stayed after school to help me complete my financial aid package. (G.R.)

2. I never did well in grade school. After three years of school, I still hadn't learned to read or add. My friends did fine. Good grades were, to me, meaningless. They just represented letters of the alphabet imprinted on my papers. In a class of thirty-five children, my grades ranked me "thirty-four." (K.W.)

3. Time goes by unbelievably quickly. I have completed elementary, junior high, and high school already. Here I am, accepted at a university, majoring in Biology and trying to pursue my goal. However, to continue succeeding academically, I have to attend my classes regularly, pay close attention to my professors' lectures and understand all the information contained in my textbooks. "A professor will assign five page papers." I have to keep up with all my homework and tasks, even while midterms are coming at the same time, usually one after another until the quarter ends. (L.W.)

Essay Writing Checklist

Before turning in your final essay, check the following points.

CONTENT AND ORGANIZATION

_____ 1. My thesis is clearly stated.

_____ 2. The body of my essay adequately supports my thesis.

_____ 3. My introduction captures the readers' attention.

_____ 4. My essay sufficiently answers the question or addresses the topic.

_____ 5. My essay contains original ideas.

_____ 6. I have provided sufficient information to adequately support my statements (for instance, statistics, quotes, examples).

_____ 7. My conclusion contributes to the overall coherence of my essay.

LANGUAGE

_____ 1. I have corrected grammar, punctuation, and spelling errors that were indicated by my teacher.

_____ 2. I have tried to use a variety of words and have avoided using the same words again and again.

_____ 3. I have chosen words that express my ideas precisely.

Additional Readings for Module 2

The following readings complement this module. You may want to use some or all of them as resources. (In addition to the following two readings, related readings are in Module 1, "The Misery of Silence," by Maxine Hong Kingston, and in Module 3, "Graduation," by Maya Angelou and "Stereotypes and the Female College Student" by Monir Shirazi.)

The Long Transition to Adulthood

Ellen Goodman

In this essay, Goodman compares and contrasts education in the past and present. She is especially interested in how schools prepared and prepare students to be adults. The point she makes is that society nowadays does not give children and adolescents enough good opportunities to try to be adults and to learn how to be adults. She says that "we have left schools the job of producing adults but schools are where the young are kept, not where they grow up." Has your schooling prepared you to be an adult? If so, how? If not, why not?

(1) "When I was a child, I spake as a child, I understood as a child, I thought as a child. But when I became a man, I put away childish things." —1 Corinthians[1]

(2) What about the years in between childhood and adulthood? How do we speak then? How do we think? How do we become men and women?

[1]This is a passage from the Bible. "Spoke" is used in everyday English instead of "spake."

(3) For most of history, there was no in-between, no adolescence as we know it. There was no such lengthy period of semi-autonomy, economic "uselessness," when the only occupation of a son or daughter was learning.

(4) In the eighteenth century, Americans weren't legally adults until they turned twenty-one, but they did important work on farms by seven or eight. When they were physically grown, at only thirteen or sixteen, they had virtually the same jobs as any other adult.

(5) In those days, education was irregular at best, but each child had his or her own vocational guidance teacher: the family. So the transition to adulthood was handled—though not always easily or without tension— through a long apprenticeship, on the farm or in a craft, by people who could point out a direct social path to adulthood.

(6) It was industrialization that changed all that. In the nineteenth century, mills and factories replaced farms, and cities replaced the countryside. Children didn't automatically follow their parents' occupations and so family relations became less important for job training than something called school.

(7) In that century, the need for child labor on farms diminished and the horrors of industrial child labor became widespread. So we passed laws against child labor and in favor of mandatory education. Decade by decade we have raised both ages.

(8) School has replaced work not just out of our benevolence. There are also deep economic reasons. In 1933, at the height of the Depression[2], the National Child Labor Committee put it as baldly as this: "It is now generally accepted that the exploitation of children, indefensible on humanitarian grounds, has become a genuine economic menace. Children should be in school and adults should have whatever worthwhile jobs there are."

(9) School became the place of reading and writing and certification. It provided the necessary paper for employment. School not only kept young people out of the marketplace but promised "better" jobs if they stayed and studied.

(10) The result of all this is clear: today, school is what young people do for a living.

(11) In 1870, less than five percent of the high school age group were in high school. In 1976, 86.1 percent of those fourteen to seventeen were in school. In 1977, nearly one-third of the eighteen to twenty-one-year-olds were in college.

(12) There has been a 129 percent increase in college enrollment in

[2]The Depression (1929 to 1935) was a period in American history in which the economy was terrible and many people were out of work.

this country since 1960. In many places today, community colleges are entered as routinely as high schools.

(13) While a high school diploma or a college degree no longer guarantees a job, there are more and more jobs you can't even apply for without them. So the payoff is less certain, but the pressure is even greater to go to school longer and longer, to extend the state of semi-autonomy further and further.

(14) The irony is that society worries more when the young try to grasp at adult "privileges" than when they remain in the passive fraternity-house state of mind. We worry about teenage drinking and driving and pregnancy—all perhaps misguided attempts at "grown-up behavior." Yet we offer few alternatives, few meaningful opportunities for adulthood training. We have virtually allowed sex, drinking, and driving to become rites of passage.

(15) School just isn't enough. It demands only one skill, tests only one kind of performance. From a pre-med dorm to an Animal House, it is a youth ghetto where adults are only authority figures, where students don't get the chance to test their own identities, their own authority, their own responsibilities to others.

(16) Without enough alternatives, we have left schools the job of producing adults. But schools are where the young are kept, not where they grow up.

(17) Adolescence isn't a training ground for adulthood now. It is a holding pattern for aging youth.

Vocabulary Gloss

The definitions given here are intended to aid your comprehension. Numbers in parentheses refer to the paragraphs in which the words appear. (Since you are not expected to understand each word in the preceding reading passage, not all the words you do not know are glossed. You will need to guess the meaning of other words you do not understand.)

adolescence	(3)	(n.)	period of life between childhood and adulthood
semi-	(3)	(prefix)	partly
autonomy	(3)	(n.)	self-government
virtually	(4)	(adv.)	in reality; being in fact or acting as what is described, but not accepted openly in that way
vocational	(5)	(adj.)	related to a person's trade or profession
guidance	(5)	(n.)	advice; leadership

apprenticeship	(5)	(n.)	the time of being an apprentice, a learner of a trade who has agreed to work for a number of years in return for being taught the trade
industrialization	(6)	(n.)	the process of developing and expanding industry, the branch of business that emphasizes manufacturing, often mechanical manufacturing
labor	(7)	(n.)	physical or mental work
to diminish	(7)	(v.)	to reduce; to become less
mandatory	(7)	(adj.)	required
benevolence	(8)	(n.)	desire to do good; activity in doing good
exploitation	(8)	(n.)	the state of using something selfishly or for one's own profit
indefensible	(8)	(adj.)	not able to be defended; not able to be supported
humanitarian	(8)	(adj.)	describing something that supports the welfare of all human beings by reducing suffering, reforming laws about punishment, etc.
grounds	(8)	(n.)	reasons for saying, doing, or believing something
menace	(8)	(n.)	danger; threat
worthwhile	(8)	(adj.)	of true value
certification	(9)	(n.)	written or printed statement, used as proof of having completed or done something
irony	(14)	(n.)	event, situation, etc., which is the opposite of what one would expect or desire
to grasp	(14)	(v.)	try to seize; try to take hold or possession of
misguided	(14)	(adj.)	mistaken; misdirected
alternative	(14)	(adj.)	choice between two or more possibilities
rites of passage	(14)	(n.)	ceremonies which separate one stage of life from another (e.g., adolescence to adulthood)

ghetto	(15)	(n.)	section of a town or city lived in by people who are members of a minority (usually racial, ethnic, or religious)
authority	(15)	(n.)	power or right to give orders and make others obey
training ground	(17)	(n.)	a place where people are taught and given practice in order to bring them to a desired standard of behavior
holding pattern	(17)	(n.)	a state in which all parts are kept in the same position (e.g., planes waiting to land at an airport)

Remote Regimen
Most Learning at Independent Study School Takes Place Outside Classroom
Maria Newman

The following abridged newspaper article describes an alternative high school system. It is a system which emphasizes individualized learning. The system provides the teachers and the materials. It is up to the students to provide the motivation. Do you think you would do well in a system in which all the responsibility to learn is on you? Why or why not?

(1) At Monte Vista High School in California, there are no junior or senior proms, no pep rallies, no class clowns, no mass crowds in the hallway between classes. Teachers do not lecture in front of a roomful of students.

(2) Instead, there is a quiet calm over the campus, where just eight teachers toil away in one wing of what was once an elementary school. No more than two students sit in the hour long classes at a time, except for math labs, where there are four.

(3) Graduation for many students is a trip to the school's office, where the registrar plops a red mortarboard on their heads and finds them a matching gown, so she can shoot a couple of snapshots of the graduate standing in the middle of the school's courtyard, a diploma in hand.

TEACHERS FOLLOW UP WITH CALL HOME

(4) On each teacher's desk is a telephone so the instructor can call students to find out why they failed to make it to class or why school work was not turned in.

(5) But for Monte Vista students, most of the learning takes place outside the classroom. The high school is an independent study program that enables students to complete high school requirements at their own pace, while they concentrate on jobs or other projects.

(6) One boy gets his assignments by FAX machine in the South Pacific where his family is on a one-year vacation. Another girl with a modeling assignment in Barbados mails in her homework. Other students are from single-parent homes and have to work to contribute to the family income.

(7) "There is no state rule [on who can go through independent study], but our rule is that a youngster must have a good reason why he can't attend school on a regular daily basis," Principal Carole Castaldo said. "We try to discourage a student who wants to go surfing or lie on the beach."

ENROLLMENT DOUBLES EACH YEAR

(8) Programs such as Castaldo's have been around for twelve years, since the State Legislature allowed school districts to offer independent study. But lately, enrollment in such programs has been booming. Each year since Monte Vista was set up, Castaldo said, enrollment has doubled. There are now 350 students in the program; 134 were graduated last year.

(9) Statewide, enrollment in independent study programs has increased almost 50% in the last five years, according to Lynn Hartzler of the State Department of Education's alternative education unit.

(10) Some of these students, Castaldo said, "are a result of a new generation of parents, parents that didn't necessarily follow a straight and narrow path. And now they're raising kids who are saying, 'We don't want a traditional program' . . . I think that's why attendance is growing—and it sure is growing."

(11) "With a statewide dropout rate of more than 30%, educators have been forced to develop alternative education programs, such as independent study, to reach students whom traditional schools do not seem to touch," said William Hebermehl, assistant superintendent of the local Department of Education.

(12) For some students, learning is more successful if education is stripped down to its most basic components: a student, books and self-motivation to learn, with a little guidance from a teacher.

'BEAT OF A DIFFERENT DRUMMER'

(13) "At many of the alternative education programs, you'll find many very polite kids, kids with very high IQs who just kind of walk to the beat of a different drummer," Hebermehl said. "They don't learn well in the confines of a 30-to-1 teaching-ratio classroom. They want a 1-on-1 or 3-on-1 situation. In these programs, they thrive."

(14) Castaldo was quick to point out that Monte Vista is not "an easy way out" or "a quick way to graduate."

(15) "It is not a school for losers," she said. "It takes a lot of self-discipline and responsibility to be successful at this."

(16) Two prerequisites for Monte Vista are that students be at least sixteen and demonstrate good reasons why they cannot attend a regular high school on a daily basis, either because of a job or other activity that will keep them busy.

(17) Another requirement for independent study—the strictest one—is that students and their parents or guardians must sign a contract stating that the student will complete a certain amount of work during a set period. If that work is not submitted on time, the student is dropped from Monte Vista three weeks after the deadline.

COURSES OF FOUR TO FIVE WEEKS

(18) Each course lasts about four to five weeks and is the equivalent of a semester. Digesting so much material in that short time might be difficult, especially because it is done almost entirely independent of teachers, Beverly Smith, a math and algebra teacher, said. But that is no excuse for failure.

(19) "Eventually, they should start reaching stumbling blocks," she said about students' lessons. "But I am here every day. It is up to them to find a friend or a relative or an enemy, or us, and ask us for help."

(20) "I tell my students I'm here to walk the path with them. But if they're not here when they should be, I will call boyfriends, girlfriends, mothers or fathers about why they are not here," Smith said.

(21) The school offers almost every course found in traditional high school: English, algebra, economics, psychology, French, German, history, geography, physical science—the list goes on.

(22) That is because the philosophy at Monte Vista is that if a student is interested in a particular subject, and the course is not offered, the school will try to provide that course.

TEACHER: 'WE'RE MISFITS'

(23) It helps to have a teaching staff with a wide background and interests. The eight teachers at Monte Vista say they are as untraditional as their students.

(24) "We're misfits," Smith said, describing her colleagues.

(25) Jo Black, an English and drama teacher, for example, frequently appears in local theater productions and has performed on the New York stage.

(26) Fred Grade, a language teacher, played in a chamber orchestra

in Europe. The others have also done interesting things with their own lives that students can use for models.

(27) Teachers said this system is not a guaranteed success for students, but failure seldom happens here because individualized attention is available. Also, the pace for courses is, for the most part, the student's option.

(28) "We have the distinct advantage of putting the game ball where it belongs: with the student," history teacher Marc Katz said. "To us, it's not the teacher who teaches. We're more the learning facilitators."

(29) "We tell the students: 'The job of educating you is now your job.' "

Vocabulary Gloss

The definitions given here are intended to aid your comprehension. Numbers in parentheses refer to the paragraphs in which the words appear. (Since you are not expected to understand each word in the preceding reading passage, not all the words you do not know are glossed. You will need to guess the meaning of other words you do not understand.)

remote	(title)	(adj.)	Far away; distant in relationship
regimen	(title)	(n.)	set of rules for diet, exercises, etc. for improving one's health and well-being
prom	(1)	(n.)	party (usually formal dance) held by a graduating class in a high school or college
pep rally	(1)	(n.)	a gathering to encourage and give support to a team (usually a sports team)
to toil	(2)	(v.)	to work hard for long hours
mortarboard	(3)	(n.)	square cap, often worn by graduates and certain academic leaders during graduation ceremonies
snapshot	(3)	(n.)	photograph
pace	(5)	(n.)	speed; rate of walking or moving
FAX machine	(6)	(n.)	a machine which can send copies to a distant location within seconds
to discourage	(7)	(v.)	to try to prevent someone from doing something
to boom	(8)	(v.)	to have a sudden increase in activity
a straight and narrow path	(10)	(n.)	a traditional path

alternative	(11)	(adj.)	describing something which is different from the traditional choice
to be stripped down	(12)	(v.)	to have all extra parts removed; to be reduced to the most essential parts
components	(12)	(n.)	parts that make up a whole
self-motivation	(12)	(n.)	encouragement that comes from within someone
guidance	(12)	(n.)	advice; leadership
walk to the beat of a different drummer	(13)	(idiom)	be untraditional; make life choices choices which are different from those made by the average person
confines	(13)	(n.)	limits; borders; boundaries
ratio	(13)	(n.)	a math term describing the relation between two amounts
to thrive	(13)	(v.)	to succeed; to grow strong and healthy
self-discipline	(15)	(n.)	self-control
prerequisite	(16)	(n.)	something required beforehand as a condition for something else
deadline	(17)	(n.)	fixed date for finishing or doing something
to digest information	(18)	(v.)	to take something into one's mind; to make something part of one's knowledge
stumbling block	(19)	(n.)	barrier; obstacle; something that prevents progress
untraditional	(23)	(adj.)	unusual; different from the beliefs, customs, opinions, characteristics that are passed on by the majority
misfits	(24)	(n.)	people who do not fit in with their surroundings; people who are very different from those around them (and whose differences may cause them and others to be uncomfortable)
colleague	(24)	(n.)	co-worker
option	(27)	(n.)	choice
to put the game ball (with someone)	(28)	(idiom)	put the responsibility with someone
facilitator	(28)	(n.)	someone who lessens the difficulty of doing something; someone who assists in a process to make it easier

Module 3:

❑ *Stereotypes*

CONTENTS

Stereotypes are overgeneralizations about individuals on the basis of their membership in a specific group. In this module, you will be reading about others' ideas and experiences with stereotyping. In addition, you will be examining your own attitudes toward and experiences with stereotyping. Some of the questions you will consider in this module include:

- What causes people to stereotype?
- Can stereotyping be avoided? How?
- Who does stereotyping hurt?
- How has stereotyping affected me in my life?

In this module, your final task will be to write an essay with multiple drafts expressing your views about stereotypes and the effects they have had on you and others. Specific assignments are on page 246. All the readings and activities in this module are designed to prepare you for this final task by providing you with appropriate ideas and language.

KEEPING A JOURNAL

There are many different types of writing and many different reasons to write. One type of writing is journal writing. This writing is for the writer, not for an audience (although the journals of many people have been published). You will be asked to keep a journal when you use this book. Keep the following guidelines in mind when writing your journal:

1. Write at least one page a day.
2. Do not write a list of events. Your journal will be more meaningful if you see it as a place to put your thoughts and reactions. Rather than writing everything that happened in a day, perhaps you might write about one thought that really struck you, or about something you read or saw.
3. Your journal is for you. Do not be overly concerned with grammar or style. Your goal should be to get your ideas down. Your journal will not be checked for grammar.
4. In your journal, approximately half of your entries will be "free," that is, on the topic of your choice. The other half will be in response to questions in this book or additional questions that your teacher gives you.

Enjoy writing in your journal. Enjoy the conversation with yourself. (Refer to Appendix A to read reflections by two famous authors on their own journals.)

JOURNAL TOPICS

The general topic for this module is stereotypes. Here are some suggested journal topics. (As part of this module's journal writing assignments, choose three of the following questions to answer each week.)

1. Look at the following categories.

CATEGORY 1: GENDER	CATEGORY 2: ETHNICITY	CATEGORY 3: MISCELLANEOUS CHARACTERISTICS
female	Black	obese
male	Arab	illiterate
	Japanese	engineering student
	Mexican	wealthy
	White	gay
	Chinese	wheelchair-bound
	Korean	blind
	Vietnamese	deaf

Choose one item from each category. Choose items which do *not* represent you. For example, if you are a Korean male, you might choose "female, Black, wealthy." With these three characteristics, create a person in your mind. You will "become" that person. Spend five minutes with your eyes closed and try to see the world through that person's eyes (your new eyes!).

From your (new) point of view, in your new identity, discuss how people's prejudgments or stereotypes affect your life.

2. The following item is from a <u>Los Angeles Times</u> news story. React to the situation or ideas expressed. You might consider how you would feel, what you would do, what you would say, etc., if you were in the same situation.

A banker said to a Black couple applying for a business loan, "We have histories of Blacks owning barbecue businesses, running shoeshine stands and limousine services. We don't associate your background with success in the import business because no one of your race has done this." (Aug. 2, 1987)

3. The following item is from a <u>Los Angeles Times</u> news story. React to the situation or ideas expressed. You might consider how you would feel, what you would do, what you would say, etc., if you were in the same situation.

> A Jewish woman starting her first important job recounts how she began each workday in humiliation. The boss would buzz her on the intercom with a JAP (Jewish American Princess) joke. After delivering the punch line, she says, "He'd roar with laughter, and I'd just sit there. I didn't know if it was funny or not, but I knew I didn't like it."

4. What stereotypes have you heard about a group that you belong to? This group can be an ethnic group (e.g., Chinese, Japanese, Mexican), a gender group (male or female), a class-based group (rich, poor), a group based on sexual orientation (homosexual, heterosexual), a group based on roles (engineering student, mother), etc. How do you react to these stereotypes?

5. Asians have been called "the model minority." Why do you think they have been called this? Is it a stereotype? Does this label have both negative and positive effects? Explain.

6. Do stereotypes play a useful function? Explain.

7. How do stereotypes contribute to racism and discrimination?

8. Can you avoid stereotyping? If so, how? If not, why is it inevitable?

Reading Unit 3A

Don't Let Stereotypes Warp Your Judgment
Robert L. Heilbroner

In this essay, Heilbroner talks about stereotypes: what they are, why they occur, how they harm and help people, and what can be done to avoid stereotyping. Before reading this essay, consider the following questions: Where have you learned your stereotypes? Do your stereotypes help you or others? Do they harm you or others? How?

(1) Is a girl called Gloria <u>apt</u> to be better-looking than one called Bertha? Are criminals more likely to be dark than blond? Can you tell a good deal about someone's personality from hearing his voice briefly over the phone? Can a person's nationality be pretty accurately guessed from his photograph? Does the fact that someone wears glasses imply that he is intelligent?

(2) The answer to all these questions is obviously, "No."

(3) Yet, from all the evidence at hand, most of us believe these things. Ask any college boy if he'd rather take his chances with a Gloria or a Bertha, or ask a college girl if she'd rather blinddate a Richard or a Cuthbert. In fact, you don't have to ask: college students in questionnaires have revealed that names conjure up the same images in their minds as they do in yours—and for as little reason.

(4) Look into the favorite suspects of persons who report "suspicious characters" and you will find a large percentage of them to be "swarthy" or "dark and foreign-looking"—despite the testimony of criminologists that criminals do *not* tend to be dark, foreign, or "wild-eyed." Delve into the main asset of a telephone stock swindler and you will find it to be a marvelously confidence-inspiring telephone "personality." And whereas we all think we know what an Italian or a Swede looks like, it is the sad fact that when a group of Nebraska students sought to match faces and nationalities of 15 European countries, they were scored wrong in 93 percent of the identifications. Finally, for all the fact that horn-rimmed glasses have now become the standard television sign of an "intellectual," optometrists know that the main thing that distinguishes people with glasses is just bad eyes.

(5) Stereotypes are a kind of gossip about the world, a gossip that makes us prejudge people before we ever lay eyes on them. Hence, it is not surprising that stereotypes have something to do with the dark world of prejudice. Explore most prejudices (note that the word means prejudgment) and you will find a cruel stereotype at the core of each one.

(6) For it is the extraordinary fact that once we have typecast the world, we tend to see people in terms of our standardized pictures. In another demonstration of the power of stereotypes to affect our vision, a number of Columbia and Barnard students were shown 30 photographs of pretty but unidentified girls, and asked to rate each in terms of "general liking," "intelligence," "beauty," and so on. Two months later, the same group were shown the same photographs, this time with fictitious Irish, Italian, Jewish, and "American" names attached to the pictures. Right away, the ratings changed. Faces which were now seen as representing a national group went down in looks and still farther down in likability, while the "American" girls suddenly looked decidedly prettier and nicer.

(7) Why is it that we stereotype the world in such irrational and harmful fashion? In part, we begin to typecast people in our childhood years. Early in life, as every parent whose child has watched a TV Western knows, we learn to spot the Good Guys from the Bad Guys. Some years ago, a social psychologist showed very clearly how powerful these stereotypes of childhood vision are. He secretly asked the most popular youngsters in an elementary school to make errors in their morning gym exercises. After-

wards, he asked the class if anyone had noticed any mistakes during gym period. Oh, yes, said the children. But it was the *unpopular* members of the class—the "bad guys"—they remembered as being out of step.

(8) We not only grow up with standardized pictures forming inside of us, but as grown-ups, we are constantly having them thrust upon us. Some of them, like the half-joking, half-serious stereotypes of mothers-in-law, or country yokels, or psychiatrists, are drummed into us by the stock jokes we hear and repeat. In fact, without such stereotypes, there would be a lot fewer jokes. Still other stereotypes are perpetuated by the advertisements we read, the movies we see, the books we read.

(9) And finally, we tend to stereotype because it helps us make sense out of a highly confusing world, a world which William James once described as "one great, blooming, buzzing confusion." It is a curious fact that if we don't *know* what we're looking at, we are often quite literally unable to *see* what we're looking at. People who recover their sight after a lifetime of blindness actually cannot at first tell a triangle from a square. A visitor to a factory sees only noisy chaos where the superintendent sees a perfectly synchronized flow of work. As Walter Lippman has said, "For the most part, we do not first see, and then define; we define first, and then we see."

(10) Stereotypes are one way in which we "define" the world in order to see it. They classify the infinite variety of human beings into a convenient handful of "types" towards whom we learn to act in a stereotyped fashion. Life would be a wearing process if we had to start from scratch with each and every human contact. Stereotypes economize on our mental effort by covering up the blooming, buzzing confusion with big recognizable cut-outs. They save us the "trouble" of finding out what the world is like—they give it its accustomed look.

(11) Thus, the trouble is that stereotypes make us mentally lazy. As S. I. Hayakawa, the authority on semantics, has written: "The danger of stereotypes lies not in their existence, but in the fact that they become for all people some of the time, and for some people all the time, *substitutes for observation.*" Worse yet, stereotypes get in the way of our judgment, even when we do observe the world. Someone who has formed rigid preconceptions of Latins as "excitable," or all teenagers as "wild," doesn't alter his point of view when he meets a calm and deliberate Genoese, or a serious-minded high school student. He brushes them aside as "exceptions that prove the rule." And, of course, if he meets someone true to type, he stands triumphantly vindicated. "They're all like that," he proclaims, having encountered an excited Latin, an ill-behaved adolescent.

(12) Hence, quite aside from the injustice which stereotypes do to others, they impoverish ourselves. A person who lumps the world into simple categories, who typecasts all labor leaders as "racketeers," all

businessmen as "reactionaries," all Harvard men as "snobs," and all French-men as "sexy," is in danger of becoming a stereotype himself. He loses his capacity to be himself—which is to say, to see the world in his own absolutely <u>unique</u>, <u>inimitable</u>, and independent fashion.

(13) Instead, he votes for the man who fits his standardized picture of what a candidate "should" look like or sound like, buys the goods that someone in his "situation" in life "should" own, lives the life that others define for him. The mark of the stereotyping person is that he never surprises us, that we do indeed have him "typed." And no one fits this <u>strait-jacket</u> so perfectly as someone whose opinions about *other people* are fixed and <u>inflexible</u>.

(14) Impoverishing as they are, stereotypes are not easy to get rid of. The world we typecast may be no better than a Grade B movie, but at least we know what to expect of our stock characters. When we let them act for themselves in the strangely unpredictable way that people do act, who knows but that many of our fondest <u>convictions</u> will be proved wrong?

(15) Nor do we suddenly drop our standardized pictures for a blind-ing vision of the Truth. Sharp swings of ideas about people often just substitute one stereotype for another. The true process of change is a slow one that adds bits and pieces of reality to the pictures in our heads, until gradually they take on some of the <u>blurriness</u> of life itself. Little by little, we learn not that Jews and Negroes and Catholics and Puerto Ricans are "just like everybody else"—for that, too, is a stereotype—but that each and every one of them is unique, special, different, and individual. Often we do not even know that we have let a stereotype <u>lapse</u> until we hear someone saying, "all so-and-so's are like such-and-such," and we hear ourselves saying, "Well—maybe."

(16) Can we speed the process along? Of course we can.

(17) First, we can become *aware* of the standardized pictures in our heads, in other peoples' heads, in the world around us.

(18) Second, we can become suspicious of all judgments that we allow exceptions to "prove." There is no more <u>chastening</u> thought than that in the vast intellectual adventure of science, it takes but one tiny exception to <u>topple</u> a whole edifice of ideas.

(19) Third, we can learn to be <u>chary</u> of generalizations about people. As F. Scott Fitzgerald once wrote: "Begin with an individual, and before you know it you have created a type; begin with a type, and you find you have created—nothing."

(20) Most of the time, when we typecast the world, we are not in fact generalizing about people at all. We are only revealing the embarrassing facts about the pictures that hang in the <u>gallery</u> of stereotypes in our own heads.

Vocabulary Gloss

The definitions given here are intended to aid your comprehension. Numbers in parentheses refer to the paragraphs in which the words appear. (Since you are not expected to understand each word in the preceding reading passage, not all the words you do not know are glossed. You will need to guess the meaning of other words you do not understand.)

to warp	(title)	(v.)	twist or bend out of shape; distort
apt	(1)	(adj.)	likely
swarthy	(4)	(adj.)	having dark skin (used to describe some Caucasians)
testimony	(4)	(n.)	statement (often made in court) by a witness
criminologist	(4)	(n.)	person who studies criminal behavior
to delve into	(4)	(v.)	dig deeply, as in study
asset	(4)	(n.)	anything valuable or useful
swindler	(4)	(n.)	someone who cheats people out of money
optometrist	(4)	(n.)	a doctor who tests vision and prescribes glasses
gossip	(5)	(n.)	careless talk about other people and their private affairs, often involving rumors
prejudice	(5)	(n.)	hatred or negative feelings toward a particular group, without logic or knowledge or examination of facts
core	(5)	(n.)	center; innermost or most important part of something
to typecast	(6)	(v.)	to put someone in a role based on physical characteristics
irrational	(7)	(adj.)	not logical
out of step	(7)	(adj.)	unusual; not following the group behavior
to thrust	(8)	(v.)	to push with force
to perpetuate	(8)	(v.)	to make something exist for a longer time
chaos	(9)	(n.)	a condition or place of total disorder or confusion

synchronized	(9)	(adj.)	describing something whose parts operate together with perfect timing
infinite	(10)	(adj.)	having no limits; beyond any known number
wearing	(10)	(adj.)	tiring; exhausting
to start from scratch	(10)	(v.)	to start from the beginning; to start anew
to economize	(10)	(v.)	to try to save resources, such as money, materials, or work
rigid	(11)	(adj.)	not flexible; fixed
preconception	(11)	(n.)	an opinion or idea formed in advance of actual knowledge
to alter	(11)	(v.)	to change
to brush something aside	(11)	(v.)	to ignore something because it is considered unimportant
vindicated	(11)	(adj.)	justified or supported
ill-behaved	(11)	(adj.)	poorly behaved; acting badly
adolescent	(11)	(n.)	a person in a period of development between puberty and maturity (often referring to young teenagers)
to impoverish	(12)	(v.)	to make poor; to take away natural strength
unique	(12)	(adj.)	special; one of a kind
inimitable	(12)	(adj.)	something that cannot be copied
straitjacket	(13)	(n.)	a long-sleeved jacketlike piece of clothing used to hold the arms tightly against the body in order to restrain a person; any tight restriction
inflexible	(13)	(adj.)	rigid; fixed; not bendable
conviction	(14)	(n.)	strongly held belief
blurriness	(15)	(n.)	the state of being unclear, indistinct in appearance
to lapse	(15)	(v.)	to be no longer in force because of disuse or the passage of time
chastening	(18)	(adj.)	moderating; restraining; describing something that makes one less extreme

to topple	(18)	(v.)	to make something fall over
chary	(19)	(adj.)	very cautious
gallery	(20)	(n.)	a building or hall in which artwork is shown

Comprehension Check

Fill in the blanks on the left with a "T" if the statement is true or an "F" if the statement is false. Write the number of a paragraph which includes information to support your answer if the answer is explicitly stated in the article.

1. _____ Most people have stereotypes about people's names. (¶ __)

2. _____ According to Heilbroner, stereotypes are related to prejudice. (¶ __)

3. _____ People's attitudes toward an individual can be affected by that individual's ethnicity. (Inference)

4. _____ Heilbroner thinks that we begin stereotyping as adults. (¶ __)

5. _____ Heilbroner suggests that jokes, advertisements, movies, and books perpetuate stereotypes. (¶ __)

6. _____ Heilbroner believes that it would be exhausting if we didn't have any stereotypes. (¶ __)

7. _____ According to Heilbroner, we use stereotypes in order to make sense of the confusing world. (¶ __)

8. _____ Stereotypes, according to Heilbroner, make people physically lazy. (¶ __)

9. _____ Hayakawa believes that stereotypes are in themselves dangerous. (¶ __)

10. _____ According to Heilbroner, stereotypes are dangerous because they keep us from judging our observations of the world accurately. (¶ __)

11. _____ Heilbroner believes stereotyping harms the stereotyper. (¶ __)

12. _____ Heilbroner suggests that people who stereotype become less independent and unique. (¶ __)

13. _____ Heilbroner says that people can get rid of stereotypes easily. (¶ __)

14. _____ According to Heilbroner, if we drop our stereotypes too suddenly, we will just substitute one stereotype for another.   (¶ ___)

15. _____ One way we can get rid of stereotypes more quickly is to become more aware of the generalizations we make, according to Heilbroner.   (¶ ___)

Interaction Activity

Work in groups of three to answer the following questions. Choose one member of the group to lead the discussion and keep it moving, one member to take notes on the discussion, and one member of the group to present your group's ideas to the class.

1. Heilbroner suggests that certain names for men and women carry different connotations, (e.g., some names bring up images of someone smart, other names bring up images of someone beautiful). Why do you think certain names get these positive or negative connotations?

2. Heilbroner says that we learn stereotypes early in our lives—from TV, from ads, from movies, from books. Discuss how "men" and "women" have been stereotyped in these media. Can you think of specific ads, movies, books, and TV programs which support your point?

3. Heilbroner says that stereotypes help us make sense out of a "highly confusing world." In what situations have stereotypes been helpful to you?

4. Look at the organization of "Don't Let Stereotypes Warp Your Judgment." Write in the paragraph numbers that apply.

¶ ___ to ¶ ___   Introduction
¶ ___   Definition of "stereotypes"
¶ ___ to ¶ ___   Causes of stereotypes
¶ ___ to ¶ ___   Problems of stereotypes
¶ ___ to ¶ ___   Getting rid of stereotypes

Vocabulary Acquisition

One way to learn vocabulary is to make a commitment to yourself to learn a certain number of words per week. In this chapter, you will use a certain form to learn words of your own choosing.

Your page will be divided into four columns. In the first column, you will list the word you want to learn. In the second column, you will copy the sentence in which you found the word. In the third column, you will copy a short dictionary definition of the word. In the fourth column, you will use the word in your own sentence.

Choose ten words that you would like to learn from "Don't Let Stereotypes Warp Your Judgment."

EXAMPLE

WORD	CONTEXT	DEFINITION	OWN SENTENCE
apt	Is a girl called Gloria <u>apt</u> to be better looking than one called Bertha?	likely	Athletes are <u>apt</u> to be healthier than non-athletes.

SHORT WRITING: RESPONDING TO IDEAS IN AN ARTICLE

Choose one idea from Heilbroner's article and react to it. Discuss this idea in relation to your own experiences and beliefs. Before writing your own reaction, read the peer writing samples and do the peer editing exercises which follow.

Peer Writing Sample

Read the following student's writing sample and discuss whether you have a similar or different reaction.

> *According to Heilbroner, many people behave the way they feel they should, rather than the way they think they should. They follow their unconscious minds rather than their analytical ones. As a result, they fall into the trap of stereotyping. They become lazy since they fail to closely observe those around them. They define others in terms of stereotypes and are unwittingly guided by these stereotypes. In contrast are those who examine life analytically. They observe those around them carefully and construct definitions of others. Their definitions are constantly changing depending on their observations, the situations in which they find themselves, and their experiences interacting with others. Clearly, observing others carefully requires more time and energy than most people have. Since most people are basically lazy, I believe that most people prejudge others before seeking to understand them. (R.P.)*

Peer Editing

1. The following student sample contains five errors involving passive versus active verb forms. Read the paragraph and correct the errors.

> A stereotype is a kind of image that set in our mind and causes us to prejudge people who we don't even know. People begin to stereotype others in their childhood. The environment in which children brought up has a critical impact on how children feel about people who are different from them. For instance, a person who grew up in Los Angeles, California probably is able to cope with different ethnic groups better than the person who grew up in an area that is not ethnically diverse. A friend of mine who is name Martha grew up interacting with individuals of diverse ethnic backgrounds. She rarely stereotypes. Unthinking individuals who stereotype others make erroneous generalizations about others. They have what is call a "one track mind." Their minds are never able to explore the whole world as long as stereotypes exist within themselves. In my opinion, the problem of stereotyping must be resolve. (M.N.)

2. In the following student sample, there are six errors involving noun forms. Read the sample and correct the errors.

> We should have pities on the person who is just a slave of stereotypes. When I was a child, I had a lot of curiosities about the world and individual. But now I lack the time to observe other closely. I hold many stereotypes. For example, if my friends wear glass and study a lot, I expect them to be "nerd." Stereotypes have affected my ability to distinguish right from wrong. (N.C.)

3. The following student sample contains seven errors of verb tense. (These words are underlined for you.) Read the sample and correct the errors.

> Sometimes the act of stereotyping is hidden and unrecognized. It is possible that people do not even realize that others are stereotyping them. I have experienced this situation when I first came to the United States in the fourth grade. I remembered that my classmates sometimes joke about my appearance and laugh at the way I talk, but I did not realize that they had stereotyped me because I am new to the United States. They think all foreigners talk funny. I was the target of their jokes. Later in life, I realized that my classmates had unfairly stereotyped me. (M.A.R.)

ADDITIONAL JOURNAL TOPICS

Your journal will continue on the topic of stereotyping. However, you may want to go into greater depth and focus specifically on issues raised in the readings in this module. Following are the suggested journal topics for "Don't Let Stereotypes Warp Your Judgment."

1. Why does Heilbroner believe that people stereotype other groups? Do you stereotype other groups? Which ones? Why?

2. Would Heilbroner's recommendations for getting rid of stereotypes work for you? Why or why not?

Reading Unit 3B

Desirée's Baby

Kate Chopin

This story, written by a nineteenth century American author, takes place in Louisiana during the days of slavery. At that time, there was a great deal of French influence in Louisiana so the names of the characters and some of the expressions they use are French. This particular story is a powerful one, showing how stereotypes and racism can harm everyone: the stereotyper and the stereotyped. Before reading, consider how a stereotyper can harm him or herself. Have you ever stereotyped someone and hurt yourself by doing that? Consider how the stereotyped person is harmed. Have you, yourself, ever been hurt by a stereotype? How?

(1) As the day was pleasant, Madame Valmondé drove over to L'Abri to see Desirée and the baby.

(2) It made her laugh to think of Desirée with a baby. Why, it seemed but yesterday that Desirée was little more than a baby herself when Monsieur in riding through the gateway of Valmondé had found her lying asleep in the shadow of the big stone pillar.

(3) The little one awoke in his arms and began to cry for "Dada." That was as much as she could do or say. Some people thought she might have strayed there of her own accord, for she was of the toddling age. The prevailing belief was that she had been purposely left by a party of Texans, whose canvas-covered wagon, late in the day, had crossed the ferry that Coton Mais kept, just below the plantation. In time Madame Valmondé abandoned every speculation but the one that Desirée had been sent to her by a beneficent Providence to be the child of her affection, seeing that she was without child of the flesh. For the girl grew to be beautiful and gentle, affectionate and sincere,—the idol of Valmondé.

(4) It was no wonder, when she stood one day against the stone pillar in whose shadow she had lain asleep, eighteen years before, that Armand Aubigny riding by and seeing her there, had fallen in love with her. That was the way all the Aubignys fell in love, as if struck by a pistol shot. The wonder was that he had not loved her before; for he had known her since his father brought him home from Paris, a boy of eight, after his mother died there. The passion that awoke in him that day, when he saw her at the gate, swept along like an avalanche, or like a prairie fire, or like any·thing that drives headlong over obstacles.

(5) Monsieur Valmondé grew practical and wanted things well consid·ered: that is, the girl's obscure origin. Armand looked into her eyes and did not care. He was reminded that she was nameless. What did it matter about a name when he could give her one of the oldest and proudest in Louisiana. They were married.

(6) Madame Valmondé had not seen Desirée and the baby for four weeks. When she reached L'Abri she shuddered at the first sight of it, as she always did. It was a sad looking place, which for many years had not known the gentle presence of a mistress, old Monsieur Aubigny having married and buried his wife in France, and she having loved her own land too well ever to leave it. The roof came down steep and black, reaching out beyond the wide galleries that encircled the yellow stuccoed house. Big solemn oaks grew close to it, and their thick-leaved, far-reaching branches shadowed it. Young Aubigny's rule was a strict one, too, and un·der it his negroes[1] had forgotten how to be gay, as they had been during the old master's easygoing and indulgent lifetime.

[1]Most Black Americans now prefer to be called "African Americans" or "Black

(7) The young mother was recovering slowly, and lay full length upon a couch. The baby was beside her, upon her arm, where he had fallen asleep, at her breast. The yellow nurse woman sat beside a window, fanning herself.

(8) Madame Valmondé bent her portly figure over Desirée and kissed her, holding her an instant tenderly in her arms. Then she turned to the child.

(9) "This is not the baby!" she exclaimed, in startled tones.

(10) "I knew you would be astonished," laughed Desirée, "at the way he has grown. Look at his legs, mamma, and his hands and fingernails—real fingernails. Zandrine had to cut them this morning. Isn't it true, Zandrine?"

(11) The woman bowed her turbaned head majestically, "Mais si,[2] Madame."

(12) "And the way he cries," went on Desirée, "is deafening. Armand heard him the other day as far away as La Blanche's[3] cabin."

(13) Madame Valmondé had never removed her eyes from the child. She lifted it and walked with it over to the window that was lightest. She scanned the baby narrowly, then looked as searchingly at Zandrine, whose face was turned to gaze across the fields.

(14) "Yes, the child has grown, has changed," said Madame Valmondé, slowly, as she replaced it beside its mother. "What does Armand say?"

(15) Desirée's face became suffused with a glow that was happiness itself.

(16) "Oh, Armand is the proudest father in the parish, I believe, chiefly because it is a boy, to bear his name; though he says not,—that he would have loved a girl as well. But I know it isn't true. I know he says that to please me. And mamma," she added, drawing Madame Valmondé's head down to her, and speaking in a whisper, "he hasn't punished one of them—not one of them—since baby is born. Even Negrillon, who pretended to have burnt his leg so he might rest from work—he only laughed, and said Negrillon was a great scamp. Oh, mamma, I'm so happy; it frightens me."

(17) What Desirée said was true. Marriage, and later the birth of his son had softened Armand Aubigny's nature greatly. This was what made the gentle Desirée so happy, for she loved him desperately. When he frowned she trembled, but loved him. When he smiled, she asked no greater blessing of God. But Armand's dark, handsome face had not often been disfigured by frowns since the day he fell in love with her.

Americans" or "Black" rather than "Negro." However, during the time period of this story, the word "Negro" was commonly used.

[2]Mais si: (French) Of course.

[3]La Blanche: (French) used as a nickname here; literally means "The White Woman."

(18) When the baby was about three months old, Desirée awoke one day to the conviction that there was something in the air menacing her peace. It was at first too subtle to grasp. It had only been a disquieting suggestion; an air of mystery among the blacks; unexpected visits from far-off neighbors who could hardly account for their coming. Then a strange, an awful change in her husband's manner, which she dared not ask him to explain. When he spoke to her, it was with averted eyes, from which the old love-light seemed to have gone out. He absented himself from home; and when there, avoided her presence and that of her child, without excuse. And the very spirit of Satan seemed suddenly to take hold of him in his dealings with the slaves. Desirée was miserable enough to die.

(19) She sat in her room, one hot afternoon, listlessly drawing through her fingers the strands of her long, silky brown hair that hung about her shoulders. The baby, half naked, lay asleep upon her own great mahogany bed. One of La Blanche's little quadroon[4] boys—half naked too—stood fanning the child slowly with a fan of peacock feathers. Desirée's eyes had been fixed absently and sadly upon the baby, while she was striving to penetrate the threatening mist that she felt closing about her. She looked from her child to the boy who stood beside him, and back again; over and over. "Ah!" It was a cry that she could not help; which she was not conscious of having uttered. The blood turned like ice in her veins, and a clammy moisture gathered upon her face.

(20) She tried to speak to the little quadroon boy; but no sound would come, at first. When he heard his name uttered, he looked up, and the mistress was pointing to the door. He laid aside the great, soft fan, and obediently stole away, over the polished floor on his bare tiptoes.

(21) She stayed motionless, with gaze riveted upon her child, and her face the picture of fright.

(22) Presently her husband entered the room, and without noticing her, went to a table and began to search among some papers which covered it.

(23) "Armand," she called to him, in a voice which must have stabbed him, if he was human. But he did not notice. "Armand," she said again. Then she rose and tottered towards him. "Armand," she panted once more, clutching his arm, "look at our child. What does it mean? Tell me."

(24) He coldly but gently loosened her fingers from about his arm and thrust the hand away from him. "Tell me what it means!" she cried despairingly.

(25) "It means," he answered lightly, "that the child is not white; it means that you are not white."

[4]Quadroon: a term used to describe a person who is one-quarter Black, particularly used in the race-conscious times of slavery.

(26) A quick conception of all that this <u>accusation</u> meant for her nerved her with unwonted courage to <u>deny</u> it. "It is a lie; it is not true, I am white! Look at my hair, it is brown; and my eyes are gray, Armand, you know they are gray. And my skin is fair," seizing his wrist. "Look at my hand; whiter than yours, Armand," she laughed <u>hysterically</u>.

(27) "As white as La Blanche's," he returned cruelly; and went away leaving her alone with their child.

(28) When she could hold a pen in her hand, she sent a despairing letter to Madame Valmondé.

(29) "My mother, they tell me I am not white. Armand has told me I am not white. For God's sake, tell them it is not true. You must know it is not true. I shall die. I must die. I cannot be so unhappy, and live."

(30) The answer that came was as brief:

> "My own Desirée: Come home to Valmondé; back to your mother who loves you. Come with your child."

(31) When the letter reached Desirée she went with it to her husband's study, and laid it open upon the desk before which he sat. She was like a stone image: silent, white, motionless after she placed it there.

(32) In silence he ran his cold eyes over the written words. He said nothing. "Shall I go, Armand?" she asked in tones sharp with agonized suspense.

(33) "Yes, go."

(34) "Do you want me to go?"

(35) "Yes, I want you to go."

(36) He thought Almighty God had dealt cruelly and unjustly with him; and felt, somehow, that he was <u>paying</u> Him back <u>in kind</u> when he stabbed thus into his wife's soul. Moreover he no longer loved her, because of the unconscious <u>injury</u> she had brought upon his home and his name.

(37) She turned away like one stunned by a blow, and walked slowly toward the door, hoping he would call her back.

(38) "Good-by, Armand," she moaned.

(39) He did not answer her. That was his last <u>blow</u> at fate.

(40) Desirée went in search of her child. Zandrine was pacing the somber gallery with it. She took the little one from the nurse's arms with no word of explanation, and descending the steps, walked away, under the live-oak branches.

(41) It was an October afternoon; the sun was just sinking. Out in the still fields, the negroes were picking cotton.

(42) Desirée had not changed the thin white garment nor the slippers which she wore. Her hair was uncovered and the sun's rays brought a golden gleam from its brown meshes. She did not take the broad, beaten road which

led to the far-off plantation of Valmondé. She walked across a deserted field, where the stubble bruised her tender feet, so delicately shod, and tore her thin gown to shreds.

(43) She disappeared among the reeds and willows that grew thick along the banks of the deep sluggish bayou⁵; and she did not come back again.

(44) Some weeks later there was a curious scene enacted at L'Abri. In the center of the smoothly swept back yard was a great <u>bonfire</u>. Armand Aubigny sat in the wide hallway that commanded a view of the spectacle; and it was he who dealt out to a half dozen negroes the material which kept his fire ablaze.

(45) A graceful <u>cradle</u> was laid upon the <u>pyre</u>. Then there were silk gowns, and velvet and satin ones added to these; laces, too, and embroideries; bonnets and gloves.

(46) The last thing to go was a tiny bundle of letters; innocent little scribblings that Desirée had sent to him during the days of their espousal. There was the <u>remnant</u> of one back in the drawer from which he took them. But it was not Desirée's; it was part of an old letter from his mother to his father. He read it. She was thanking God for the blessing of her husband's love:

(47) "But, above all," she wrote, "night and day, I thank the good God for having so arranged our lives that our dear Armand will never know that his mother, who adores him, belongs to the race that is <u>cursed</u> with the brand of slavery."

Vocabulary Gloss

The definitions given here are intended to aid your comprehension. Numbers in parentheses refer to the paragraphs in which the words appear. (Since you are not expected to understand each word in the preceding reading passage, not all the words you do not know are glossed. You will need to guess the meaning of other words you do not understand.)

to stray	(3)	(v.)	to wander away
of her own accord	(3)	(adv. phrase)	of her own free will
to toddle	(3)	(v.)	to walk with short, unsteady steps, like a baby just learning to walk

⁵Bayou: a swamp-like body of water that stems from a lake or river (a term most commonly used in Louisiana).

prevailing	(3)	(adj.)	most common
plantation	(3)	(n.)	a large piece of land on which crops (such as tea, sugar, cotton) are grown
to abandon	(3)	(v.)	to leave completely and forever
speculation	(3)	(n.)	thoughts without facts to lead to a definite conclusion
Providence	(3)	(n.)	a special event showing God's care or the kindness of fate
idol	(3)	(n.)	an image worshipped as a god; a person or thing greatly loved and admired
passion	(4)	(n.)	strong, deep, often uncontrollable feeling
avalanche	(4)	(n.)	a large mass of snow and ice crashing down the side of a mountain
obstacle	(4)	(n.)	something which stands in the way and prevents action or success
obscure	(5)	(adj.)	vague; unclear
origin	(5)	(n.)	starting point; parents and conditions of early life
to shudder	(6)	(v.)	to shake uncontrollably for a moment, as from fear or strong dislike; to tremble
startled	(9)	(adj.)	very surprised; shocked
to scan	(13)	(v.)	to examine closely, especially in search of something; to look something over
scamp	(16)	(n.)	a trouble-making but usually playful child
to frown	(17)	(v.)	to draw the eyebrows together especially in anger or effort, or to show disapproval, causing lines to appear on the forehead
conviction	(18)	(n.)	strong and firm belief
to menace	(18)	(v.)	to threaten
subtle	(18)	(adj.)	hardly noticeable; indirect; hard to see
disquieting	(18)	(adj.)	anxiety-producing

to account for something	(18)	(v.)	to explain the reason for an event
averted	(18)	(adj.)	turned away (as one's eyes, or one's thoughts)
to strive	(19)	(v.)	to struggle hard for something
to penetrate	(19)	(v.)	to enter, cut, or force a way (into or through something)
mist	(19)	(n.)	thick fog; (an area of) clouds of very small drops of water floating in the air, near or reaching to the ground
to utter	(19)	(v.)	to speak (especially for a short time, saying a word or two)
to steal away	(20)	(v.)	to move quietly and secretly
gaze	(21)	(n.)	a steady, fixed look
to stab	(23)	(v.)	to strike forcefully with a pointed weapon (such as a knife)
accusation	(26)	(n.)	a charge of doing wrong
to deny	(26)	(v.)	to declare something untrue
hysterically	(26)	(adv.)	wildly, in an uncontrolled manner
pay . . . in kind	(36)	(v.)	to pay someone back with the same treatment
injury	(36)	(n.)	damage to a living thing; harm
blow	(39)	(n.)	a hard strike with the open or closed hand, a weapon, etc.
bonfire	(44)	(n.)	a large fire built in the open air
cradle	(45)	(n.)	a small bed for a baby, especially one that can be moved gently from side to side
pyre	(45)	(n.)	a mass of wood (usually used for the ceremonial burning of a dead body)
remnant	(46)	(n.)	a part that remains
to be cursed with something	(47)	(v.)	to be the owner or receiver of something which causes misfortune, suffering, or harm

Comprehension Check

Fill in the blanks on the left with a "T" if the statement is true or an "F" if the statement is false. Write the number of a paragraph which includes information to support your answer if the answer is explicitly stated in the story.

1. _____   Madame Valmondé gave birth to Desirée.   (¶ ___)

2. _____   Desirée was found by Monsieur Valmondé when she was a toddler.   (¶ ___)

3. _____   Madame Valmondé loved Desirée as a daughter because she had no children of her own.   (¶ ___)

4. _____   Desirée and Armand met for the first time when Desirée was eighteen.   (¶ ___)

5. _____   Armand fell in love instantly on the day he saw Desirée at the pillar.   (¶ ___)

6. _____   Armand had spent his whole life at L'Abri.   (¶ ___)

7. _____   Monsieur Valmondé and Armand were both worried before the wedding about Desirée's obscure origins.   (¶ ___)

8. _____   L'Abri had a cheerful appearance.   (¶ ___)

9. _____   Armand Aubigny had treated the slaves on his plantation worse than his father had.   (¶ ___)

10. _____   When Madame Valmondé saw the baby, she was startled because it had such long fingernails. (Inference)

11. _____   Armand was happy with the baby when it was first born.   (¶ ___)

12. _____   Desirée felt a change for the worse in her household when the baby was three months old.   (¶ ___)

13. _____   Armand's behavior toward the slaves on his plantation remained the same, regardless of the events in his life.   (¶ ___)

14. _____   Desirée first realized that her child looked part Black when she compared him to a little boy who was one-quarter Black.   (¶ ___)

15. _____   Armand believed that Desirée was part Black.   (¶ ___)

16. _____ When Desirée wrote her mother, her mother responded by saying that it was impossible for Desirée to be part Black.   (¶ ___)

17. _____ Armand was self-centered. (Inference)

18. _____ Desirée returned to Valmondé after she left Armand. (Inference)

19. _____ While Armand was burning Desirée's and the baby's possessions, he found a letter from his own mother to his own father.   (¶ ___)

20. _____ It was Armand who was part Black. (Inference)

Interaction Activity

Work in small groups to discuss the following questions.

1. At the end of the story there is a surprise "twist." How did the author make you think that Desirée was the one who was part Black? What clues did you miss that might have "tipped you off" that Armand was the one who was part Black?

2. This story takes place at a time when slavery existed in the United States. How do stereotypes relate to inhumane systems such as slavery?

Vocabulary Acquisition

One way to learn vocabulary is to make a commitment to yourself to learn a certain number of words per week. In this chapter, you will use a certain form to learn words of your own choosing.

Your page will be divided into four columns. In the first column, you will list the word you want to learn. In the second column, you will copy the sentence in which you found the word. In the third column, you will copy a short dictionary definition of the word. In the fourth column, you will use the word in your own sentence.

Choose ten words that you would like to learn from "Desirée's Baby."

EXAMPLE

WORD	CONTEXT	DEFINITION	OWN SENTENCE
to stray	Some people thought that she might have strayed there of her own accord, for she was of a toddling age.	to wander	Don't stray too far from the crowd; you may get lost.

SHORT WRITING: VARYING THE POINT OF VIEW

Write an account of this event from the point of view of Zandrine, La Blanche, or the "quadroon" boy. Before writing your account, read the peer writing sample and do the peer editing exercise which follows.

Peer Writing Sample

Read the following student sample and decide whether you think it could be a realistic portrayal of La Blanche's perspective.

God works in amazing ways. The master of this plantation has always given us a hard time (even though he was a bit nicer when the baby was born). He never questioned his right to own slaves or to control us. He never questioned why the color of our skin should make a difference. He simply looked down on us because of our black skin.

Actually, our skin had nothing to do with it. My skin is as light as the skin of many white people. (There's a lot of white blood among us slaves because our masters and other white men frequently "used" our bodies for their own pleasure.)

Now, Monsieur Aubigny is discovering that he is part negro—one-half negro in fact. (That may even be more than me!) I wonder how he is going to handle himself now. How is he going to deal with his new image of himself? How is he going to treat us?

He is going to have to do a lot of rethinking of his old ideas. Perhaps, he'll finally realize that the individual, not the skin color, is what matters. (R.N.)

Peer Editing

The following student sample contains five errors demonstrating confusion between the simple and continuous tenses. Read the sample and correct the errors.

> *I have been seeing so much in my life. The events of the past few months have been one of the strangest of all. Yesterday, Desirée, my mistress, was taking the baby from me suddenly and walked away from this plantation. She was seeming to be in a state of shock; she was crying.*
>
> *I have been knowing for a long time about the baby. However, Desirée, the wife of the plantation owner, wasn't figuring it out until yesterday. Poor woman. I hear her husband was very cruel to her.*
>
> *It seems as if race matters to everyone around here. To me, a baby is a baby; a human being is a human being. Who cares about the color? (C.P.)*

SHORT WRITING: RESPONDING AS A CHARACTER

Write Armand's journal entry for that last day. Before writing the entry, read the peer writing samples and do the peer editing exercises which follow.

Peer Writing Samples

Read the following student samples of Armand's journal entry for that last day and discuss whether you think Armand would react in these ways.

> 1. *This cannot be! How can God be so cruel to me? What have I done to deserve this? I'm white. Yes, I'm white. I read that letter. This is only a dream. Maybe if I pinch myself, I'll wake up from this dreadful nightmare.*

Maybe I didn't pinch myself hard enough. Once more, just once more and I'll return to reality. I think I want to scream.

Okay, be calm now, Armand. So what if you're negro? You're wealthy. You have enough money to last the rest of your lifetime.

Yeah, but what about my name in society? I'll forever be known as a negro. I'll be stepped on and discriminated against. I won't stand for it. I can't stand it. NO!!

So what am I going to do now? What do I want to do now? All my servants know I belong to their race. Soon word will spread.

STOP IT!!!

If I stop, what am I going to do? Shut myself up in this luxurious bedroom forever? I can't do that.

Okay, okay, okay. Let me think this over rationally. I can overcome this disastrous nightmare.

First of all, I have to believe that it's not a nightmare. The situation is not going to go away.

Okay. It's not going to be easy, but I can handle it. I'm black. This is not a nightmare.

Next, I've got to clean myself up and go out to look for my wife. No matter what price I have to pay, I have to find her. I was wild with anger before, but my shame has tamed me. I must explain to Desirée that I am responsible for her grief. She will understand the situation if I tell her. I can't let my wife and child leave me. I'll go quickly and I won't return as narrow-minded as before. (S.R.)

2. *I remember all those times that I treated slaves so badly. I realize now that I have been discriminating against my own race. I never thought that I could be one of them. I still cannot believe that I belong to the race which I hate the most. Why did I have to find that letter and discover my past? Why couldn't God just leave me alone?*

Now that I have found out who I really am, I feel so miserable about my life. I looked down upon negros because I thought I was superior to them, but not anymore. I have become part of the so-called inferior group of people. How much more does God want me to suffer? I just cannot believe what is happening to me.

What will other people think of me when they discover my negro origin? Those blacks that I have been

discriminating against are going to laugh at me when
they find out about my past.
And what about Desirée? (J.E.)

Peer Editing

1. The following student sample contains four subject–verb agreement errors. Read the sample and correct the errors.

    Why do the world treat me so cruelly? I have driven
    my wife and child away. Our happy family have been
    broken apart, and I have caused this devastation. I am no
    better than my field workers who labors all day in the hot
    sun. The color of our baby have come from me, not my wife.
    (X.P.)

2. The following student sample contains five preposition errors. (These are underlined.) Read the sample and correct the errors.

    How could I blame it <u>to</u> my poor innocent baby? I
    discriminated _____ blacks all my life. When I look back
    _____ the time when the baby was born, I realize that those
    days were the best in my life. I feel guilty that Desirée and
    the baby are gone. I wish I could see my wife again so I
    could apologize _____ her. I am so ashamed <u>to</u> myself.
    (R.P.)

ADDITIONAL JOURNAL TOPIC

Your journal will continue on the topic of stereotyping. However, you may want to go into greater depth and focus specifically on issues raised in the readings in this module. Following is the suggested journal topic for "Desirée's Baby."

> *Discuss how stereotypes harmed all the characters in the*
> *story. Who were the victims of the stereotypes—that is, were*
> *the members of the stereotyped groups the only victims or*
> *were the stereotypers (the people who made the stereotype)*
> *also victimized? Support your answer.*

Reading Unit 3C

Graduation
Maya Angelou

**Maya Angelou, an African American, is well-known for her autobiographi-
cal writings. The following abridged excerpt is from her book about her
childhood years in Stamps, Arkansas (in the southern part of the U.S.) in
the 1940s. This particular story is about a graduation ceremony which was
almost ruined by stereotypes. Before reading this story, you may want to
think about your own graduation experiences. How did you feel? How did
others treat you? What happened on the day of your graduation?**

(1) The children in Stamps trembled visibly with anticipation. Some
adults were excited too, but to be certain the whole young population had
come down with graduation epidemic. Large classes were graduating from
both the grammar school and the high school. Even those who were years
removed from their own day of glorious release were anxious to help with
preparations. The graduating classes themselves were the nobility. Like
travelers with exotic destinations on their minds, the graduates were remark-
ably forgetful. They came to school without their books, or tablets or even
pencils. Volunteers fell over themselves to secure replacements for the
missing equipment. When accepted, the willing workers might or might
not be thanked, and it was of no importance to the pregraduation rites.

Even teachers were respectful of the now quiet and aging seniors, and tended to speak to them, if not as equals, as beings only slightly lower than themselves.

(2) Unlike the white high school, Lafayette County Training School distinguished itself by having neither lawn, nor hedges, nor tennis court, nor climbing ivy. Its two buildings (main classrooms, the grade school and home economics) were set on a dirt hill with no fence to limit either its boundaries or those of bordering farms. There was a large expanse to the left of the school which was used alternatively as a baseball diamond or basketball court. Rusty hoops on swaying poles represented the permanent recreation equipment.

(3) Over this rocky area relieved by a few shady tall persimmon trees the graduating class walked. The girls often held hands and no longer bothered to speak to the lower students. There was a sadness about them, as if this old world was not their home and they <u>were bound for</u> higher ground. The boys, on the other hand, had become more friendly, more outgoing. A decided change from the closed attitude they projected while studying for finals. Now they seemed not ready to give up the old school, the familiar paths and classrooms. Only a small percentage would be continuing on to college—one of the South's A & M (agricultural and mechanical) schools, which trained Negro[1] youths to be carpenters, farmers, handymen, masons, maids, cooks, and baby nurses. Their future rode heavily on their shoulders, and blinded them to the collective joy that had pervaded the lives of the boys and girls in the grammar school graduating class.

(4) Parents who could afford it had ordered new shoes and ready-made clothes for themselves. They also engaged the best <u>seamstresses</u> to make the floating graduating dresses and to cut down <u>secondhand</u> pants which would be pressed to a military slickness for the important event.

(5) Oh, it was important, all right. Whitefolks would attend the ceremony, and two or three would speak of God and home, and the Southern way of life, and Mrs. Parsons, the principal's wife, would play the graduation march while the lower-grade graduates paraded down the aisles and took their seats below the platform. The high school seniors would wait in empty classrooms to make their dramatic entrance.

(6) I was the person of the moment. The center.

(7) My class was wearing butter-yellow dresses. I was going to be lovely. A walking model of all the various styles of fine hand sewing and it didn't worry me that I was only twelve years old and merely graduating from the

[1]Most Black Americans now prefer to be called "African Americans" or "Black Americans" or "Black" rather than "Negro." However, when Angelou wrote her book, and while she was growing up, "Negro" was commonly used.

eighth grade. Besides, many teachers in Arkansas Negro schools had only that diploma and were licensed to impart wisdom.

(8) As a member of the winning team (the graduating class of 1940) I had outdistanced unpleasant sensations by miles. I was headed for the freedom of open fields.

(9) My work alone had awarded me a top place and I was going to be one of the first called in the graduating ceremonies. On the classroom blackboard, as well as on the bulletin board in the auditorium, there were blue stars and white stars and red stars. No absences, no tardinesses, and my academic work was among the best of the year. I had memorized the Presidents of the United States from Washington to Roosevelt in chrono-logical as well as alphabetical order.

(10) Louise and I had rehearsed the exercises until we tired out ourselves. Henry Reed was class valedictorian. He was a small, very black boy with hooded eyes, a long, broad nose and an oddly shaped head. I had admired him for years because each term he and I vied for the best grades in our class. Most often he bested me, but instead of being disappointed I was pleased that we shared top places between us. Like many Southern Black children, he lived with his grandmother, who was as strict as Momma and as kind as she knew how to be. He was courteous, respectful, and soft-spoken to elders, but on the playground he chose to play the roughest games. I admired him. Anyone, I reckoned, sufficiently afraid or sufficiently dull could be polite. But to be able to operate at a top level with both adults and children was admirable.

(11) His valedictory speech was entitled "To Be or Not to Be." The rigid tenth-grade teacher had helped him write it. He'd been working on the dramatic stresses for months.

(12) Among Negroes the tradition was to give presents to children going only from one grade to another. How much more important this was when the person was graduating at the top of the class. Uncle Willie and Momma had sent away for a Mickey Mouse watch like Bailey's.[2] Louise gave me four embroidered handkerchiefs. Mrs. Sneed, the minister's wife, made me an undershirt to wear for graduation, and nearly every customer gave me a nickel or maybe even a dime with the instruction "Keep on moving to higher ground," or some such encouragement.

(13) Amazingly the great day finally dawned and I was out of bed before I knew it. I threw open the back door to see it more clearly, but Momma said, "Sister, come away from that door and put your robe on."

(14) I hoped the memory of that morning would never leave me. In my robe and barefoot in the backyard, I gave myself up to the gentle warmth

---

[2]Bailey is Marguerite's brother.

and thanked God that no matter what evil I had done in my life He had allowed me to live to see this day.

(15) Bailey came out in his robe and gave me a box wrapped in Christmas paper. He said he had saved his money for months to pay for it. It felt like a box of chocolates, but I knew Bailey wouldn't save money to buy candy when we had all we could want under our noses.

(16) He was as proud of the gift as I. It was a soft-leather-bound copy of a collection of poems by Edgar Allan Poe, or, as Bailey and I called him, "Eap." I turned to "Annabel Lee" and we walked up and down the garden rows, the cool dirt between our toes, reciting the beautifully sad lines.

(17) Momma made a Sunday breakfast although it was only Friday. After we finished the blessing, I opened my eyes to find the watch on my plate. It was a dream of a day. Everything went smoothly and to my credit. I didn't have to be reminded or scolded for anything. I was too <u>jittery</u> to attend to <u>chores</u>, so Bailey volunteered to do all before his bath.

(18) Days before, we had made a sign for the store, and as we turned out the lights Momma hung the cardboard over the doorknob. It read clearly: CLOSED. GRADUATION.

(19) My dress fitted perfectly and everyone said that I looked like a sunbeam in it. On the hill, going toward the school, Bailey walked behind with Uncle Willie.

(20) The school blazed without <u>gaiety</u>. The windows seemed cold and unfriendly from the lower hill. A sense of <u>ill-fated</u> timing crept over me, and if Momma hadn't reached for my hand I would have drifted back to Bailey and Uncle Willie, and possibly beyond. She made a few slow jokes about <u>my feet getting cold</u>, and tugged me along to the now-strange building.

(21) Around the front steps, <u>assurance</u> came back. There were my fellow "greats," the graduating class. Hair brushed back, legs oiled, new dresses and pressed pleats, fresh pocket handkerchiefs and little handbags, all homesewn. I joined my comrades and didn't even see my family go in to find seats in the crowded auditorium.

(22) The school band struck up a march and all classes filed in as had been <u>rehearsed</u>. We stood in front of our seats, as assigned, and on a signal from the choir director, we sat. No sooner had this been accomplished than the band started to play the national anthem. We rose again and sang the song, after which we recited the pledge of allegiance. We remained standing for a brief minute before the choir director and the principal signaled to us, rather <u>desperately</u> I thought, to take our seats. The command was so unusual that our carefully rehearsed and smooth-running machine was thrown off. For a full minute we fumbled for our chairs and bumped into each other awkwardly. Habits change or solidify under

pressure, so in our state of nervous tension we had been ready to follow our usual assembly pattern: the American national anthem, then the pledge of allegiance, then the song every Black person I knew called the Negro National Anthem. All done in the same key, with the same passion and most often standing on the same foot.

(23) Finding my seat at last, I was overcome with a presentiment of worse things to come. Something unrehearsed, unplanned, was going to happen, and we were going to be made to look bad. I distinctly remember being explicit in the choice of pronoun. It was "we," the graduating class, the unit, that concerned me then.

(24) The principal welcomed "parents and friends" and asked the Baptist minister to lead us in prayer. His invocation was brief and punchy, and for a second I thought we were getting on the high road to right action. When the principal came back to the dais, however, his voice had changed. It had not been in my plan to listen to him, but my curiosity was piqued and I straightened up to give him my attention.

(25) He was talking about Booker T. Washington, our "late great leader." Then he said a few vague things about friendship and the friendship of kindly people to those less fortunate than themselves. With that his voice nearly faded away. Like a river diminishing to a stream and then to a trickle. But he cleared his throat and said, "Our speaker tonight, who is also our friend, came from Texarkana to deliver the commencement address, but due to the irregularity of the train schedule, he's going to, as they say, 'speak and run.' " He said that we understood and wanted the man to know that we were most grateful for the time he was able to give us and then something about how we were willing always to adjust to another's program, and without more ado—"I give you Mr. Edward Donleavy."

(26) Donleavy looked at the audience once (on reflection, I'm sure that he only wanted to reassure himself that we were really there), adjusted his glasses and began to read from a sheaf of papers.

(27) He was glad "to be here and to see the work going on just as it was in the other schools."

(28) He told us of the wonderful changes we children in Stamps had in store. The Central School (naturally, the white school was Central) had already been granted improvements that would be in use in the fall. A well-known artist was coming from Little Rock to teach art to them. They were going to have the newest microscopes and chemistry equipment in their laboratory. Mr. Donleavy didn't leave us long in the dark over who made these improvements available to Central High. Nor were we to be ignored in the general betterment scheme he had in mind.

(29) He said that he had pointed out to people at a very high level that one of the first-line football tacklers at Arkansas Agricultural and Mechanical College had graduated from good old Lafayette County Training School.

(30) He went on to praise us. He went on to say how he had bragged that "one of the best basketball players at Fisk sank his first ball right here at Lafayette County Training School."

(31) The white kids were going to have a chance to become Galileos and Madame Curies and Edisons and Gauguins[3], and our boys (the girls weren't even in on it) would try to be Jesse Owenses and Joe Louises.[4]

(32) Owens and the Brown Bomber[5] were great heroes in our world, but what school official had the right to decide that those two men must be our only heroes? Who decided that for Henry Reed to become a scientist he had to work like George Washington Carver, as a bootblack, to buy a lousy microscope?.

(33) The man's dead words fell like bricks around the auditorium and too many settled in my belly. Constrained by hard-learned manners, I couldn't look behind me, but to my left and right, the proud graduating class of 1940 had dropped their heads. Every girl in my row had found something new to do with her handkerchief. Some folded the tiny squares into love knots, some into triangles, but most were wadding them, then pressing them flat on their yellow laps.

(34) On the dais, Professor Parsons sat, a sculptor's reject, rigid. His large, heavy body seemed devoid of will or willingness, and his eyes said he was no longer with us. The other teachers examined the flag (which was draped stage right) or their notes, or the windows which opened on our now-famous playing diamond.

(35) Graduation, the hush-hush magic time of frills and gifts and congratulations and diplomas, was finished for me before my name was called. The accomplishment was nothing. The meticulous maps, drawn in three colors of ink, learning and spelling decasyllabic words, memorizing *The Rape of Lucrece*[6]—it was for nothing. Donleavy had exposed us.

(36) We were maids and farmers, handymen and washerwomen, and anything higher that we aspired to was farcical and presumptuous.

[3]Galileo, Madame Curie, and Edison were white scientists. Gauguin was a white artist.
[4]Jesse Owens and Joe Louis were Black sports figures.
[5]The Brown Bomber was a nickname for Joe Louis.
[6]*The Rape of Lucrece* is a poem with 1,855 lines by Shakespeare.

(37) Then I wished that Gabriel Prosser and Nat Turner[7] had killed all whitefolks in their beds and that Abraham Lincoln had been assassinated before the signing of the Emancipation Proclamation,[8] and that Harriet Tubman[9] had been killed by that blow on her head and Christopher Columbus had drowned on the *Santa Maria*.

(38) It was awful to be a Negro and have no control over my life. It was brutal to be young and already trained to sit quietly and listen to charges brought against my color with no chance of defense. We should all be dead. I thought I should like to see us all dead, one on top of the other. A pyramid of flesh with the whitefolks on the bottom, as the broad base, then the Indians with their silly tomahawks and teepees and wigwams and treaties, the Negroes with their mops and recipes and cotton sacks and spirituals sticking out of their mouths. The Dutch children should all stumble in their wooden shoes and break their necks. The French should choke to death on the Louisiana Purchase (1803) while silkworms ate all the Chinese with their stupid pigtails. As a species, we were an abomination. All of us.

(39) Donleavy was running for election, and assured our parents that if he won we could count on having the only colored paved playing field in that part of Arkansas. Also, we were bound to get some new equipment for the home economics building and the workshop.

(40) He finished and [a] tall white man who was never introduced joined him at the door. They left with the attitude that now they were off to something really important.

(41) The ugliness they left was palpable. An uninvited guest who wouldn't leave. The choir was summoned and sang a modern arrangement of "Onward, Christian Soldiers," with new words pertaining to graduates seeking their place in the world. But it didn't work. Elouise, the daughter of the Baptist minister, recited "Invictus,"[10] and I could have cried at the impertinence of "I am the master of my fate, I am the captain of my soul."

(42) My name had lost its ring of familiarity and I had to be nudged to go and receive my diploma. All my preparations had fled. I neither marched up to the stage like a conquering Amazon,[11] nor did I look in the audience for Bailey's nod of approval. Marguerite Johnson, I heard

---

[7]Gabriel Prosser and Nat Turner led slave rebellions in the early 1800s.

[8]The Emancipation Proclamation is the government document that declared all slaves to be free.

[9]Harriet Tubman led slaves to freedom on the "Underground Railroad."

[10]"Invictus" is a poem by William Ernest Henley, a nineteenth century poet.

[11]In Greek myth, the Amazons were a group of women known for their strength and warrior ability.

the name again, my honors were read, there were noises in the audience of appreciation, and I took my place on the stage as rehearsed.

(43) I thought about colors I hated: ecru, puce, lavender, beige, and black.

(44) There was shuffling and rustling around me, then Henry Reed was giving his valedictory address, "To Be or Not to Be." Hadn't he heard the whitefolks? We couldn't *be*, so the question was a waste of time. Henry's voice came out clear and strong. I feared to look at him. Hadn't he got the message? When the ceremony was over, I had to tell Henry Reed some things. That is, if I still cared.

(45) Henry had been a good student in elocution. His voice rose on tides of promise and fell on waves of warnings. To be a man, a doer, a builder, a leader, or to be a tool, an unfunny joke. I <u>marveled</u> that Henry could go through with the speech as if we had a choice.

(46) I had been listening and silently <u>rebutting</u> each sentence with my eyes closed; then there was a <u>hush</u>, which in an audience warns that something unplanned is happening. I looked up and saw Henry Reed, the conservative, the proper, the A student, turn his back to the audience and turn to us (the proud graduating class of 1940) and sing, nearly speaking,

> *"Lift ev'ry voice and sing*
> *'Till earth and heaven ring*
> *Ring with the harmonies of Liberty . . . "*

It was the poem written by James Weldon Johnson. It was the music composed by J. Rosamond Johnson. It was the Negro national anthem. Out of habit we were singing it.

(47) Our mothers and fathers stood in the dark hall and joined the hymn of encouragement. A kindergarten teacher led the small children onto the stage and they tried to follow:

> *"Stony the road we <u>trod</u>*
> *<u>Bitter</u> the <u>chastening rod</u>*
> *Felt in the days when hope, unborn, had died.*
> *Yet with a steady beat*
> *Have not our <u>weary</u> feet*
> *Come to the place for which our fathers sighed?"*

(48) Each child I knew had learned that song with his ABC's. But I personally had never heard it before. Never heard the words, despite the thousands of times I had sung them. Never thought they had anything to do with me.

(49) And now I heard, really for the first time:

"We have come over a way that with tears has been watered,
We have come, treading our path through the blood of the slaughtered."

(50) While echoes of the song shivered in the air, Henry Reed bowed his head, said "Thank you," and returned to his place in the line. The tears that slipped down many faces were not wiped away in shame.

(51) We were on top again. As always, again. We survived. The depths had been icy and dark, but now a bright sun spoke to our souls. I was no longer simply a member of the proud graduating class of 1940; I was a proud member of the wonderful, beautiful Negro race.

Vocabulary Gloss

The definitions given here are intended to aid your comprehension. Numbers in parentheses refer to the paragraphs in which the words appear. (Since you are not expected to understand each word in the preceding reading passage, not all the words you do not know are glossed. You will need to guess the meaning of other words you do not understand.)

to tremble	(1)	(v.)	to shake, as from fear or cold
anticipation	(1)	(n.)	excited expectation of a future event
epidemic	(1)	(n.)	an outbreak of a disease that spreads rapidly
nobility	(1)	(n.)	a class of people with higher status; ruling class
to be bound for somewhere	(3)	(v.)	to be heading toward somewhere; to be directed in a particular way
seamstress	(4)	(n.)	woman who sews
secondhand	(4)	(adj.)	previously used by another; not new
chronological	(9)	(adj.)	arranged in order of time of occurrence
valedictorian	(10)	(n.)	a student, usually the one receiving the highest academic honors, who delivers the farewell speech at the graduation ceremony
to vie for something	(10)	(v.)	to compete to reach or achieve something

jittery	(17)	(adj.)	nervous; shaking from anxiety or nervousness
chore	(17)	(n.)	routine or daily task
gaiety	(20)	(n.)	cheerfulness; joyfulness
ill-fated	(20)	(adj.)	marking or causing an unlucky future; likely to fail or to come to a bad end
to have cold feet	(20)	(idiom)	to become afraid and, for this reason, not complete an action
assurance	(21)	(n.)	self-confidence; a feeling of certainty
to rehearse	(22)	(v.)	to practice in preparation for a public performance
desperately	(22)	(adv.)	acting in a way showing hopelessness; done with a sense of urgency
presentiment	(23)	(n.)	a sense of something about to occur; a feeling about something before it occurs
late	(25)	(adj.)	dead, often recently dead
fortunate	(25)	(adj.)	lucky
to fade	(25)	(v.)	to lose strength, brightness, or loudness gradually; to disappear slowly
grateful	(25)	(adj.)	thankful
reflection	(26)	(n.)	consideration; reexamination
to be/have in store	(28)	(v.)	to have in one's future
to leave in the dark	(28)	(v.)	to keep a secret or knowledge from
bootblack	(32)	(n.)	someone who shines shoes as a job
rigid	(34)	(adj.)	fixed; not flexible; not moving
devoid	(34)	(adj.)	empty; completely lacking
to expose	(35)	(v.)	to reveal the true nature of someone or something
to aspire	(36)	(v.)	to desire strongly; to hope for; to aim toward a goal

farcical	(36)	(adj.)	ridiculous; like a farce (a show in which the improbability of plot and characters creates a humorous effect)
presumptuous	(36)	(adj.)	overly confident; arrogant
to assassinate	(37)	(v.)	to murder, usually an important person
brutal	(38)	(adj.)	cruel; harsh
charge	(38)	(n.)	accusation; words suggesting someone's wrongdoing
defense	(38)	(n.)	words in support or justification of something or someone
species	(38)	(n.)	a biological term defining a specific classification of organisms; a group of living things
abomination	(38)	(n.)	something that brings about great dislike or disgust
palpable	(41)	(adj.)	capable of being touched or felt; obvious
impertinence	(41)	(n.)	irrelevance; something not related to the matter at hand
fate	(41)	(n.)	that which will happen to someone in the future
to marvel	(45)	(v.)	to be amazed
to rebut	(46)	(v.)	to present opposing evidence or arguments
hush	(46)	(n.)	quiet, silence or stillness, especially after noise
to tread ("trod" = past tense)	(47)	(v.)	to walk on, under or along
bitter	(47)	(adj.)	harsh; severe
chastening	(47)	(adj.)	describing something which is used to punish, either morally or physically
rod	(47)	(n.)	a short thin piece of material such as metal or wood (often used to hit people or animals as punishment)
weary	(47)	(adj.)	extremely tired

to slaughter	(49)	(v.)	to kill a large number of people in a violent and brutal manner

Comprehension Check

Fill in the blanks on the left with a "T" if the statement is true or an "F" if the statement is false. Write the number of a paragraph which includes information to support your answer if the answer is explicitly found in the story.

1. _____   This story takes place in a small town in Arkansas near the beginning of the school year. (Inference)

2. _____   People in Stamps thought graduation was unimportant because they were Black and had few dreams for their future. (Inference)

3. _____   Lafayette County Training School was a new and modern school. (¶ ___)

4. _____   People in Stamps treated the graduating class the same as usual. (¶ ___)

5. _____   Most of the graduating class were bound for college. (¶ ___)

6. _____   The graduating class felt the "weight" of the future. (¶ ___)

7. _____   The narrator, Marguerite, was graduating from the eighth grade. (¶ ___)

8. _____   Marguerite had been an average student. (¶ ___)

9. _____   The valedictorian, Henry, planned to give a speech entitled "To Be or Not to Be." (¶ ___)

10. _____   Marguerite received candy from her brother for a graduation present. (¶ ___)

11. _____   Marguerite had a presentiment that something was going to go wrong before she entered the school for the graduation ceremony. (¶ ___)

12. _____   The graduation ceremony began with a march, the national anthem, the pledge of allegiance, and the Negro national anthem. (¶ ___)

13. _____   Donleavy, the white speaker, talked about improving the science facilities at Lafayette County Training School. (¶ ___)

14. _____ Donleavy praised the academic work of the graduating class.   (¶ ___)

15. _____ Donleavy's speech made the graduating class feel special.   (¶ ___)

16. _____ Marguerite hated only whites because of what Donleavy had said.   (¶ ___)

17. _____ After Donleavy's speech, Marguerite questioned the relevance of the songs at graduation that encouraged the graduates to take control of their lives.   (¶ ___)

18. _____ Henry changed his plan and led the Negro national anthem to bring back the pride of his people in their ability to overcome hardship.   (¶ ___)

19. _____ The Negro national anthem is a song about the difficulties the Blacks had faced and their ability to overcome those difficulties.   (¶ ___)

20. _____ Marguerite never regained her pride in her graduating class or race.   (¶ ___)

Interaction Activity

Work in groups of three to discuss the following questions.

1. Why do you think graduation was especially important to the Blacks in a small town in the American South in the 1940s?
2. The valedictorian's speech was entitled "To Be or Not to Be." Why was this especially ironic and important in this story?
3. After Donleavy's speech, Marguerite says that "Donleavy had exposed us." What does she mean?

Vocabulary Acquisition

One way to learn vocabulary is to make a commitment to yourself to learn a certain number of words per week. In this chapter, you will use a certain form to learn words of your own choosing.

Your page will be divided into four columns. In the first column, you will list the word you want to learn. In the second column, you will copy the sentence in which you found the word. In the third column, you will copy a short dictionary definition of the word. In the fourth column, you will use the word in your own sentence.

Choose ten words that you would like to learn from "Graduation."

EXAMPLE

WORD	CONTEXT	DEFINITION	OWN SENTENCE
anticipation	The children of Stamps trembled visibly with anticipation.	the sense of expectation	Anticipation of tests is often worse than the test, itself.

SHORT WRITING: VARYING THE POINT OF VIEW

The narrator of this story is clearly Marguerite. She is speaking from the point of view of an adult looking back at childhood events. Marguerite, the adult, remembers how Marguerite, the child, felt and acted. Marguerite, the adult, is telling the story the way Marguerite, the child, experienced it. Write about these events from someone else's point of view: the school principal? the valedictorian? the white guest speaker? Marguerite's mother? The events will remain the same, but the experience of those events will change. Before writing your version of the story, read the peer writing samples and do the peer editing exercises which follow.

Peer Writing Samples

Read the following student writing samples and determine whose point of view is discussed.

1. *The ceremony was both a disaster and a success. I will never forget the way the graduates looked after Donleavy finished his speech. It was as if they accepted Donleavy's words as the truth. It hurt me to see them so affected on their graduation day. That was supposed to be their day to be proud and optimistic about their future.*

    I've tried to raise my grandson to believe that he can be somebody, that he has choices in this world. I'm not the only one. This whole town tries to teach its children that they are important and that we are proud of their successes. Almost everyone in town was at the graduation ceremony.

    I'm so proud of my grandson. I've raised him to be good and smart. I've also raised him to be proud of being a Negro. He really turned everything around at the ceremony. He overcame the stereotypes of the white speaker when he started singing the Negro national anthem. As everyone sang and regained their confidence, I felt tears start to form in my eyes. I raised him well. (M.N.)

2. *I feel proud of my students and myself. When I heard Donleavy, the speaker at the day's event, say he was going to speak and run, I immediately grew depressed. Graduation is supposed to be a special day for my students but that white speaker almost ruined their day. When he came and said he was in a rush, I didn't even give my students time to sing the Negro national anthem. I behaved this way because I wanted to make friends with the man; I wanted him and his white friends to support this school and have a good relationship with us. Therefore, I let the speaker make his speech before singing the Negro national anthem.*

   In his speech, Donleavy mentioned only trivial matters such as the Central School's new equipment. He noted how great our sports facilities could be. Didn't he know that such a speech would sadden our graduates?

   After he finished his speech, our valedictorian came to the platform and made his presentation "To Be or Not to Be." Unexpectedly, Henry followed that speech with the Negro national anthem, a song that always gives us strength. The song was sung by the students and the audience; I saw some people crying during the song. I think people realized the greatness and importance of being black, of being ourselves.

   I am proud of my students. I am proud of Henry. I am proud of my race. Henry has taught me a lesson. He made the graduation meaningful for all of us. (S.L.)

Peer Editing

1. The following writing sample contains ten errors involving number (singular/plural, countable/uncountable). Read the sample and correct the errors.

   To us, the student, graduation means a lot. Graduation is an accomplishment achieved through years of hard works. It is a great pleasure to share my graduation with my classmates, especially my best friend, Marguerite.

In our graduation ceremony, I believe I wasn't the only one who felt the excitements rise and fall and then rise again. I wonder if graduation means the same to every graduates in America? Does graduation mean something different to a white person and to a Negro? I'm sure one of our speaker believed that graduation is experienced differently. I think he believes that one of the difference between the races is how much each group can achieve in their lives. We, Negroes, are not expected to continue our educations. Why is it that our school is given sports equipments while the white people's school is getting microscopes and books? Are we only expected to be gold medalist in the next Olympics? Are white people expected to be the only Nobel Prize winner?

I don't know Henry well but I respect him. He made it clear that we can overcome others' low expectations.
(D.C.)

2. The following writing sample contains five relative clause errors. Before correcting the sample, practice correcting relative clause errors by doing this exercise.

   Relative Clauses   Correct the following sentences.
   a. That is the building which it is going to be one of the tallest in the world.
   b. There is a book has an interesting plot.
   c. The man has an interesting background will be coming to visit tomorrow.

   Despite some moments of tension, the graduation ceremony at Lafayette County Training School was quite successful and emotional for all of the graduating students and their parents.

As the principal of the school, I was honored to welcome the graduating class, their parents, and friends. Throughout the ceremony, I could feel the students' excitement. The terrible moment came when our guest speaker had to "speak and run" delivered his speech. That speech almost ruined the occasion is supposed to be so special. I personally regret inviting him.

Still, the rest of the ceremony was quite sensational. The valedictorian, a conservative student named Henry Reed who he was raised by his grandmother, presented his speech, "To Be or Not to Be." He encouraged everyone to sing that song has always given us strength. There wasn't anyone in the audience had a dry eye after that song. Even I felt a tear or two streaming down my face.

I'm proud of those kids. They are growing stronger and taller every day. They are the masters of their fate. (C.H.)

3. The following writing sample contains six errors of word form. (For example, an adjective is used where an adverb should be used.) Read the sample and correct the errors.

Throughout my career, I have made a lot of speeches. I took every one of those speeches very serious. Those occasions made me feel very honor.

However, the speech I was about to make that day was very different from all the others. It was the speech for the graduation ceremony at a Negro school. My usual feeling of honor was replaced by a sense of humiliating. I was afraid that my white colleagues would catch me speaking to a Negro audience and they would criticize me for wasting my words in front of an audience that could not understand a sophisticate speech. I tried to leave the scene as quick as possible.

While I was there, I did give them some good advise. I hope they appreciated it. (K.L)

SHORT WRITING: VARYING THE POINT OF VIEW

Write an editorial that Marguerite or Henry might have written for the Lafayette County Training School newspaper a week after the graduation. Before writing your editorial, read the peer writing samples and do the peer editing exercises which follow.

Peer Writing Samples

Read the following student writing samples and decide which editorial you like best.

1. *What is graduation? To me, it is a time of joy and a time of great accomplishment. This year's graduation class has accomplished nothing less than a momentous task. Those students deserve all the great joy and happiness in the world. This year's graduation class has not only overcome a difficult task in life, but they have also overcome obstacles placed in front of the Negro race.*

   So many times I have been told that the world is a "white man's world" and a Negro man's world is working in the field and being a handyman for someone else. The world is as much a Negro man's world as it is a white man's world, or any race's world, for that matter. It is not up to white men to tell us what we can or can't be. It is up to us. We are the ones who should choose our fate.

   You, the graduating class of 1940, have proved that anything is possible. Keep looking ahead and don't look back. You need not be somebody's field worker or handyman. You can be what you want to be and nothing less. Good luck and best wishes for your future success. (M.F.)

2. *Graduation is a time of sadness and joy. With tears in our eyes, we have painfully said our last goodbyes to our friends, teachers, and school. Goodbyes that mean "we will be going on different roads but maybe someday our roads will cross again." Those words will always be in my heart, but the words spoken by our white speaker at our graduation will always plague my soul. Never will I let these memories leave me, the memory of humiliation and success.*

What right did that white man have to throw those cruel words at us? I know the challenge we all have to confront is great, but we have to show our strength. As I said in my speech "To Be or Not to Be," every one of us is capable of being anything we choose to be. We can climb the highest mountain, we can swim the deepest sea, we can cross the hottest desert, we can be lawyers, we can be doctors. The choice is ours, not others'. But we must make the choice to "be." We just need determination. We have both. We can do it.

I hope that by our ten-year class reunion, you will have reached your goals, made your dreams come true, overcome the obstacles we, as Negro people, have to confront. Together, we overcame those obstacles at graduation. We can keep on overcoming them. (A.V.N.)

3. *There comes a time in everyone's life that changes everything. The graduation day at Lafayette High School just might have been that day for me and many of my classmates. We went into the ceremony as innocent youths and came out as determined young adults.*

That day was unlike any other. It has changed our views, attitudes, and aspirations. At first, we were just proud to be members of the graduating class of 1940. Now, we are proud members of the Negro race.

The challenge of being Black in this society is great. Still, we will prove ourselves to be the masters of our own fate. This graduating class of 1940 will show the world that Negroes can be scientists, lawyers, and doctors. Nothing can stop our determination and destiny.

Yesterday, we were thought of as property. Today, we are considered "separate but equal." Tomorrow, we will be judged by our values and morals and not by our skin color. No doubt, the struggle will be long and difficult; however, we will rise to the occasion and be victorious. Persistence is what we need to achieve equality and justice.

Yes. Graduation day was special indeed. (R.B.)

Peer Editing

The following writing sample contains nine verb form errors. Read the sample and correct the errors.

We have finally graduate. Throughout the years, we have learned, we have cried, we have laugh, and finally, we have growed. We have learned not to be ashamed of our race but to be proud of it. We have cried inside when we did realize that the world was nothing but a hopeless place for us. However, we have also smiled and be proud.

Our valedictorian, Henry Reed gave us a reason to be proud yesterday. When he started to sing the Negro national anthem at the end of the graduation ceremony, we all could realized that there was hope for us.

As long as we are willing to try, we can accomplish our goals. The world is not ready to see us as leaders, but we know that we can do it. We will grow from our tears and pain.

This is what we should have learn from the graduation. The experience involved more than just receive a diploma and hear a speech. (T.C.)

ADDITIONAL JOURNAL TOPICS

Your journal will continue on the topic of stereotyping. However, you may want to go into greater depth and focus specifically on issues raised in the readings in this module. Following are the suggested journal topics for "Graduation."

1. Angelou's story shows how stereotypes can affect people. In Angelou's case, the Black stereotypes expressed by the white speaker at the graduation ceremony made the students lose their self-confidence, their belief in their own power to rise above stereotypes. This effect of stereotyping is very common. Describe an incident in which someone's stereotype caused you to lose your belief in your own uniqueness and ability.

2. Angelou's story shows how one group of people rose above stereotypes and racism. Describe an incident in which you or someone you know had to deal with stereotypes and came out a "winner."

Reading Unit 3D

Are Movies Ready for Real Asians?
David Hwang

In this abridged article, Hwang looks at American films to see how they portray Asians. He looks at the portrayals from older movies and asks whether there has been great change in recent movies. He claims that stereotypes of Asians have existed and still exist in movies and that it is essential that movies strive to portray "three-dimensional" Asian characters, not "two-dimensional" stereotypes. Prior to reading his article, think about movies that you have seen with Asian characters. What were the characters' roles? How did they behave? Were they stereotyped in any way? Have you ever seen movies containing stereotyped characters?

(1) It was at the movies that my father first saw America. In Shanghai cinemas, he watched "North by Northwest" and "It's a Wonderful Life," whetting <u>his appetite</u> to cross an ocean. Years later, as his Chinese-American son, I sat in southern California theaters, and saw an America that did not include me—an exciting land, a romantic land, but not my land.

(2) On the few occasions when people who looked like me appeared

on the screen, it was a foreigner who was <u>on</u> <u>display</u>. These Asians spoke English like <u>goofy</u> children. Leaving the theater, I imagined all eyes upon me.

(3) How far has Hollywood come toward bringing to the screen <u>three-dimensional</u> Asian characters?

(4) Among the earliest Asian film stars were Anna May Wong and Sessue Hayakawa. Miss Wong often <u>portrayed</u> characters of mystery and dark sexuality, as in "Shanghai Express." Her <u>persona</u> is <u>consistent</u> with the movies' portrayal of Asian women as <u>feminine</u> to an extreme.

(5) Hayakawa was a silent-film star who rose to stardom with "The Cheat" and enjoyed a long career that <u>culminated in</u> his portrayal of the camp commander in "Bridge Over the <u>River Kwai</u>." As an example of an Asian male in the cinema, Hayakawa is <u>atypical</u>. In his silent films, he presents Japanese men with <u>sex</u> <u>appeal</u>, a view that has rarely been <u>duplicated</u>. If the Asian female is typed as feminine to the point of <u>caricature</u>, her male equivalent has been systematically <u>emasculated</u> by American media. The roles usually associated with Asian men are feminine ones: cooks, house-boys, laundrymen. Over the years, Asian men have gone from being laboring <u>coolies</u> to technical coolies: the white lab coat, the pocket calculator and the business suit are among our images in the 80's.

(6) Asian men are <u>sympathetic</u> when they are unthreatening to white men. The most popular Asian male of the movies of an earlier day was probably Charlie Chan. But though he was often cleverer than both his <u>adversaries</u> and his fellow detectives, he, too, was unthreatening to white men. The image, that of a dumpy, middle-aged man who tended to speak lines straight out of a fortune cookie, was <u>benign</u>. Chan was <u>servile</u>, nonsexual, irritatingly ingratiating, and never used the word "I."

(7) More recently, Bruce Lee leaped into the American consciousness and demonstrated a <u>box-office</u> appeal in <u>martial</u> <u>arts</u> films that continues to this day. The late Mr. Lee, an attractive figure who was both powerful and <u>principled</u> in his screen personae, <u>made</u> some <u>headway</u> toward creating a more positive <u>cinematic</u> image of Asians. But he spent many years in America trying to <u>ignite</u> his career. Only in Hong Kong was he able to appear in the films that have become classics. His death in 1973, concurrent with the release of "Enter the Dragon," which went on to become one of the top money-making films of all time, left many questions unanswered. One is why he has never appeared in a love scene, though it would seem almost <u>obligatory</u> for heroes in the action adventure <u>genre</u>.

(8) The United States has been at war almost continuously with one Asian nation or another since 1941, and from these experiences have come a wealth of films that have gone a long way toward determining the public's <u>perception</u> of the Asian as enemy. The average Japanese soldier seen in

World War II films, for instance, is of a particular cut—short, nearsighted, babbling, <u>sadistic</u>, and violent—in short, less than human. An exception might be Hayakawa's role in "The Bridge On the River Kwai;" his character was no less the enemy for being three-dimensional and capable of feeling pain.

(9) Louis Malle recently attempted a sympathetic portrayal of a Vietnamese immigrant's struggle against Texas fishermen in the film "Alamo Bay." Yet, again, the Vietnamese character seemed more a child than a man—<u>unassertive</u>, <u>passive</u>, <u>persecuted</u>. Without a true human being at the <u>core</u> of the film, the dilemmas of all the characters came off as too <u>contrived</u>.

(10) This <u>depiction</u> is an example of my fundamental <u>objection</u> to the way Asians have been treated in American films. A sympathetic <u>two-dimensional</u> Asian is only slightly better than the same cutout designed to be hated. Directors attempting to make movies with Asian characters need only ask themselves one question: if this character were white, would he or she seem to be a fully fleshed-out creation? If the answer is no, then minorities are being used as little more than set decorations or special effects, and the film makers are enforcing a <u>double standard</u> that <u>implies</u> that Asians are less than fully human.

(11) In the absence of such humanity, all we see on screen is a foreign face. A completely good character does little more to <u>elicit</u> understanding than one who is completely evil. Neither seems like someone you could lunch with, whose home you could visit, whose life you could value.

(12) I would like to think that audiences are becoming too <u>sophisticated</u> to <u>buy into</u> the old Asian stereotypes, and that Hollywood would encourage this awareness by shopping for fresh, new stories with a ring of truth.

Vocabulary Gloss

The definitions given here are intended to aid your comprehension. Numbers in parentheses refer to the paragraphs in which the words appear. (Since you are not expected to understand each word in the preceding reading passage, not all the words you do not know are glossed. You will need to guess the meaning of other words you do not understand.)

to whet one's appetite	(1)	(v.)	to make one eager to do something
to be on display	(2)	(v.)	to be presented as part of a show or spectacle to amuse others; to be exhibited or shown
goofy	(2)	(adj.)	silly
three-dimensional	(3)	(adj.)	having height, width, and depth

to portray	(4)	(v.)	to act out; to play a role
persona, personae (pl.)	(4)	(n.)	character; personality
consistent	(4)	(adj.)	something that follows easily or fits well with its context
feminine	(4)	(adj.)	characterized by or possessing qualities generally associated with women
to culminate in	(5)	(v.)	to end in
atypical	(5)	(adj.)	unusual; uncommon; different
sex appeal	(5)	(n.)	sexual attractiveness to others
to duplicate	(5)	(v.)	to copy
caricature	(5)	(n.)	exaggeration; ridiculous cartoon-like image
to emasculate	(5)	(v.)	to weaken; to make less masculine
coolie	(5)	(n.)	worker who does hard labor for low pay
sympathetic	(6)	(adj.)	agreeable; likeable
adversary	(6)	(n.)	foe; enemy
benign	(6)	(adj.)	friendly and harmless; not dangerous
servile	(6)	(adj.)	humble; subservient; acting as an obedient slave does toward his master
box office	(7)	(n.)	entrance to a theatre; (box-office appeal: a performer's or performance's power to attract)
martial arts	(7)	(n.)	techniques for self-defense (such as kung fu, tai chi, judo)
principled	(7)	(adj.)	motivated by moral or ethical values
to make headway	(7)	(v.)	to progress; to move forward toward one's goal
cinematic	(7)	(adj.)	having to do with movies
to ignite	(7)	(v.)	to set fire to something; to excite
obligatory	(7)	(adj.)	necessary; required
genre	(7)	(n.)	style of writing or of presenting an idea
perception	(8)	(n.)	view; attitude

sadistic	(8)	(adj.)	cruel; vicious; enjoying doing harm to others
unassertive	(9)	(adj.)	hesitant; shy; not actively putting forth one's needs
passive	(9)	(adj.)	not active; not participating; not responding
persecuted	(9)	(adj.)	made to suffer; oppressed
core	(9)	(n.)	center or deepest part
contrived	(9)	(adj.)	obviously false, unrealistic
depiction	(10)	(n.)	image; portrait
objection	(10)	(n.)	complaint; disagreement
two-dimensional	(10)	(adj.)	flat; having no depth
double standard	(10)	(n.)	separate set of rules, distinct from the normal, usual rules, designed exclusively to treat a specific group of people or things
to imply	(10)	(v.)	to hint at; to state indirectly
to elicit	(11)	(v.)	to bring out; to call forth
sophisticated	(12)	(adj.)	knowledgeable of the ways of the world
to buy into something	(12)	(v.)	to accept and agree with someone else's idea (especially a false one)

Comprehension Check

Fill in the blanks on the left with a "T" if the statement is true or an "F" if the statement is false. Write the number of a paragraph which includes information to support your answer.

1. _____ Hwang's father saw American movies in China. (¶ ___)

2. _____ Hwang says that movies he saw in American theaters as a child made him feel part of America. (¶ ___)

3. _____ When Hwang saw Asians on the screen when he was a child, he felt connected to the character. (¶ ___)

4. _____ Hwang says that Asian women have been stereotyped as being feminine to an extreme. (¶ ___)

5. _____ Hwang says that Asian men have been stereotyped as having a great deal of sex appeal. (¶ ___)

6. _____ Hwang says that a common stereotype of Asian men

in the 1980s was someone who worked nonstop in a technical job.   (¶ ___)

7. _____ Hwang says that Asian male characters are liked when they are not a threat to white men.   (¶ ___)

8. _____ An example of a nonthreatening Asian stereotype, according to Hwang, is Sessue Hayakawa.   (¶ ___)

9. _____ According to Hwang, Bruce Lee made some progress in creating a positive movie image of Asians because he was strong and had a clear sense of values.   (¶ ___)

10. _____ Bruce Lee's films were especially valued in the United States.   (¶ ___)

11. _____ Most action-adventure pictures include a love scene and Hwang wonders why Bruce Lee never appeared in one.   (¶ ___)

12. _____ Hwang does not discuss any movies which present Asians as three-dimensional characters.   (¶ ___)

13. _____ According to Hwang, war movies often present Asians as subhuman.   (¶ ___)

14. _____ Hwang would not mind stereotyped characters if they were positive stereotypes.   (¶ ___)

15. _____ Hwang hopes that audiences will stop supporting stereotypes of Asians and that Hollywood will stop portraying stereotyped images of Asians.   (¶ ___)

Interaction Activity

Work in small groups to discuss the following questions.

1. Hwang's essay is designed to show how movies have portrayed Asian characters. Summarize his examples in this chart.

ACTOR OR CHARACTER	WAS THIS A A STEREOTYPED CHARACTER? YES OR NO	WHAT TYPE OF STEREOTYPES WERE PORTRAYED BY THIS CHARACTER, IF ANY?
Anna May Wong		
Sessue Hayakawa's role as commander in "The Bridge On the River Kwai"		

Charlie Chan

Bruce Lee

Average WWII
Japanese soldier

Vietnamese
character in "Alamo
Bay"

2. How are other ethnic groups stereotyped in movies? How are women stereotyped in movies? What other stereotypes have you noticed in movies?

3. Are stereotyped characters in movies harmful? To whom? How?

4. Some ethnic groups have taken action against stereotyped portrayals of their group in the movies. They have organized pickets and protests in front of the movie theater and encouraged people not to see the movie. Do you think this type of reaction is a good idea? Why or why not? If not, what would you suggest doing in response to stereotyped images in the cinema?

Vocabulary Acquisition

One way to learn vocabulary is to make a commitment to yourself to learn a certain number of words per week. In this chapter, you will use a certain form to learn words of your own choosing.

Your page will be divided into four columns. In the first column, you will list the word you want to learn. In the second column, you will copy the sentence in which you found the word. In the third column, you will copy a short dictionary definition of the word. In the fourth column, you will use the word in your own sentence.

Choose ten words that you would like to learn from "Are Movies Ready for Real Asians?"

EXAMPLE

WORD	CONTEXT	DEFINITION	OWN SENTENCE
to be on display	It was a foreigner who was on display.	to be exhibited or shown	The artwork was on display in the gallery.

SHORT WRITING: RESPONDING TO IDEAS IN AN ARTICLE

Choose one point made by Hwang and react to it based on your own experiences and knowledge. Before writing your reaction, read the peer writing sample and do the peer editing exercises which follow.

Peer Writing Sample

Read the following student writing sample. Do you have a similar perspective and/or have you had similar experiences?

> *I reacted to Hwang's essay with mixed emotions. On the one hand, I was amused; on the other hand, I felt sad. Stereotypes, whether taught through the media or schools, cause pain. Hwang's essay made me recall my own suffering which resulted from Asian stereotypes.*
>
> *Hwang said that he imagined all eyes upon him when he was leaving the theater after watching a movie which portrayed Asians as goofy children who spoke broken English. I know too well what Hwang meant by this. His description of movies' portrayals of Asians brought back my own recollections of my high school history teacher's image of Asians. I had just been in the United States a few days, and there were no other Asians in my class. My teacher made broad, sweeping generalizations about Asians. He said we were shy and intelligent and never talked. By the time he had finished describing Asians, I felt like a complete nerd. When the teacher had finished his lecture, my classmates stared at me as if they knew everything there was to know about me. They seemed to take in the teacher's every word. Hwang's essay brought back my own feelings of the discomfort and embarrassment which can result from stereotypes. As I left my classroom that day, I, too, felt that all eyes were on me. (J.M.)*

Peer Editing

1. The following student sample contains four verb tense errors. (These words are underlined for you.) Read the sample and correct the errors.

> *Hwang's essay explored a question I <u>examine</u> for many months: why are Asians treated so poorly by the American*

media? I frequently see Asian actors in the movies who play the roles of violent gang members. The James Bond series still <u>included</u> karate killers. Asian actors <u>were</u> only used for "effect." Asian actors never <u>played</u> central roles in movies; rather they just add ethnic flavor and a mood of violence. In the future, I hope there will be more films with Asian actors who play the lead characters and portray less violent aspects of Asian culture. (W.L.)

2. In the following student sample, there are five errors involving subject/verb agreement. Locate these errors and correct them.

> *As Hwang points out, there is many movies that have characters with less than fully developed personalities. Consider, for instance, the movie "Black Rain." The characters in this movie portray Asians negatively; the few Asian characters in the movie is shown only as violent and uncaring individuals. The movie is about an American detective who chase a Japanese teenager from New York to Tokyo. The Japanese character has only one goal in mind: revenge.*
>
> *This movie is bad because it show repeated crimes such as murders. Rather than depicting real Asians, it portray only stereotypical violent ones. (E.S.K.)*

ADDITIONAL JOURNAL TOPIC

Your journal will continue on the topic of stereotyping. However, you may want to go into greater depth and focus specifically on issues raised in the readings that you have done or will do in this module. Following is the suggested journal topic for "Are Movies Ready for Real Asians?"

> *Choose one movie which you have seen recently. Discuss whether any stereotypical characters are portrayed in the movie. (For example, are all men portrayed as*

courageous? Are all women beautiful? Are all Asians studious? Are all wives housewives? Are all the secretaries women?) If you believe that the movie did not portray stereotypes, describe the movie and why each character was an individual, not a "type."

ESSAY WRITING: TOPICS

Select one of the following topics for this module's essay. To write this essay, you may use the readings in this module as resources, along with your journal entries. You will need to write at least two or three drafts of this essay, along with the final version. The drafts will be read, commented on, and evaluated by your instructor and your peers.

Alternative 1

"Stereotypes harm the stereotyper and the stereotyped person equally." Do you agree or disagree? Support your answer with your own ideas and experiences, and with quotes and examples from the stories and articles.

Alternative 2

Angelou in "Graduation" describes an event in her life to show how stereotypes affected her and how she, and her graduating class, overcame these stereotypes. Describe an event in your life in which you were faced with other people's stereotypes and discuss what you learned from this experience.

Before beginning to write your essay, read and discuss the composing process of two students who respond to these topics. The composing process for Essay Alternative 1 begins next. The composing process for Essay Alternative 2 begins on page 248.

Essay Alternative 1: The Composing Process

To help you see the changes that one student made when gathering ideas, revising, and editing, we have included one student's brainstorming activity, first and second drafts, and final version for this essay (see pages 248–255). This material is intended for discussion purposes and is not to be used as a model. In the following section, you will discuss questions pertaining to this student's composing process. Refer to the student's writing when indicated.

DISCUSSION QUESTIONS

Work in groups of three to discuss the following questions.

1. *Look at the brainstorming activity* (page 248).
   a. Discuss other factors the student might have included.
   b. Do you think the student has done sufficient brainstorming? Why or why not?

2. *Read the first draft* (pages 249–250).
   a. There are many grammatical errors in the first draft. Why doesn't the instructor correct them?
   b. The instructor comments that the introduction is "great." Why does the instructor say this? Do you agree?
   c. The instructor notes twice that something is off-topic. Do you agree?
   d. The instructor comments that repeating the word "harm" three times seems redundant. How might the writer change this? The instructor also suggests another word for "trying." What word is suggested?
   e. The instructor asks for an example to support the writer's point that "the most damaging negative effect of exposure to negative stereotypes is that it can lead to the person believing the stereotype is true." Can you think of an example to support this?
   f. In the second to last paragraph, the writer says, "the harm done to stereotypers is not equivalent to the harm done to the stereotyped person." This is also the writer's thesis in the first paragraph. What's the problem?
   g. Look at the peer review sheet on pages 250–251. Do you agree with the peers' ratings on the content and organization of the first draft? What types of suggestions for improving the first draft do the peers make? Do you agree with these suggestions? What would you suggest?

3. *Read the second draft of this essay* (pages 251–253). (In this draft, the instructor has indicated the grammar mistakes.)
   a. How did the writer avoid the redundancy of the word "harm"?
   b. How many reasons does the author give for believing that the stereotyped groups get hurt? List those reasons. What examples does the author give for each reason?
   c. The author's thesis is that the stereotyped group is harmed more

by stereotypes even though both the stereotyper and the stereotyped are harmed. In the first draft, the author did not really support this. However, in the second draft, she gives a clear reason why the stereotyper is hurt more. What is her reason?

    d. The teacher comments that the conclusion is "excellent." Why?

    e. Before reading the final version, see if you can correct the grammar mistakes.

4. *Read the final version* (pages 253–255).

    a. On a scale from 1 to 10, rate this final version for content and originality (with 10 indicating excellent content and a high degree of originality, and 1 indicating poor content and little originality).

    b. On a scale from 1 to 10, rate this final version for organization (with 10 indicating excellent organization, and 1 indicating poor organization).

    c. There is a saying that a composition is never finished . . . it is only abandoned. This means that a composition can continually be revised. The writer of this essay chose to stop after writing two drafts. If she wanted to continue revising, what might she work on?

BRAINSTORMING

Stereotyping

1. What is stereotyping?

    Description / Examples

      Banker / Black Couple

      Boss / Jewish Woman

2. What harm does stereotyping cause

    Analysis

Types of Harm	Harm to stereotypers	Harm to stereotyped
Economic	could lose $ movies could lose workers	could lose $ could lose jobs
Emotional	Might be stereotyped themselves embarrassed	Might lose self-esteem Might become depressed, anxious Marguerite in Angelou's "Graduation"

3. Who suffers the most from stereotyping?

    The stereotyped!

      powerless, without choice, no voice, little protection

DRAFT 1

A banker said to a Black couple applying for a business loan, "We have histories of Blacks owning barbecue businesses, running shoeshine stands, and limousine services. We don't associate your background with success in the import business because no one of your race has done this."

A Jewish woman starting her first important job recounts how she began each day in humiliation. The boss would buzz her on the intercom with a JAP (Jewish American Princess) joke. After delivering the punchline, she says, "He'd roar with laughter and I'd just sit there. I didn't know if it was funny or not, but I knew I didn't like it."

Great introduction! This caught my attention.

Very informal. Do you want to use the first-person pronoun "I" here?

I read about these events in the *Los Angeles Times* newspaper. They demonstrate about two incidents that hurt stereotyped people. In neither case does the stereotyper suffer equal harm. I know because I was stereotyped once and it hurt my feelings. It is true that stereo-

Is something missing here?

Off-topic. You never mention this topic again.

types do harm the stereotyper (as Heilbroner says). But the more damaging harms are done to the stereotyped person.

This seems redundant

In the examples given, the stereotyped people suffer two types of harm, economic harm and emotional harm. The Black couple may be turned down for their loan; their future economic success may be hurt. Psychologically, they cannot feel like individual. They are treated like representatives of a group and they are forced in a nar-

can you use a different word for one of the mentions of "trying"? How about "striving"?

row compartment. The banker is trying to prevent them from being who they are and trying to get what they want. The Jewish woman is being hurt financially because she knows that if she refuse to listen to all the jokes that humiliate her, she can lose her first important job like my cousin lost his job two or three days ago. However, if she continues listening to the jokes which make fun of her ethnic group, she could feel depressed and hurt emotionally.

Off-topic. You do not mention your cousin again.

Very informal

In addition to these examples, people who are stereotyped suffer in big way. Lots of exposure to negative stereotypes can weaken a person's self-esteem. Exposure to negative stereotypes can make the stereotyped person feel trapped, unable to leave the molds that society puts them in. Marguerite, in Angelou's story "Graduation" is a good example of this. After hearing the white speaker's words at her graduation (and the indirect message that Blacks are not expected to do well in school), she begins to feel frustrated and angry that all their talk about "to be or not to be" is just fake. The most damaging negative effect of exposure to negative stereotypes is that it can lead to the person believing the stereotype is true.

Why? Could you say more here? An example would be helpful.

The stereotyped people are not the only ones who get hurt. Stereotypes also hurt the stereotyper. As Heilbroner says, people who stereotypes is "in danger of becoming stereotyped themselves when they stop seeing the world in their own unique, inimitable way." In addition, there can be financial consequences of stereotyping. However, the harm done to stereotypers is not equivalent to the harm done to the stereotyped person.

In what ways? Examples would help the reader understand your essay.

Good idea, but you do not show this in your essay.

What are these consequences?

In conclusion, I think there is harm done on both sides. The stereotyper hurts in psychological and economical ways, but the harm goes deeper for the stereotyped groups, touching on self-esteem, identity, and human potential. (X.L.)

This conclusion is a bit weak. Could you expand on the first sentence just a bit?

I like this sentence

PEER REVIEW OF DRAFT 1

Reviewers ___T.G._____ and ___H.V._____
Paper which is being reviewed: ___X.L._____

What do you believe the author's purpose was in writing this essay? (For example, the author wanted to show how ...; the author wanted to describe an event to entertain us; the author wanted to convince us that ...; the author wanted to explain ...)

The author tried to convince us that stereotyping is wrong and that it hurts the stereotyped more than the stereotyper.

On a scale from 1 to 10, rate the essay for content (with 10 indicating excellent content and a high degree of originality, and 1 indicating poor content and little originality).

Rating for content: ___8___

Reasons for giving this rating:

We liked reading this essay. The introduction got us interested.

What would you suggest? (Be specific. For instance, if a certain paragraph needs more detail, state which paragraph you are talking about.)

Improve the conclusion. It does not match the great introduction.

On a scale from 1 to 10, rate this essay for organization (with 10 indicating excellent organization, and 1 indicating poor organization).

Rating for organization: ___6___

Reasons for giving this rating: The essay has an introduction, body and conclusion, but the introduction seems weak. Also the writer seems to include a lot of details which do not support his thesis.

What would you suggest?

Delete the sections of this essay which wander.

DRAFT 2

This essay is much better! you have eliminated all parts of your essay that do not address the thesis!

A banker said to a Black couple applying for a business loan, "We have histories of Blacks owning barbecue businesses, running shoeshine stands, and limousine services. We don't associate your background with success in the import business because no one of your race has done this."

A Jewish woman starting her first important job recounts how she began each work day in humiliation. The boss would buzz her on the intercom with a JAP (Jewish American Princess) joke. After delivering the punchline, she says, "He'd roar with laughter and I'd just sit there. I didn't know if it was funny or not, but I knew I didn't like it."

These two events were reported in the *Los Angeles Times* ~~newspaper.~~

They demonstrate two incidents in which stereotypes caused harm to the stereotyped person. In neither case does the stereotyper suffer equivalent harm. It is true that stereotypes do harm the stereotyper (as Heilbroner says); however, the more damaging harms are done to the stereotyped person.

[margin note: mass noun — subject/verb agreement error]

In the examples given, the stereotyped people suffer both economic and emotional harm. The Black couple may be turned down for their loan; their future economic success may be hurt. Psychologically, they cannot feel like individual. They are treated like representatives of a group and they are forced in a narrow compartment. The banker is trying to prevent them from being who they are and striving to get what they want. The Jewish woman is being hurt financially because she knows that if she refuse to listen to all the jokes that humiliate her, she can lose her first important job. However, if she continues listening to the jokes which make fun of her ethnic group, she could feel depressed and hurt emotionally.

[margin note: agreement]
[margin note: into]
[margin note: subject/verb agreement error]

[margin note: Can you use a more vivid word here?]

In addition to these examples, people who are stereotyped suffer in big way. Repeated exposure to negative stereotypes can weaken a person's self-esteem. Women, for example, who are repeatedly given the message that they should not be too intelligent may lose their self-confidence. In addition, exposure to negative stereotypes can make the stereotyped person feel trapped, unable to leave the molds that society puts him in. Marguerite, in Angelou's story, "Graduation," is a good example of this. After hearing the white speaker's words at her graduation (and the indirect message that Blacks are not expected to do well in school), she begins to feel frustrated and angry that all their talk about "to be or not to be" is just farcical. The most damaging negative effect of exposure to negative stereotypes is that it can lead to the person believing the

[margin note: Perhaps you could say "...it can lead to the internal-ization of the stereotype so that the stereotyped]

stereotype is true. Women, for example, who are told that men are more intelligent than women, may actually start believing that a woman can't be President of the United States.

person actually begins to believe the stereotype".?

The stereotyped people are not the only ones who get hurt. Stereotypes do hurt the stereotyper. As Heilbroner says, people who ~~stereotypes~~ is "in danger of becoming stereotyped themselves when they stop seeing the world in their own unique, inimitable way." *agreement* In addition, there can be financial consequences of stereotyping. The banker in the story may end up losing money because he may lose the Black couple's business. The joke-telling boss may end up losing a good secretary because of his bad jokes. A movie producer who uses Asian stereotypes in his movies may lose money from audiences who refuse to support such movies. However, the harm done to stereotypers is not equivalent to the harm done to the stereotyped group. In all cases, the stereotypers are in control. They have a choice about whether to stereotype or not. They can decide whether the losses (or harm) outweigh their will to stereotype. The stereotyped groups do not have this choice.

In conclusion, I think there is harm done on both sides. The stereotyper hurts himself in psychological and economical ways. However, the harm done to the stereotyped group is stronger because the stereotypes imposed on them; they have less control over the situation. For the stereotyped group, the harm goes much deeper, touching on issues of self-esteem, identity, and human potential. (X.L.)

much better conclusion. this brings your ideas to a natural end.

missing verb

FINAL VERSION

A banker said to a Black couple applying for a business loan, "We have histories of Blacks owning barbecue businesses, running shoeshine stands, and limousine services. We don't associate your background with success in the import business because no one of your race has done this."

A Jewish woman starting her first important job recounts how she began each work day in humiliation. The boss would buzz her on the intercom with a JAP (Jewish American Princess) joke. After delivering the punchline, she says, "He'd roar with laughter and I'd just sit there. I didn't know if it was funny or not, but I knew I didn't like it."

These two events were reported in the *Los Angeles Times* newspaper. They demonstrate two incidents in which stereotypes caused harm to the stereotyped person. In neither case does the stereotyper suffer equivalent harm. It is true that stereotypes do harm the stereotyper (as Heilbroner says); however, the more damaging harm is done to the stereotyped person.

In the examples given, the stereotyped people suffered both economic and emotional harm. The Black couple may be turned down for their loan; their future economic success may be hurt. Psychologically, their individuality has been ignored; they have been treated as representatives of a group and forced into a narrow compartment. The banker is trying to prevent them from being who they are and striving for what they want. The Jewish woman is being hurt financially because she knows that if she refuses to listen to those jokes that humiliate her, she can lose her first important job. However, if she continues listening, she will be hurt emotionally by jokes that make fun of her ethnic group.

In addition to these examples, people who are stereotyped suffer in profound ways. Repeated exposure to negative stereotypes can weaken a person's self-esteem. Women, for example, who are repeatedly given the message that they should not be too intelligent may lose their self-confidence. In addition, exposure to negative stereotypes can make the stereotyped person feel trapped, unable to escape the molds that society has placed him in. Marguerite, in Angelou's story "Graduation," is a good example of this. After hearing the white speaker's words at her graduation (and the indirect message that Blacks weren't expected to do well in school), she began to feel frustrated and angry that all their talk about "to be or not to be" was just farcical. The most damaging negative effect of exposure to negative stereotypes is that it can lead to internalization of the stereotype so that the stereotyped person actually begins to believe the stereotype. Women, for example, who are told that men are more intelligent than women, may actually start believing that a woman can't be President of the United States.

The stereotyped people are not the only ones who get hurt. Stereotypes do hurt the stereotyper. As Heilbroner said, people who stereotype are "in danger of becoming stereotyped themselves when they stop seeing the world in their own unique, inimitable way." In addition, there can be financial consequences of stereotyping. The banker in the initial story may end up losing money because he may lose the Black couple's business. The joke-telling boss may end up losing a good secretary because of his insensitive jokes. A movie producer who uses Asian stereotypes in his movies may lose money from audiences who refuse to support such movies. However, the harm done to stereotypers is not equivalent to the harm done to the stereotyped group. In all cases, the stereotypers are in control. They have a choice about whether to stereotype or not. They can decide whether the losses (or harm) outweigh their will to stereotype. The stereotyped groups do not have this choice.

In conclusion, I think there is harm done on both sides. The stereotypers hurt themselves in psychological and economical ways. However, the harm done to the stereotyped group is stronger because the stereotypes are imposed on them; they have less control over the situation. For the stereotyped group, the harm goes much deeper, touching on issues of self-esteem, identity, and human potential. (X.L.)

Essay Alternative 2: The Composing Process

To help you see the changes that one student made when gathering ideas, revising, and editing, we have included one student's brainstorming activity, first and second drafts, and final version for this essay (see pages 257–265). This material is intended for discussion purposes and is not to be used as a model. In the following section, you will discuss questions pertaining to this student's composing process. Refer to the student's writing when indicated.

DISCUSSION QUESTIONS

1. *Look at the brainstorming activity* (page 257).
   a. Discuss other factors the student might have included.
   b. Do you think the student has done sufficient brainstorming? Why or why not?

2. *Read the first draft* (pages 258–259).
   a. There are many grammatical errors in the first draft. Why doesn't the instructor correct them?
   b. "Nice" is a very vague word. The instructor asks whether the writer can think of a more descriptive word. What words might he use instead of "nice"?
   c. Why did the instructor cross out "I am telling you that" in ¶2?
   d. The author says that the kids tried to beat him up because he was Vietnamese and they wanted to get back at him because many American soldiers had died in Vietnam. The instructor asks, "How is this a stereotype?" What do you think? Is there a stereotype here? If so, what is it? Why does the instructor want the writer to clarify the stereotype?
   e. The instructor urges the writer to "go deeper" in the conclusion. Why? What would you suggest?
   f. The instructor comments that this is a "good narrative." What makes it a good narrative?
   g. Look at the peer review sheet on pages 259–260. Do you agree with the peers' ratings on the content and organization of the first draft? What types of suggestions for improving the first draft do the peers make? Do you agree with these suggestions? What would you suggest?

3. *Read the second draft of this essay* (pages 260–263). (In this draft, the instructor has indicated the grammar mistakes.)

   a. What word did the writer use in place of "nice"? Why is it an improvement?

   b. The teacher comments that the conclusion is "better." Why is it better?

   c. Before reading the final version, see if you can correct the grammar mistakes.

4. *Read the final version* (pages 263–265).

   a. On a scale from 1 to 10, rate this final version for content and originality (with 10 indicating excellent content and a high degree of originality, and 1 indicating poor content and little originality).

   b. On a scale from 1 to 10, rate this final version for organization (with 10 indicating excellent organization, and 1 indicating poor organization).

   c. There is a saying that a composition is never finished . . . it is only abandoned. This means that a composition can continually be revised. The writer of this essay chose to stop after writing two drafts. If he wanted to continue revising, what might he work on?

BRAINSTORMING

Stereotype experience??

School
math class
Everyone thinks
that I'm smart

Family
Always have
to be responsible,
must do hard jobs,
Cannot cry. Why?
Oldest male

School
Kids beat
me up.
Why?
Vietnamese

Sports
Play
basketball
Why?
Tall

1984 – Spring –
bus – noisy – kids follow me –
try to hit me – man watches –
tells me "fight" – kick the boys –
Stereotypes? – V.N. – hated V.N. because of war
martial arts – Bruce Lee!

Lesson?
Stereotypes helped and hurt me
Should not be stereotyped
bad

DRAFT 1

Can you think of a more descriptive word?

It was a (nice) day in Spring, 1984. The day was filled with sunshine and there was no clouds up on the horizontal. The sound of the birds singing and the children were playing in the yard. People were relaxing and enjoying the comfortable of their home. The sun was starting to descend in the west.

I had just go off the school bus and behind me were kids, who were yelling and pushing, trying to get off. It was rough being on the same bus with those kids. They were loud and so talkative even the bus driver couldn't quiet them down. The driver end up turning the radio real loud just to get back on the kids. I'm telling you that It was war on that bus among the kids and the bus driver. I couldn't stay the noises and the papers flying around on the bus, which they call it the paper's war. So I always tried to get off the bus first whenever I get the chance.

Good narrative!

That day, I was the first one who got off the bus. As walked away from the bus, I can hear the kids dispersed slowly away from the crowd and headed away to different directions. The neighborhood was once again peaceful. As I took the shortcut home, I had a feeling that someone is following me. (I always take the shortcut home just to save time from walking around the block and in time to catch my cartoon shows.) I turned around just to see who was it when I saw two of my classmates. They are the two meanest guys in class whom always making troubles. As they walking close to me, I can tell that they were up to something. I turned around and heading home in a hurry but they were faster then I was. One of the guys caught me from the shoulders and pulled me back. They started to call me names and told me to go back to where I came from. I stood there silent and thinking what I should do at that time. They begin to push me around and against the walls.

At that time, there were a man stand on his back window. He

saw that the two guys were harassing me so yell to me to fight back. I don't believe in violent so I didn't fight back. Also I was afraid that if I fight back, they both will jump me. I didn't want to fight unless I had to.

They begin to push me harder and starting to punch me. The next thing I knew was I had kicked one guy in the jaw. There were a little blood on his mouth. I began to worry that they both are going to jump on me because I had started the first blood. But this does not happen because the two guys had ran away after I kicked one guy. I was surprised and glad that they had left. At that time, I thought that they will be back and give me more problems.

The next day at school, I meet them in class. They came to me and apologized for what they had done the day before. They told me that they didn't like me before because I was Vietnamese. They want to get back on me because there many American soldiers had died in Vietnam. Now, they said, they knew it wasn't my fault.

On the same day, I also found out that they thought I knew some kind of martial arts but I didn't tell them the truth, that fear had brought me to kick one of them, just to keep myself safe.

Begin from that time, I knew what stereotype is and how it can affect the stereotyped and the stereotyper. In my case, the stereotypes both hurt and helped me. They were responsible for my getting attacked in the first place but they were also responsible for my scaring away my attackers. (C.N.)

How did they know? What made them realize this? Expand.

Can you work on this conclusion?

Is this the only lesson that you learned? What about other types of stereotypes? Are they OK? Go deeper in the conclusion.

How are these stereotypes? Expand.

PEER REVIEW SHEET

Reviewers ___L.C.___ and ___A.V.___
Paper which is being reviewed: ___C.N.___

What do you believe the author's purpose was in writing this essay? (For example, the author wanted to show how ...; the author wanted to describe an event to entertain us; the author wanted to convince us that ...; the author wanted to explain ...)

He wanted to tell us that his experience with stereotypes taught him a lesson.

On a scale from 1 to 10, rate the essay for content (with 10 indicating excellent content and a high degree of originality, and 1 indicating poor content and little originality).

Rating for content: __7__

Reasons for giving this rating:

Good story but lesson is weak. He rushed through the lesson.

What would you suggest? (Be specific. For instance, if a certain paragraph needs more detail, state which paragraph you are talking about.)

Tell more about the lesson. Did it change you? Also, why did those kids change their minds so fast?

On a scale from 1 to 10, rate this essay for organization (with 10 indicating excellent organization, and 1 indicating poor organization).

Rating for organization: __8__

Reasons for giving this rating:

Good story. We could imagine it. He led us smoothly to the conclusion.

What would you suggest?

Write a better conclusion. Say more about the lesson.

DRAFT 2

It was a summer-like day in Spring, 1984. The day was filled
agreement
with sunshine and there was no clouds up on the horizon. One could

hear the sound of the birds singing and the children were playing in the yard. People were relaxing and enjoying the comfortable of *noun*

plural

their home. The sun was starting to descend in the west.

verb form

    I had just go off the school bus and behind me were kids, who

were yelling and pushing, trying to get off. It was rough being on

the same bus with those kids. They were loud and so talkative even

verb tense

the bus driver couldn't quiet them down. The driver end up turn-

at

ing the radio real loud just to get back on the kids. It was war on

stand

that bus among the kids and the bus driver. I couldn't stay the

noises and the papers flying around on the bus, which they call

the paper's war. So I always tried to get off the bus first whenever

verb tense

I get the chance.

missing subject

    That day, I was the first one who got off the bus. As walked

verb tense

away from the bus, I can hear the kids dispersed slowly away

prep.

from the crowd and headed away to different directions. The neigh-

borhood was once again peaceful. As I took the shortcut home (which

I always take just to save time from walking around the block and

in time to catch my cartoon shows) I had a feeling that someone

embedded question order

was following me. I turned around just to see who was it when I

verb tense

saw two of my classmates. They are the two meanest guys in class

verb form   *noncount*   *verb form*   *verb tense*

whom always making troubles. As they walking close to me, I can

parallel structure problem

tell that they were up to something. I turned around and heading

home in a hurry but they were faster than I was. One of the guys

caught me by the shoulders and pulled me back. They started to

call me names and told me to go back to where I came from. I stood

verb tense

there silent thinking what I should do at that time. They begin to

push me around and against the walls.

agreement   *ing at*

    At that time, there were a man stand on his back window.

missing subject   *verb tense*

He saw that the two guys were harassing me so yell to me to fight

noun

back. I don't believe in violent so I didn't fight back. Also I was

tense   *tense*

afraid that if I fight back, they both will jump me. I didn't want

to fight unless I had to.

They begin to push me harder and starting to punch me. The
tense *tense* *agreement*
next thing I knew I had kicked one guy in the jaw. There were a
verb tense
little blood on his mouth. I began to worry that they both are going
drawn blood first
to jump on me because I had started the first blood. But this does
verb form
not happen because the two guys had ran away after I kicked one

guy. I was surprised and glad that they had left. At that time, I
verb tense
thought that they will be back and give me more problems.
verb tense
The next day at school, I meet them in class. They came to

me and apologized for what they had done the day before. They told

me that they didn't like me before because I was Vietnamese. They
verb tense *at*
want to get back on me because ~~there~~ many Americans soldiers had

died in Vietnam. The only things that they associated with Viet-

nam and Vietnamese were murder and Communism. That is how
verb form
they "saw" me. They didn't think that when I just born, the war
verb tense
has already been going on for many years and I was too young to

have anything to do with the war. They didn't think that I was a

victim of the war. That was why I had to leave my country and

immigrate to the United States. Now, the two boys said, they knew

it wasn't my fault. I wondered how they had changed their stereo-

type so suddenly. I soon got an explanation.

A few minutes later, I found out that they thought I knew

some kind of martial arts. They thought that all Asian people know

a little about martial arts. They thought of Bruce Lee, a powerful
O *missing relative pronoun*
martial arts expert and movie star, had gave people the impres-
verb form
sion that all Asian people know a little about martial arts. I didn't

tell them the truth (that I don't really know any kind of martial

arts); I didn't tell them that fear had brought me to kick one of them

just to keep myself safe.
verb form *plural agreement* *unclear referent*
Begin from that time, I knew what stereotype is and how it

can affect the stereotyped and the stereotyper. In my case, the

stereotypes both hurt and helped me. They were responsible for my getting attacked in the first place but they were also responsible for my scaring away my attackers.

This event taught me a major lesson. It taught me that we can make wrong assumptions if we rely on stereotypes. I myself will try my best not to make this mistake because people can get hurt very badly. As Heilbroner says, stereotype make us "mentally lazy." I now believe it is important to use our brains and our eyes and ears and judge people by what they do and say, not by our preconceived ideas about their ethnic group. (C.N.)

plural

FINAL VERSION

It was a summer-like day in Spring, 1984. The day was filled with sunshine and there were no clouds on the horizon. One could hear the sound of the birds singing and the children playing in the yard. People were relaxing and enjoying the comfort of their homes. The sun was starting to descend in the west.

I had just gotten off the school bus and behind me were kids who were yelling and pushing, trying to get off. It was rough being on the same bus with those kids. They were loud and so talkative even the bus driver couldn't quiet them down. The driver ended up turning the radio on very loud just to get back at the kids. It was war on that bus among the kids and the bus driver. I couldn't stand the noise and the papers flying around on the bus (a so-called "paper war") so I always tried to get off the bus first whenever I got the chance.

That day, I was the first one who got off the bus. As I walked away from the bus, I could hear the kids disperse slowly away from the crowd and head away to different directions. The neighborhood was once again peaceful. As I walked home, I had a feeling that someone was following me. I turned around just to see who it was when I saw two of my classmates. They were the two meanest guys in class who were always making trouble. As they walked close to me, I could tell that they were up to something. I turned around and headed home in a hurry but they were faster than I was. One of the guys caught me by the shoulders and pulled me back. They started to call me names and told me to go back to where I came from. I stood there silent, thinking about what to do. They began to push me around and against the walls.

At that time, there was a man who was standing at his back window. He saw that the two guys were harassing me so he yelled to me to fight back. I don't believe in violence so I didn't fight back. I was also afraid that if I fought back, they both would jump me. I didn't want to fight unless I had to.

They began to push me harder and started to punch me. The next thing I knew was that I had kicked one guy in the jaw. There was a little blood on his mouth. I began to worry that they both were going to jump on me because I had drawn the first blood. However, this did not happen because the two guys ran away after I kicked one guy. I was surprised and glad that they had left. At that time, I thought that they would be back and give me more problems.

The next day at school, I met them in class. Surprisingly, they came to me and apologized for what they had done the day before. They told me that, at first, they didn't like me because I was Vietnamese. They wanted to get back at me because many American soldiers had died in Vietnam. The only things that they associated with Vietnam and the Vietnamese were murder and Communism. That is how they "saw" me. They didn't think that when I was just born, the war had already been going on for many years and I was too young to have anything to do with the war. They didn't think that I was a victim of the war. That was why I had to leave my country and immigrate to the United States. Now, the two boys said, they knew it wasn't my fault. I wondered why they had changed their stereotype so suddenly. I soon got an explanation.

A few minutes later, I found out that they thought I knew some kind of martial arts. They thought that all Asian people knew a little about martial arts. They thought of Bruce Lee, a powerful martial arts expert and movie star, who had given people the impression that all Asian people know a little about martial arts. I didn't tell them the truth (that I don't really know any kind of martial arts); I didn't tell them that fear had brought me to kick one of them just to keep myself safe.

Beginning from that time, I realized what stereotypes were and how they can affect the stereotyped person and the stereotyper. In my case, the stereotypes both hurt and helped me. They were responsible for my getting attacked in the first place but they were also responsible for my scaring away my attackers.

This event taught me a major lesson. It taught me that we can make wrong assumptions if we rely on stereotypes. I myself will try my best not to make this mistake because people can get hurt very badly. As Heilbroner says, stereotypes make us "mentally lazy." I now believe it is important to use our brains and our eyes and ears and judge people by what they do and say, not by our preconceived ideas about their ethnic group. (C.N.)

Writing and Developing the Thesis Statement

Before writing your essay for this module, do the following exercises to "fine-tune" your abilities to write a clear thesis and develop that thesis logically.

The thesis statement establishes the subject of the essay, clarifies the writer's view toward the subject, and gives the reader a sense of how the essay will be developed. The thesis statement must not be too narrow or too broad. If the thesis statement is too broad, the essay will be too general; if the thesis statement is too narrow, the essay will be repetitive.

In the sample essay on page 256, the thesis is "It is true that stereotypes do harm the stereotyper; however, the more damaging harm is done to the stereotyped person." The writer has established her subject ("stereotypes"), has clarified her view toward the subject (that stereotypes "do harm the stereotyper" but that "the more damaging harm is done to the stereotyped person"), and has given the reader a sense of how the essay will be developed (most likely by presenting the harm done to both the stereotyped and the stereotyper and demonstrating why the harm done to the stereotyped is worse).

EXERCISES

1. Decide whether the following sentences meet the criteria for good theses. If not, discuss why not.
   a. Society needs to fight against stereotypes wherever they are found.
   b. There are many stereotypes in the world.
   c. Stereotypes both harm and help individuals.
   d. I have many stereotypes.

2. How might the following thesis sentences be developed in the body of an essay?
   a. The existence of stereotypes is inevitable.
   b. Society needs to fight against stereotypes wherever they are found.
   c. Stereotypes dominate Hollywood's portrayals of Arabs.
   d. Stereotypes harm the stereotyper and the stereotyped equally.
   e. Stereotypes of Jewish women abound in the literary work of Philip Roth.
   f. Stereotypes of women have changed since the 1950s.

Essay Writing Checklist

Before turning in your final essay, check the following points.

CONTENT AND ORGANIZATION

_____ 1. My thesis is clearly stated.

_____ 2. The body of my essay adequately supports my thesis.

_____ 3. My introduction captures the reader's attention.

_____ 4. My essay sufficiently answers the question or addresses the topic.

_____ 5. My essay contains original ideas.

_____ 6. I have provided sufficient information to adequately support my statements (for instance, statistics, quotes, examples).

_____ 7. My conclusion contributes to the overall coherence of my essay.

LANGUAGE

_____ 1. I have corrected grammar, punctuation, and spelling errors that were indicated by my teacher.

_____ 2. I have tried to use a variety of words and have avoided using the same words again and again.

_____ 3. I have chosen words that express my ideas precisely.

Additional Readings for Module 3

The following readings complement this module. You may want to use some or all of them as resources. (In addition to these readings, there is a related reading in Module 1: "Why Couldn't My Father Read?" by Enrique Lopez.)

Stereotypes and the Female Student

Monir Shirazi

Monir Shirazi wrote this essay as an undergraduate student at the University of California at Irvine. Prior to reading this essay, think about your experiences in higher education. Do you believe that women receive an inferior education compared to men?

(1) Do women and men receive an equal education? Although women go to the same lectures, listen to the same professors, take the same notes, and study the same texts as men, their education is inferior. This educational inequality stems from a number of factors, some of which are related to stereotypes.

(2) Adrienne Rich, a well-known author and advocate for women's rights, suggests that "the content of education itself validates men even as it invalidates women."[1] Rich believes that education teaches students that "men have been the shapers and thinkers of the world and that this is only natural." Education is biased, she believes, and this bias is white, male, racist and sexist.

[1]Rich Adrienne, 1975. "Toward a woman-centered university." In *Women and the Power to Change.* Florence Hall (ed.) New York: McGraw-Hill, 15-46.

(3) I think of my own classes. In my English literature survey course, only one or two female authors were presented. In my philosophy class, men, and men alone, were presented as the great philosophers. No one questioned why there was no female author's work worthy of being in the curriculum. No one questioned why there were no female philosophers discussed in the class.

(4) By focusing almost exclusively on men, the educational system is perpetuating stereotypes. Men are doers. Men are the thinkers. Men are rational. Men produce masterpieces. Men are capable of genius. Men achieve great goals. What messages do the female students receive? Women are *not* doers. Women are *not* thinkers. And so on. How can female students receive an equal education if they are receiving those messages? What do those messages do to a female student who has dreams of success or achievement?

(5) Stereotypes begin affecting the female student long before she reaches higher education. A girl is told (from a young age) that relationships are more important than work, that how she dresses is more important than how well she does in school, that she will not get married if she is too intelligent, that the most important job she can do is serve her husband and children, that women should be quiet and unassertive. A female student, thus, feels many conflicts about speaking up in class, excelling in class, taking time away from others to pursue her selfish goals. With all of these messages built up inside of her over the years, how can she receive an equal education?

(6) Rich asks her readers to watch male and female behavior:

> Look at a classroom: look at the many kinds of women's faces, postures, expressions. Listen to the women's voices. Listen to the silences, the unasked questions, the blanks. Listen to the small, soft voices, often courageously trying to speak up, voices of women taught early that tones of confidence, challenge, anger, or assertiveness are unfeminine. Listen to voices of the women and the men. Observe the space men allow themselves, physically and verbally, the male assumption that people will listen, even when the majority of the group is female. Look at the faces of the silent and of those who speak.[2] (Rich 1979, p. 241.)

(7) I asked earlier whether males and females receive an equal education. Women may sit in the same classrooms as men, but the education that they receive is inferior because of the stereotypes women face. As long

[2]Rich, Adrienne, 1979. "Taking Women Students Seriously." In *On Lies, Secrets and Silence: Selected Prose* 1966-1978. New York: W. W. Norton, 237-245.

as stereotypes of men and women perpetuate educational inequality and men and women fail to question these stereotypes, inequality of education will persist.

Vocabulary Gloss

The definitions given here are intended to aid your comprehension. Numbers in parentheses refer to the paragraphs in which the words appear. (Since you are not expected to understand each word in the preceding reading passage, not all the words you do not know are glossed. You will need to guess the meaning of other words you do not understand.)

inequality	(1)	(n.)	absence or lack of equality
to validate	(2)	(v.)	to support on a sound basis
sexist	(2)	(adj.)	biased against women
to perpetuate	(4)	(v.)	to make last for a long time
rational	(4)	(adj.)	sensible, logical, based on reasoning
masterpiece	(4)	(n.)	something made or done with very great skill
unassertive	(5)	(adj.)	not having or showing confidence; not expressing oneself forcefully
assertiveness	(6)	(n.)	the ability to have or show confidence; the ability to express oneself forcefully

We Talk, You List...

Vine Deloria, Jr.

Vine Deloria, Jr., was born in 1933 on the Pine Ridge I
in Martin, South Dakota. He has been on the Board of
National Office for the Rights of the Indian and has served
tive Director of the National Congress of American Indians. In t..
article, Deloria shows how Indians have been stereotyped in the mo...
to reading this article, think about the movies you have seen. Ho **ave**
American Indians been <u>portrayed</u>? How might these stereotypes have
affected their lives?

(1) One reason that Indian people have not been heard from until recently is that we have been completely covered up by movie Indians. Western movies have been such favorites that they have <u>dominated</u> the public's <u>conception</u> of what Indians are. It is not all bad when one thinks about the handsome Jay Silverheels <u>helping</u> the Lone Ranger <u>out of a jam</u>, or Ed Ames rescuing Daniel Boone with some clever Indian trick. But the other mythologies that have wafted skyward because of the movies have blocked out any idea that there might be real Indians with real problems.

(2) Other minority groups have fought tenaciously against stereotyping, and generally they have been successful. Italians quickly quashed their image as mobsters that television projected in "The Untouchables."

Blacks have been successful in getting a more realistic picture of the Black man in a contemporary setting because they have had stand-out performers like Bill Cosby and Sidney Poitier to represent them.

(3) Since stereotyping was highlighted by modern pictures, it would probably be well to review the images of minority groups projected in the movies in order to understand how the situation looks at the present. Perhaps the first aspect of stereotyping was the tendency to exclude people on the basis of their inability to handle the English language. Not only were racial minorities excluded, but immigrants arriving on these shores were soon whipped into shape by ridicule of their English. Indians were always devoid of any English whatsoever. They were only allowed to speak when an important message had to be transmitted on the screen. For example, "many pony soldiers die" was meant to indicate that Indians were going to attack the peaceful settlers who happened to have broken their three hundredth treaty moments before. Other than that, Indian linguistic ability was limited to "ugh."

(4) The next step was to acknowledge that there was a great American dream to which any child could aspire. The great American dream was projected in the early World War II movies. The last reel was devoted to a stirring proclamation that we were going to win the war and it showed factories producing airplanes, people building ships, and men marching in uniform to the transports. There was a quick pan of a black face before the scene shifted to scenes of orchards, rivers, Mount Rushmore, and the Liberty Bell as we found out what we were fighting for.

(5) The new images expressed a profound inability to understand why minority groups couldn't "make it" when everybody knew what America was all about—freedom and equality. By projecting an image of everyone working hard to win the war, the doctrine was spread that America was just one big happy family and that there really weren't any differences so long as we had to win the war.

(6) World War II movies were entirely different for Indians. Each platoon of red-blooded white American boys was equipped with his own set of Indians. When the platoon got into trouble and was surrounded, its communications cut off except for one slender line to regimental headquarters, and that line tapped by myriads of Germans, Japanese, or Italians, the stage was set for the dramatic episode of the Indians.

(7) John Wayne, Randolph Scott, Sonny Tufts, or Tyrone Power would smile broadly as he played his ace, which until this time had been hidden from view. From nowhere, a Navajo, Comanche, Cherokee, or Sioux[1] would appear, take the telephone, and in some short and inscrutable phraseology communicate such a plentitude of knowledge to his fellow tribesman

---

[1]Navajo, Comanche. Cherokee, and Sioux are names of American Indian tribes.

(fortunately situated at the general's right hand) that fighting units thousands of miles away would instantly <u>perceive</u> the situation and rescue the platoon. The Indian would disappear as mysteriously as he had come, only to reappear the next week in a different battle to perform his <u>esoteric rites</u>. Anyone watching war movies during the 40's would have been convinced that without Indian telephone operators, the war would have been lost irretrievably, in spite of John Wayne.

Vocabulary Gloss

The definitions given here are intended to aid your comprehension. Numbers in parentheses refer to the paragraphs in which the words appear. (Since you are not expected to understand each word in the preceding reading passage, not all the words you do not know are glossed. You will need to guess the meaning of other words you do not understand.)

to portray	(intro.)	(v.)	to show
to dominate	(1)	(v.)	to control
conception	(1)	(n.)	general idea
to help out of a jam	(1)	(v.)	to help (someone) overcome a problem
to whip into shape	(3)	(v.)	to drive into the desired condition of being obedient or well-behaved
ridicule	(3)	(n.)	the act of exposing to laughter or mockery
to be devoid of	(3)	(v.)	to lack
to aspire	(4)	(v.)	to try to accomplish a particular goal
reel	(4)	(n.)	a revolvable device on which film is wound
proclamation	(4)	(n.)	public statement
profound	(5)	(adj.)	deep
to make it	(5)	(v.)	to be successful
platoon	(6)	(n.)	a subdivision of a military unit
to tap	(6)	(v.)	to cut in on (a telephone or telegraph wire) to get information
to set the stage	(6)	(v.)	to make preparations for what follows

to play one's ace	(7)	(v.)	to be in a position of power because one uses a secret advantage
to perceive	(7)	(v.)	to see or observe
esoteric	(7)	(adj.)	relating to knowledge which is restricted to a small group
rite	(7)	(n.)	ceremonial act or action

Suggestions for Parents

Paula Poindexter-Wilson, Ph.D., and Mary Ellen House

In this list, taken from an article entitled "Recognizing Diversity: A Resource for Parents and Teachers to Fight Prejudice, Build Pride, Respect Diversity," Poindexter-Wilson and House suggest ways that parents might help prepare their children to confront prejudice and discrimination. Before reading their list, consider what suggestions you would make to parents. What suggestions would you make to teachers? administrators? legislators?

Here are ways that parents can help to prepare children to confront prejudice and discrimination.

(1) BUILD AND NURTURE YOUR CHILDREN'S SELF-ESTEEM EVERY DAY. Set aside a minimum of 10 minutes each day for uninterrupted, supportive time with them. Identify and praise their unique qualities. Build a minimum of 10 positives into your conversation every day. Compliment your children when they do something that makes them feel competent. Avoid being overly critical.

(2) TEACH YOUR CHILDREN POSITIVE VALUES. Provide values that will lay the foundation for success in life regardless of color, ethnic or religious group. Values include importance of an education and lifelong learning, self-discipline, perseverance, respect for people and their differences, commitment to excellence, sense of humor, love of family, friends, and those not so fortunate, honesty, fairness, curiosity, cooperation, capacity to risk, willingness to teach and help others, courage and strength, an ability to set and pursue goals, a capacity to dream, a desire to make things better.

(3) TEACH YOUR CHILDREN HONESTLY, OPENLY, AND LOVINGLY ABOUT THEIR ETHNIC GROUP. Help them understand that they are different and the world is filled with people who are different and that's OK.

(4) TEACH YOUR CHILDREN TO APPRECIATE AND RESPECT PEOPLE WHO ARE DIFFERENT. Encourage them to learn about people who come from other countries, speak other languages, have a different culture.

(5) TEACH YOUR CHILDREN TO FEEL PROUD OF THE UNIQUENESS OF THEIR ETHNIC STATUS. Include dolls and books in their toy collection and library that represent their ethnic group. Teach about historical, contemporary and family heroes. Provide biographies on members of minority groups who have been successful in the fields of politics, education, business, science, media, publishing, entertainment, fine arts, music, culture and sports. Expose your children to art, literature, and cultural programs that represent their racial, ethnic, or religious group.

(6) TEACH YOUR CHILDREN THAT PREJUDICE AND DISCRIMINATION EXIST BUT THEY ARE WRONG AND UNFAIR. Make your children aware of their rights and opportunities, and the rights of others. Help them to identify racism when it exists. Do not permit them to use minority group status as an excuse for inferior performance.

(7) TEACH YOUR CHILDREN WHAT TO DO WHEN FACED WITH PREJUDICE, DISCRIMINATION OR A RACIAL SLUR. Children need to have a repertoire of ways to respond to discimination. Sometimes they might feel like crying. Other times the best response is to ignore the incident. And there are times when they should speak out against it. Mostly, children need to know it's important to discuss their experiences with you. Children should always stand with their heads high and never feel ashamed of being a member of a racial or ethnic group.

(8) TEACH YOUR CHILDREN NOT TO PREJUDGE. Encourage them to evaluate people on their inner qualities, not on their appearance.

(9) BECOME ACTIVELY INVOLVED IN THE ELIMINATION OF PREJUDICE AND DISCRIMINATION. Encourage your children to speak up and work toward the elimination of prejudice and discrimination.

Vocabulary Gloss

The definitions given here are intended to aid your comprehension. Numbers in parentheses refer to the paragraphs in which the words appear. (Since you are not expected to understand each word in the preceding reading passage, not all the words you do not know are glossed. You will need to guess the meaning of other words you do not understand.)

to nurture	(1)	(v.)	to care for; to nourish
self-esteem	(1)	(n.)	the state of valuing or caring about oneself
competent	(1)	(adj.)	capable; qualified
uniqueness	(5)	(n.)	individuality; distinctiveness
to expose (someone) to (something)	(5)	(v.)	to exhibit; display, show something to someone
inferior	(6)	(adj.)	lower in rank, social position, importance, quality, etc.
slur	(7)	(n.)	a remark or comment which speaks of something as unimportant or unworthy

Appendix A: Journal Excerpts from Famous Writers

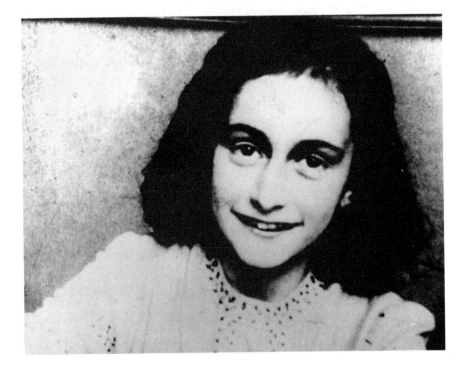

Anne Frank: A Diary of a Young Girl

(journal entry, Saturday, June 20, 1942)

Anne Frank was a Jewish teenager during the Nazi years. Although Anne eventually died in a concentration camp, her memory lives on through her diary. The diary begins when Anne first received the diary from her father before the family went into hiding. Most of the diary recounts Anne's thoughts and experiences during the years that her family remained in hiding. This excerpt describes Anne's reaction to receiving the diary as a gift. Prior to reading this excerpt, you might consider why someone might want to keep a diary[1].

---

[1]Excerpt from Anne Frank: *A Diary of a Young Girl* (journal entry, Saturday, June 20, 1942)

(1) It's an odd idea for someone like me to keep a diary; not only because I have never done so, but because it seems to me that neither I— nor for that matter anyone else—will be interested in the unbosomings of a thirteen-year-old schoolgirl. Still, what does that matter? I want to write, but more than that, I want to bring out all kinds of things that lie buried deep in my heart.

(2) There is a saying that "paper is more patient than man"; it came back to me on one of my slightly <u>melancholy</u> days, while I sat chin in hand, feeling too bored and <u>limp</u> even to make up my mind whether to go out or stay at home. Yes, there is no doubt that paper is patient and as I don't intend to show this cardboard-covered notebook, bearing the proud name "diary" to anyone, unless I find a real friend, boy or girl, probably no one cares. And now I come to the <u>root</u> of the matter, the reason for my starting a diary; it is that I have no such real friend.

(3) Let me put it more clearly, since no one will believe that a girl of thirteen feels herself quite alone in the world, nor is it so. I have dar-ling parents and a sister of sixteen. I know about thirty people whom one might call friends—I have <u>strings</u> of boy friends anxious to catch a <u>glimpse</u> of me and who, failing that, <u>peep</u> at me through mirrors in class. I have relations, aunts and uncles, who are darlings too, a good home, no—I don't seem to <u>lack</u> anything. But it's the same with all my friends, just fun and joking, nothing more. I can never bring myself to talk of anything outside the common round. We don't seem able to get any closer, that is the root of the trouble. Perhaps I lack confidence, but anyway, there it is, a stubborn fact and I don't seem to be able to do anything about it.

(4) <u>Hence</u>, the diary. In order to <u>enhance</u> in my mind's eye the pic-ture of the friend for whom I have waited so long, I don't want to set down a series of <u>bold</u> <u>facts</u> in a diary like most people do, but I want this diary to be my friend, and I shall call my friend Kitty.

Vocabulary Gloss

The definitions given below are intended to aid your comprehension. Numbers in parentheses refer to the paragraphs in which the words appear. (Since you are not expected to understand each word in the read-ing, not all the words you do not know are glossed. You will need to guess the meaning of other words you do not understand.)

melancholy	(2)	(adj.)	sadness, especially over a period of time and not for any particular reason
limp	(2)	(adj.)	lacking strength or stiffness

root	(2)	(adj.)	origin; cause
strings	(3)	(n.)	a set (of words, actions, people, etc.) following each other closely
glimpse	(3)	(n.)	a quick look at or incomplete view of
to peep	(3)	(v.)	to look (at something) quickly and secretly
to lack	(3)	(v.)	to be without, not to have
hence	(4)	(conj.)	for this reason, therefore
to enhance	(4)	(v.)	to increase good things (such as value, power or beauty)
bold facts	(4)	(n.)	plain facts

On Keeping A Notebook
Joan Didion

In this abridged excerpt from *Slouching Towards Bethlehem*, Didion talks about keeping a notebook and why that is so important to her. She distinguishes a notebook from a diary, saying that in a notebook she "tells lies" (i.e. describes the world as she sees it) while in a diary, people simply report the day's events as objectively as possible. She claims that keeping a notebook helps us "keep <u>on nodding terms</u> with the people we used to be" and that this is important because otherwise, "they turn up unannounced and surprise us."

Prior to reading this excerpt, you might consider the different types of written records (e.g. diaries, journals, notebooks) that people keep. How would a 12-year-old girl's diary differ from a 40-year-old woman's diary? from a 25-year-old man's diary?[2]

(1) My first notebook was a Big Five tablet, given to me by my mother with the sensible suggestion that I stop <u>whining</u> and learn to amuse myself by writing down my thoughts. She returned the tablet to me a few years ago; the first entry is an <u>account</u> of a woman who believed herself to be freezing to death in the Arctic night, only to find, when day broke, that she had <u>stumbled</u> <u>onto</u> the Sahara Desert, where she would die of the heat before lunch. I have no idea what turn of a five year old's mind could have <u>prompted</u> so <u>exotic</u> a story, but it does reveal a certain tendency for the extreme which has stayed with me into adult life; perhaps if I were analytically inclined I would find it a truer story than any I might have told about Donald Johnson's birthday party or the day my cousin Brenda put Kitty Litter in the Aquarium.

[2]Excerpt from Joan Didion: "On Keeping A Notebook" (from *Slouching Towards Bethlehem*)

(2) So the point of my keeping a notebook has never been, nor is it now, to have an accurate factual record of what I have been doing or thinking. That would be a different impulse entirely, an instinct for reality which I sometimes envy but do not possess. At no point have I ever been able successfully to keep a diary, and on those few occasions when I have tried dutifully to record a day's events, boredom has so overcome me that the results are mysterious at best. What is this business about "shopping, typing piece, dinner with E, depressed"? Shopping for what? Typing what piece? Who is E? Was this "E" depressed, or was I depressed? Who cares?

(3) In fact, I have abandoned altogether that kind of pointless entry; instead I tell what some would call lies. "That's simply not true," the members of my family frequently tell me when they come up against the memory of a shared event. "The party was *not* for you, the spider was *not* a black widow, *it wasn't that way at all.*" Very likely they are right, for not only have I always had trouble distinguishing between what happened and what merely might have happened, but I remain unconvinced that the distinction, for my purposes, matters. The cracked crab that I recall having for lunch the day my father came home from Detroit in 1945 must certainly be embroidery, worked into the day's pattern to lend verisimilitude; I was ten years old and would not now remember the cracked crab. The day's events did not turn on cracked crab. And yet it is precisely that ficticious crab that makes me see the afternoon all over again, a home movie run all too often, the father bearing gifts, the child weeping, an exercise in family love and guilt. Or that is what it was to me. Similarly, perhaps it never did snow that August in Vermont; perhaps there never were flurries in the nightwind, and maybe no one else felt the ground hardening and summer already dead even as we pretended to bask in it, but that was how it felt to me, and it might as well have snowed, could have snowed, did snow.

(4) *How it felt to me*: that is getting closer to the truth about a notebook. I sometimes delude myself about why I keep a notebook. I imagine that the notebook is about other people. But of course it is not. I have no real business with what one stranger said to another at the hat-check counter in Pavillion. *Remember what it was to be me*; that is always the point.

(5) It is a difficult point to admit. We are brought up in the ethic that others, any others, all others, are by definition more interesting than ourselves; taught to be diffident, just this side of self-effacing. Only the very young and the very old may recount their dreams at breakfast, dwell upon self, interrupt with memories of beach picnics and favorite Liberty lawn dresses and the rainbow trout in a creek near Colorado Springs. The rest of us are expected, rightly, to affect absorption in other people's favorite dresses, other people's trout.

(6) And so we do. But our notebooks give us away, for however dutifully we record what we see around us, the <u>common</u> <u>denominator</u> of all we see is always, transparently, shamelessly, the implacable "I." We are not talking here about the kind of notebook that is patently for public <u>consumption</u>,a structural conceit for binding together a series of graceful *pensées*; we are talking about something private.

(7) And sometimes even the maker has difficulty with the meaning. There does not seem to be, for example, any point in my knowing for the rest of my life that, during 1964, 720 tons of <u>soot</u> fell on every square mile of New York City, yet there it is in my notebook, labeled "FACT." Nor do I really need to remember that Ambrose Bierce liked to spell Leland Stanford's name "£eland $tanford" or that "smart women almost always wear black in Cuba," a fashion hint without much potential for practical application. And does not the relevance of these notes seem <u>marginal</u> at best?

> In the basement museum of the Inyo County Courthouse in Independence, California, sign pinned to a mandarin coat: "This MANDARIN COAT was often worn by Mrs. Minnie S. Brooks when giving lectures on her TEAPOT COLLECTION."

> Redhead getting out of car in front of Beverly Wilshire Hotel, chinchilla stole, Vuitton bags with tags reading:

MRS. LOU FOX

HOTEL SAHARA

VEGAS

(8) Well, perhaps not entirely marginal. As a matter of fact, Mrs. Minnie S. Brooks and her MANDARIN COAT pull me back into my own childhood, for although I never knew Mrs. Brooks and did not visit Inyo County until I was thirty, I grew up in just such a world, in houses cluttered with Indian relics and bits of gold ore and ambergris and the souvenirs my Aunt Mercy Farnsworth brought back from the Orient. It is a long way from that world to Mrs. Lou Fox's world, where we all live now, and is it not just as well to remember that? Might not Mrs. Minnie S. Brooks help me to remember what I am? Might not Mrs. Lou Fox help me to remember what I am not?

(9) But sometimes the point is harder to <u>discern</u>. What was I planning to make of this line by Jimmy Hoffa: "I may have my faults, but being wrong ain't one of them"? What is a recipe for sauerkraut doing in my notebook? What kind of magpie keeps this notebook? *"He was born the night the Titanic went down."* That seems a nice enough line, and I even recall who said it, but is it not really a better line in life than it could ever be in fiction?

(10) But of course that is exactly it: not that I should ever use the line, but that I should remember the woman who said it and the afternoon I heard it. We were on her terrace by the sea, and we were finishing the wine left from lunch, trying to get what sun there was, a California winter sun. The woman whose husband was born the night the *Titanic* went down wanted to rent her house, wanted to go back to her children in Paris. I remember wishing that I could afford the house, which cost $1000 a month. "Someday you will," she said lazily. "Someday it all comes." There in the sun on her terrace it seemed easy to believe in someday, but later I had a low-grade afternoon hangover and ran over a black snake on the way to the supermarket and was flooded with inexplicable fear when I heard the checkout clerk explaining to the man ahead of me why she was finally divorcing her husband. "He left me no choice," she said over and over as she punched the register. "He has a little seven-month-old baby by her, he left me no choice." I would like to believe that my dread then was for the human condition, but of course it was for me, because I wanted a baby and did not then have one and because I wanted to own the house that cost $1000 a month to rent and because I had a hangover.

(11) It all comes back. Perhaps it is difficult to see the value in having one's self back in that kind of mood, but I do see it; I think we are well advised to keep on nodding terms with the people we used to be, whether we find them attractive company or not. Otherwise, they turn up unannounced and surprise us, come hammering on the mind's door at 4 A.M. of a bad night and demand to know who deserted them, who betrayed them, who is going to make amends. We forget all too soon things we thought we could never forget. We forget the loves and the betrayals alike, forget what we whispered and what we screamed, forget who we were. I have already lost touch with a couple of people I used to be; one of them, a seventeen-year-old, presents little threat although it would be of some interest to me to know again what it feels like to sit on a river levee drinking vodka-and-orange-juice and listening to Les Paul and Mary Ford and their echoes sing "How High the Moon" on the car radio. (You see I still have the scenes, but I no longer perceive myself among those present, no longer could even improvise the dialogue.) The other one, a twenty-three-year-old, bothers me more. She was always a good deal of trouble, and I suspect she will reappear when I least want to see her, skirts too long, shy to the point of aggravation, always the injured party, full of recriminations and little hurts and stories I do not want to hear again, at once saddening me and angering me with her vulnerability and ignorance, an apparition all the more insistent for being so long banished.

(12) It is a good idea, then, to keep in touch, and I suppose that keeping in touch is what notebooks are all about. And we are all on our own

when it comes to keeping those lines open to ourselves: your notebook will never help me, nor mine you.

(13) It all comes back. Even that recipe for sauerkraut: even that brings it back. I was on Fire Island when I first made that sauerkraut, and it was raining, and we drank a lot of bourbon and ate the sauerkraut and went to bed at ten, and I listened to the rain and the Atlantic and felt safe. I made the sauerkraut again last night and it did not make me feel any safer, but that is, as they say, another story.

Vocabulary Gloss

The definitions given below are intended to aid your comprehension. Numbers in parentheses refer to the paragraphs in which the words appear. (Since you are not expected to understand each word in the preceding reading passage, not all the words you do not know are glossed. You will need to guess the meaning of other words you do not understand.)

on nodding terms	(intro)	(idiom)	a relationship between people who recognize each other but only know each other slightly
to whine	(1)	(v.)	to complain too much in an unnecessarily sad voice
account	(1)	(n.)	a written or spoken report; description; story
to stumble onto	(1)	(v.)	to meet or discover by chance
to prompt	(1)	(v.)	to be the cause of (a thought, action, or feeling)
exotic	(1)	(adj.)	strange and unusual
impulse	(2)	(n.)	a sudden wish to do something
instinct	(2)	(n.)	natural feeling
abandoned	(3)	(adj.)	to leave or give up completely and forever
to distinguish between	(3)	(v.)	to make or recognize differences
embroidery	(3)	(n.)	a design sewn onto plain cloth in order to decorate it

verisimilitude	(3)	(n.)	the quality of seeming to be true; likeness to reality or real things
flurries	(3)	(n.)	a sudden sharp rush of wind or rain; light snowfall
to bask	(3)	(v.)	to sit or lie in enjoyable heat and light
to delude	(4)	(v.)	to mislead the mind or judgment of; deceive; trick
ethic	(5)	(n.)	a system of moral behavior
diffident	(5)	(adj.)	having or showing a lack of belief in one's own powers, and therefore, unwilling to speak or act with force
self-effacing	(5)	(adj.)	avoiding the attention of others; keeping oneself from seeming important
to affect	(5)	(v.)	to pretend to feel, have, or do
absorption	(5)	(n.)	the taking up of all one's attention, interest, time, etc.
common denominator	(6)	(n.)	the facts or characteristics that are similar among a group of items
consumption	(6)	(n.)	the act of buying and using goods and services; usage
pensées	(6)	(n.)	(French) thoughts, ideas
soot	(7)	(n.)	black powder produced by burning and carried into the air and left on surfaces by smoke
marginal	(7)	(adj.)	of small rather than central importance
to discern	(9)	(v.)	to see, notice, or understand, especially with difficulty
hangover	(10)	(n.)	the feeling of sickness the day after drinking too much alcohol
inexplicable	(10)	(adj.)	describing something which is too strange to be explained or understood
dread	(10)	(n.)	great fear, especially of some harm to come

to desert	(11)	(v.)	to leave at a difficult time or leave in a difficult position
to betray	(11)	(v.)	to be disloyal or unfaithful to
to make amends	(11)	(v.)	to make up for poor behavior toward someone
to perceive	(11)	(v.)	to have or come to have knowledge of (something) through one of the senses or through the mind
to improvise	(11)	(v.)	to make up as one is speaking
recrimination	(11)	(n.)	quarreling and blaming one another
vulnerability	(11)	(n.)	the state of being easily harmed, hurt, or wounded; sensitive
apparition	(11)	(n.)	the spirit of a dead person moving in bodily form; a ghost
to be banished	(11)	(v.)	to be sent away, especially out of the country, as a punishment

Appendix B: Grammar

CONTENTS

NOUNS: COUNTABLE AND UNCOUNTABLE NOUNS

Countable nouns describe something that we can count.

> four dollars
> three dogs
> two tables
> fifteen birds

Uncountable nouns describe something that we cannot count.

> wool
> ignorance
> stupidity
> research

1. uncountable nouns:
    have no plural
    are never used with *a* or *an*
    are used with the third person singular verb (*he, she,* or *it* verb form, as in The salt *is* on the table.)

Frequently used nouns that are uncountable in most contexts:

MASS	DISEASES	SUBJECTS OF STUDY	GAMES
furniture	measles	physics	checkers
luggage	mumps	mathematics	pool (billiards)
money	influenza	politics	baseball
vocabulary	arthritis	economics	tennis
grammar		history	
equipment		biology	
machinery		medicine	
garbage		humanities	
homework		physical sciences	
traffic			
jewelry			
scenery			
slang			

PARTICLES TOO SMALL TO COUNT	LIQUIDS	GASSES
rice	orange juice	air
hair	lemonade	fog
sand	coffee	hydrogen
sugar	tea	oxygen
salt	milk	pollution
	blood	smog
		smoke
		steam

NATURAL PHENOMENA (THINGS THAT OCCUR IN NATURE)

weather	humidity	darkness	electricity
dew	rain	daylight	fire
fog	sleet	moonlight	gravity
hail	thunder	sunlight	
heat	wind	sunshine	

ABSTRACT NOUNS

advice	fun	justice	recreation
anger	gossip	knowledge	space
beauty	happiness	laughter	stupidity
confidence	health	love	time
courage	help	luck	violence
cowardice	hospitality	peace	wealth
education	ignorance	poverty	welfare
entertainment	information	pride	
experience	intelligence	progress	

2. Some nouns can be used either as countable nouns or as uncountable nouns. Consider these examples:

I did my <u>work</u> quickly. (uncountable)

Her painting is a <u>work</u> of art. (countable)

There's a lot of <u>noise</u> in this classroom. (uncountable)

She heard a strange <u>noise</u> last night. (countable)

Maria has beautiful <u>hair</u>. (uncountable)

Is that a <u>hair</u> on your jacket? (countable)

<u>Food</u> is necessary for survival. (uncountable)

Fruit and vegetables are nutritious <u>foods</u>. (countable)

John doesn't have <u>experience</u> driving. (uncountable)

He has had many good <u>experiences</u> at school. (countable)

3. *Many* or *a lot of* is used with countable nouns.
   Much or *a lot of* is used with uncountable nouns.
   Much is generally used with negative statements and questions.
   A lot of can be used with any type of statement or question.

countable noun	How <u>many</u> dollars do you have?
uncountable noun	How <u>much</u> money do you have?

4. *A few* is used with countable nouns.
   A little is used with uncountable nouns.

countable noun	Do you have <u>a few</u> dollars?
uncountable noun	Do you have <u>a little</u> money?

5. A speaker often uses *some* with an uncountable noun when she is talking about an unspecified amount.

   I bought <u>some</u> coffee.

   (Note that the exact amount of coffee purchased is not specified.)

EXERCISE 1

Complete the sentences with the correct form—singular or plural—of the given nouns.

1. book   I bought some _____ .

2. advice   Did you get any _____ ?

3. homework   He finished a lot of _____ .

4. novel   Have you read any good _____ lately?

5. grammar   He knows a lot of _____ .

6. traffic   He was caught in a lot of _____ .

7. information   I don't have any _____ yet.

8. vocabulary   He finished studying all his _____ .

9. violence   There is a lot of _____ in this world.

10. luck   Did you have a lot of _____ ?

11. clothing   She is giving a lot of _____ to the poor.

12. computer   There were five _____ on the counter.

13. knowledge   He has a lot of _____ .

14. noise   There is a lot of _____ in here.

15. gossip   Many people like to read _____ about movie stars.

EXERCISE 2

Choose the correct word in parentheses.

1. Since it's summer, there (is, are) a lot of sunshine.
2. The physician (has, have) a lot of knowledge about medicine.
3. The advice (is, are) helpful.
4. The milk (is, are) sour.
5. Thuy's idea (is, are) good.
6. There (is, are) a lot of warm weather in the tropics.
7. The jewelry (is, are) made of gold.
8. There (is, are) many words that I don't know.
9. There (is, are) time to review the test.
10. Their hospitality (was, were) generous.
11. There (is, are) a few books on the counter.
12. A lot of the entertainment (was, were) exciting.
13. Their homework (is, are) completed.
14. Physics (is, are) my favorite subject.
15. His slang (bothers, bother) me.

NOUNS: PRONOUN REFERENCE

The word a pronoun refers to is called its *referent*. Pronouns allow you to avoid repetition.

1. The table lists the various forms of personal pronouns.

SUBJECT PRONOUNS	OBJECT PRONOUNS	POSSESSIVE ADJECTIVE	POSSESSIVE PRONOUN	REFLEXIVE PRONOUN
I	me	my	mine	myself
we	us	our	ours	ourselves
you (sing.)	you	your	yours	yourself
you (plur.)	you	your	yours	yourselves
he	him	his	his	himself
she	her	her	hers	herself
it	it	its	——	itself
they	them	their	theirs	themselves
one	one	one's	——	oneself

2. Make sure that the pronoun refers to the noun referent and agrees with it in number and gender.

   singular   The *father* is reading to *his* son.
   singular   The *mother* is reading to *her* son.
   plural   The *parents* are reading to *their* son.
   plural   The *books* are on the table. Bring *them* here.

   To refer to uncountable nouns, use *it, this* or *that.*

   The research is quite preliminary. *It* is not reliable.

   The lemonade is too sour. Throw *it* out.

3. Subject-verb agreement is determined by the noun referent.

   We each have a *coat. Mine* is red.

   We each have two *coats. Mine* are wool.

4. Indefinite pronouns include *anybody, anyone, each, either, everybody, everyone, everything, neither, no one, someone,* and *something.* They refer to nonspecific persons or things. Even though these indefinite pronouns may seem to have plural meanings, treat them as singular in formal English.

   It is important that everyone does his or her [not *their*] best.

   When someone has been drinking, he or she [not *they*] is likely to speed.

5. Ambiguous reference errors occur when the pronoun could refer to two possible referents.

When María put the book on the shelf, it fell. (What fell—the book or the shelf?)

Paul told José that he had received an A. (Who received an A—Paul or José?)

6. A pronoun must refer to a particular referent, not to a word that is implied but not present in the text.

> Incorrect: After winning, Susana thanked them for *it.* (The word *it* refers to Susana's *prize* [implied by the word *winning*], but the word *prize* did not occur in the sentence. In addition, the referent for *them* is not clear.)

7. Modifiers, including possessives, cannot serve as noun referents. These modifiers may strongly imply the noun which the pronoun refers to. However, modifiers are not nouns and cannot be noun referents.

> Incorrect: In Austen's *Pride and Prejudice, she* describes the plight of a young woman. (The pronoun *she* cannot refer to "Austen's" since "Austen's" is a possessive modifier not a pronoun.)

8. Sometimes the word *they* is used in spoken English to refer to persons who have not been specifically identified. Do not use it in this way when writing in English. Use pronouns only when the referents are specifically identified.

> Incorrect: There are many ways to help the homeless. For example, *they* could get the homeless jobs, create housing for the homeless, and give the homeless food packages. (Who is *they?* The government? the local leaders? The referent is unclear.)

9. Pronouns should not be used immediately after their referents. "The book *it* is on the table" should be "The book is on the table."

10. If a pronoun modifies a gerund or a gerund phrase, it should appear in the possessive case (*my, our, your, his/her/its, their*). (A gerund is a verb form ending in *-ing* that functions as a noun.)

My mother always permitted *our* cooking in the kitchen.
(The possessive pronoun *our* modifies the gerund *cooking.*)

11. Pronoun object forms are always used after prepositions.

John gave the book to *me.*
She sat on *it.*
He stared at *me.*

EXERCISE 1

Each of the following sentences contains a pronoun error which is under-lined. Can you correct the errors and explain why they occurred? Follow the example shown next.

> Example: He looked at I with an evil eye. (This sentence is not correct. It should be "He looked at me with an evil eye." Object pronouns follow prepositions such as *at.*)

1. Many people today they would like to move to Washington.
2. María and me are happy that we both got good grades.
3. Even though Mary and Jane failed the midterm, she managed to get an A in the course.
4. Kim and me have to see the doctor after school today.
5. He gave the book to Quang and I.
6. The five-year-olds crossed the street by themself.
7. He put on his coat and I put on mines.
8. The research is preliminary. They cannot be published yet.
9. The mother is singing to his son.
10. My father always permitted us using his workroom.

EXERCISE 2

Fill in the blanks with the appropriate pronoun or pronouns.

> Example: He is no different than most of __*us*__ (we/us) who have our own special talents.

1. Between you and _____ (me/I), I hate the professor.
2. The dog bit _____ (he and I/him and me).
3. The workers ate their sandwiches while I ate _____ (mines/mine/my).
4. My brother and _____ (I/me) have dentist appointments after school.
5. They did the work _____ (themself/himself/themselves).

6. The child took the train away from his brother because it did not belong to _____ (he/him).

7. My goal is to become a lawyer, but _____ (she's/her's/hers) is to become a doctor.

8. She wrote the book for _____ (you and I/you and me).

9. They sang to _____ (themselves/themself) in the shower.

10. My brother loves _____ (his/her/himself) car because it is the first one that he has ever owned.

EXERCISE 3

The following paragraphs come from *The Odyssey*. (Penelope has just seen her husband, Odysseus, after not seeing him for a long time.) Fill in the blanks with appropriate pronouns.

"Dear son, I can't believe (1) _____ eyes. This must be some god who wears my husband's shape and form. I dare not believe, after so long, that it's really (2) _____ . My heart aches and (3) _____ mind is numbed at the sight of him. Go, Telemachus, and all the rest of (4) _____ . Leave us here alone. If this is indeed Odysseus, then I shall soon know (5) _____ for myself."

Now husband and wife were alone. Still trembling, Penelope approached Odysseus. She ran a hand down his leg and found the scar that (6) _____ knew so well. Then (7) _____ looked up at him and spoke.

Tears streamed down both their faces as (8) _____ embraced. After twenty long years of separation (9) _____ held each other once again. For a long time (10) _____ kissed and stared into each other's eyes and said not a word.

ARTICLES: DEFINITE ARTICLES

1. In general, use *the* before nouns which have been mentioned more than once.

   I'm studying grammar. *The* grammar isn't easy.

2. *The* is also used when both the speaker and the listener are referring to the same specified object, that is, they have a common referent.

   The food at that restaurant is the best.

3. Idiomatic Usage—Note the following expressions:

NO ARTICLE	DEFINITE ARTICLE
at night	in the morning
	in the afternoon
go to church	go to the bank
go to work	go to the store
go downtown	go to the movies
go to bed	go to the beach
travel by bus/airplane/jet/train	go to the park
at college	
at school	
at work	
at home	

EXERCISE 1

Fill in the blank with "the" or "φ".

1. Although slang can be fun to learn, _____ slang that I'm learning is not.

2. Yesterday I saw a dog and a cat. _____ dog was barking at _____ cat.

3. _____ love is a wonderful feeling.

4. A mouse spotted the cat and began to run. Fortunately, _____ mouse outran _____ cat.

5. _____ haste makes waste.

6. _____ time is money.

7. I'm going to a computer store this afternoon. _____ store is on the corner.

8. An alligator can be dangerous. _____ toothless alligator at the zoo is not.

9. I had a car accident last year. _____ accident did not cause much damage.

10. I hate _____ traffic. Wasting my time frustrates me.

EXERCISE 2

Each of the sentences here contains one mistake. Find the mistakes and correct them.

1. The gold is an important metal.
2. Cat named Chester chased the mouse.
3. I'm studying book that is about geology.
4. I always exercise in morning.
5. Did you see man who is sitting next to José?
6. I always buy a gas at Joe's Gas Station.
7. I went to the bed at midnight.
8. I drank a lemonade that Gia made.
9. I drank some tea. Tea was too hot.
10. He always strives to obtain the wisdom.

ARTICLES WITH PROPER NOUNS

Proper nouns include the following:

- Names of people: John, Van, Mara
- Names of places: Millbrae, Nevada, Spain, Korea
- Names of religions (and associated words): Christianity—Christian, Hinduism—Hindu
- Names of courses in school: Electrical Engineering, History of Mexico
- Names of periods and events: the Renaissance, the American Revolution, World War II
- Styles of art and architecture: Baroque, Victorian, Gothic
- Days, months, and special holidays: Passover, Chinese New Year, March, Friday
- Titles: Mr., Mrs., Ms., Dr.

1. Proper nouns generally begin with a capital letter.

2. In general, do not use the definite article "the" with proper nouns. However, there are exceptions as follows:

Parts of the Globe	the North Pole the East, the West, the Equator
Museums, Hotels	the Hilton Hotel, the Metropolitan Art Museum
Schools (when the word "University" or "College" or "High School" comes first) Note that when these words come last, the noun phrase is not preceded by a definite article)	the University of California the University of Hawaii the High School of Fine Arts but Stanford University Vista High School Monte Vista High School
Large Bodies of Water (seas, oceans, gulfs, and rivers)	the Mississippi River the Atlantic Ocean the Seine the Mediterranean Sea
Deserts	the Sahara Desert the Mojave Desert

3. "The" is used with geographical proper nouns which end in "s."

COUNTRIES	GROUPS OF ISLANDS
the United States	the Bahamas
the Netherlands	the Falklands
the Philippines	the West Indies
GROUPS OF LAKES	**MOUNTAIN RANGES**
the Great Lakes	the Alps
the Finger Lakes	the Andes
	the Rockies

4. "The" is used to refer to groups of people of a certain nationality:
the French (people)
the Chinese (people)
the Vietnamese (people)

EXERCISE 1

Edit the following sentences. Capitalize the proper nouns when appropriate.

1. I used to speak spanish in my home.
2. One day, my teacher, mr. helman held a teacher-parent conference.
3. Mr. helman told my parents that they should only speak english to me at home.
4. He told them that by speaking english, they would be helping me to improve my grades in literature of the world and gain admittance to stanford university.
5. I will always remember that tuesday in december as long as I live.
6. My mom served mr. helman pepsi-cola.
7. Then, she asked how I was doing in algebra.
8. He told her that my grades in algebra were okay but that my work in english was not.
9. He suggested that I practice english with my friends.
10. My mom thanked mr. helman for this advice.
11. Before leaving, he asked my mom how to get to main street.
12. Secretly, I hoped that my mom would give mr. helman the wrong directions.

EXERCISE 2

Insert the noun phrases in the parentheses in the following sentences. First, determine if the noun phrase is a proper noun or not. Then, capitalize and add "the" where necessary.

1. The Toyota is produced in _____ (japan).
2. Large quantities of Toyotas are shipped to _____ _____ (united states, china, and south korea).
3. They are shipped across _____ (atlantic ocean).
4. Some are shipped to _____ (hawaiian islands).
5. Before (great depression) _____, _____ (japanese) did not ship cars.
6. At that time, mainly _____ (united states, germany, france, italy, and great britain) produced cars.

7. Nowadays, cars are produced in both _____ (east) and _____ (west).

8. In Japan, one sees German-built cars and in _____ (united states) one sees Japanese-built cars.

9. This is why it is important for Americans in _____ (united states) to learn _____ (japanese) and for _____ (japanese) in Japan to learn _____ (english).

10. From _____ (north pole) to _____ (south pole), people need to know diverse languages.

VERBS: VERB TENSE

Simple Present and Present Progressive

Verb tenses in English can either occur in the simple form or the progressive form.

I'*m driving* a Toyota today, but I usually *drive* a Chevrolet.
  (progressive)   (simple)

FORMS OF THE VERB

SIMPLE	**PROGRESSIVE**
walk	form of *be* + walk + *ing*

THE SIMPLE PRESENT TENSE

1. We use the simple present to express
   a. a habitual action
      He reads the paper every morning.
   b. a general truth which is repeated periodically
      The sun rises each morning.
   c. a condition which is not repeated but which is always true
      Michael loves math.

2. There are several verbs in English that generally occur in the simple present and not in the present progressive. The simple present is used with these nonaction verbs to indicate that something is happening now. The nonaction verbs are listed next.

NONACTION VERBS

APPEARANCE	PERCEPTION
appear (seem)	hear (perceive with the ears)
be (existence)	sound (seem)
consist	see (perceive with the eyes)
cost	smell (have a smell, not sniff)
equal	taste (perceive a taste involuntarily)
look	
resemble	
seem	

POSSESSION	INCLUSION	PREFERENCE AND DESIRE
belong (possession)	comprise	hate
have (possession)	consist	like
own	contain	love
possess	include	need
		prefer
		want
		desire
		approve
		appreciate
		mind

THOUGHTS
believe
feel (think, believe)
know
think (believe, have an opinion)
understand
doubt
guess (suppose)
imagine
mean (signify)
recognize
remember
understand
perceive

3. We often use the simple present with these words:
   always
   often
   frequently
   usually
   sometimes
   every day, week, month, and so on
   once a week, month, year, and so on
   occasionally
   seldom
   rarely
   never

THE PRESENT PROGRESSIVE

The progressive is generally used to indicate that the action is ongoing, in progress, incomplete, or temporary. It may also represent a change from a normal activity.

1. We use the present continuous tense to express:
   a. an event that is happening now
      I am now looking at this page.
   b. an event that is taking place in the near future
      I am graduating from this university in a few days.
   c. an event which is taking place temporarily
      We're living in this trailer temporarily while we are looking for a house.
   d. events which happen very frequently and about which we feel some emotion.
      She's always playing her music too loudly. (irritation)

2. The following words and expressions accompany the present progressive:

for the time being	(right) now	these days, nowadays
temporarily	at the (this) moment	today
	at present	this week, month, year
		this quarter, semester, etc.

3. Adverbs which may appear with the present progressive tense include: *gradually, slowly, soon, quickly,* and *rapidly.*
   John is recovering slowly.
   He is gradually getting better.

EXERCISE 1

Choose the word or phrase that best completes the sentence. Sometimes, there is more than one correct answer. Explain the reason for your choice.

1. The cake _____ (is tasting, tastes) delicious.

2. She _____ (is preferring, prefers) her red coat.

3. They _____ (are trying, try) to get a loan to buy a car this afternoon.

4. I _____ (am graduating, graduate) in just a few more days.

5. He _____ (is working, works) temporarily as a bank teller.

6. Jorge _____ (is owning, owns) a new Porsche.

7. She _____ (is writing, writes) her mother each Thursday.

8. I _____ (am knowing, know) all that information already.

9. My father always _____ (is telling, tells) us the truth.

10. We often _____ (are fighting, fight) at the dinner table.

EXERCISE 2

Fill in the blank with the simple present or present progressive form of the verb in the parentheses. Certain time expressions should help you decide what verb to use.

1. (sing) The man often _____ in the shower.

2. (major) For the time being, Kim _____ in Chemistry.

3. (equal) Two plus two always _____ four.

4. (go) The tired student _____ on a vacation in just a few days.

5. (cry) The child frequently _____ when his mother leaves him.

6. (impress) The art of Van Gogh always _____ me.

7. (perceive) Every time I see flowers bloom, I _____ the beauty of nature.

8. (earn) He temporarily _____ money as a writer.

9. (review) At this very moment, the students _____ verb tenses.

10. (fly) John _____ to Los Angeles this evening.

Simple Past and Present Perfect

SUMMARY CHART: When to Use Simple Past and Present Perfect

SIMPLE PAST TENSE	PRESENT PERFECT TENSE
The action started and ended in the past.	The action started in the past and continues to the present.
There was a repeated past action that is unlikely to occur again (or the emphasis is on its completion).	There was a repeated past action that may occur again.
The action occurred at a specific time in the past.	The action occurred at an unspecified time in the past.

SIMPLE PAST TENSE

1. We use the simple past tense to
   a. talk about an event or action that happened at a definite time in the past.
      The dog jumped over the fence.
      The child sang the song.
   b. express a series of past events in chronological order.
      I got up, washed my face, ate breakfast, brushed my teeth, and went to school.
2. Many times, the past tense is accompanied by a specific time reference, such as *five months ago, last March, in 1985, when they first met,* etc.

   Where is John? He was here last week.

   The children dressed up like witches last Halloween.

PRESENT PERFECT TENSE

1. The present perfect is formed by using the auxiliary verb *have* and a past participle.

| I, You, We | have | danced, jumped, left |
| He, She, It | has | dreamed, won, begun |

| There | has | been | a storm |
| There | have | been | several storms |

2. Adverbs (such as *always* and *never*) are commonly placed between the auxiliary verb and the main verb.

   They *have always done* their homework on time.
   I *have often seen* them walk home together

3. We use the present perfect in the following situations:
   - when an action starts in the past and continues into the present
     She's been studying Spanish for ten years.
     He's been studying the history of Vietnam lately.
   - when a past action may occur again
     They've had two fights this year.
     I've gone to the new shopping mall three times.
   - when the action took place at an unspecified time in the past
     We've already had some coffee today.
     I've seen two or three plays this year.

4. Most participles are the same as the past tense form. However, some verb forms are irregular. Following is a list of common irregular verb forms.

INFINITIVE	PAST TENSE	PAST PARTICIPLE
arise	arose	arisen
awake	awoke	awaken
be	was, were	been
beat	beat	beaten, beat
become	became	become
begin	began	begun
bend	bent	bent
bite	bit	bitten, bit
blow	blew	blown
break	broke	broken
bring	brought	brought
build	built	built
burst	burst	burst
buy	bought	bought
catch	caught	caught
choose	chose	chosen
cling	clung	clung
come	came	come
cost	cost	cost
deal	dealt	dealt
dig	dug	dug
dive	dived, dove	dived
draw	drew	drawn
dream	dreamed	dreamed
drink	drank	drunk
drown	drowned	drowned
eat	ate	eaten
fall	fell	fallen
fight	fought	fought
find	found	found
fly	flew	flown
forget	forgot	forgotten
freeze	froze	frozen
get	got	gotten, got
give	gave	given
go	went	gone
grow	grew	grown
hang (suspend)	hung	hung
hang (execute)	hanged	hanged
have	had	had
hear	heard	heard
hide	hid	hidden
hurt	hurt	hurt
keep	kept	kept

know	knew	known
lay (put)	laid	laid
lead	led	led
lend	lent	lent
let (allow)	let	let
lie	lay	lain
lose	lost	lost
make	made	made
mean	meant	meant
meet	met	met
prove	proved	proved, proven
read	read	read
ride	rode	ridden
ring	rang	rang
rise	rose	risen
run	ran	run
say	said	said
see	saw	seen
send	sent	sent
shake	shook	shaken
shrink	shrank	shrunk, shrunken
sing	sang	sung
sink	sank	sunk
sit	sat	sat
slay	slew	slain
sleep	slept	slept
speak	spoke	spoken
spin	spun	spun
spring	sprang	sprung
stand	stood	stood
steal	stole	stolen
sting	stung	stung
strike	struck	struck, stricken
swear	swore	sworn
swim	swam	swum
swing	swung	swung
take	took	taken
teach	taught	taught
throw	threw	thrown
wake	woke, waked	waked, woken
wear	wore	worn
wring	wrung	wrung
write	wrote	written

EXERCISE 1

Circle the letter that matches the correct words to fill in the blanks.

1. Jan and Joe _____ absent since last week.
   a. were   b. had   c. have been   d. has been

2. Ever since Ken _____ to the United States in 1980, he has experienced difficulty getting a job.
   a. has come   b. come   c. came   d. have come

3. How many soft drinks _____ today?
   a. you have drunk   b. did you drunk   c. drank   d. have you drunk

4. Jessie _____ a doctor for eight years.
   a. been   b. is   c. has been   d. have been

5. I'd like some more cake. So far, I _____ one piece of cake.
   a. have only eaten   b. ate   c. eat   d. has eaten

6. Last year, I _____ French, but this year I am studying German.
   a. studied   b. study   c. have studied   d. had studied

7. Last weekend, John _____ to the library.
   a. has gone   b. have gone   c. went   d. go

8. I _____ geography since I was in high school.
   a. have not studied   b. don't study   c. has not studied
   d. didn't study

9. Mary _____ the professor since last March.
   a. knew   b. know   c. have known   d. has known

10. Mr. Vu _____ his country four years ago.
    a. leave   b. have left   c. left   d. has left

EXERCISE 2

Fill in the blanks with the correct form of the verb in parentheses. Use the simple past or present perfect tense.

1. I _____ Taiwan several years ago. (leave)

2. María _____ to New Orleans last year. She hopes to return. (go)

3. Ever since Jorge was a child, he _____ to be a teacher. He still hopes to become one. (want)

4. Lately, James' writing _____ a lot. (improve)

5. Last year, there _____ a terrible fire in a factory on Hope Street. (be)

6. I _____ to my homeland since 1984. (not return)

7. When I was in France in 1983, I _____ French. I have not spoken a word of French since that time. (study)

8. Last weekend, Diep _____ to Maine. (fly)

9. So far, Thuy _____ enough money to visit her aunt in New York, but not enough to visit her relatives in Switzerland. (save)

10. When Charles _____ in Taiwan last year, he studied engineering. (live)

11. Ann _____ karate from 1982 to 1985. (study)

12. They _____ Los Angeles three times last summer before returning to Mexico. (visit)

13. Rosina _____ this textbook ever since her English class first began. (use)

14. Up to now, we _____ three tests this semester. (have)

15. The crime rate in the major cities _____ over the last five years. It will probably continue to increase. (double)

16. Last June, we _____ the Grand Canyon. (see)

17. Mike _____ the United States five years ago. (leave)

THE PAST PERFECT

The past perfect is formed with an auxiliary verb, *had,* and a past participle.

We	had	spoken	French.
She	had	learned	the truth.
I	had	moved	the table.

1. The past perfect means that an action was completed before a particular moment in the past. Use the past perfect when an earlier event is mentioned in relation to a later one.

   Before Pablo came to the United States (in 1982), he had already learned English.

2. If *when* is used with the past perfect in the main clause, it means that the action in the main clause occured earlier than the action introduced by *when*.

> When Pablo came to the U.S., he had already studied English. (Pablo had studied English before he came to the U.S.)

> When Pablo came to the U.S., he studied English. (Pablo began to study English when he came to the U.S.)

3. The past perfect can be used in a sentence with *before, after,* and *until,* but the simple past tense is usually more common, particularly in spoken English.

> He had studied abroad for two years until he came to the United States.

> He studied abroad for two years until he came to the United States.

4. *Just, already, never (not ever),* and *for* + a time period are often used with the past perfect.

> Michelle looked as though she had just seen a ghost.
> School had already started by the time he arrived.

> When the teacher told the students to turn in their papers, they had not yet finished writing.

> Kim had had her dog for only ten days when it was hit by a car.

EXERCISE 1

Determine whether the following sentences are correct (C) or incorrect (I). Circle the appropriate letter.

1. Jaime played the piano until last year. C   I
2. I had finished my term project by the time my teacher requested it. C   I
3. Sam did not yet finish his homework by the time I saw him. C   I
4. By the time Halloween came, the children already made beautiful costumes. C   I

5. I had not begun to wash the dishes when the phone had rung. C   I
6. Before World War II, radio shows had been popular in the United States. C   I

EXERCISE 2

Fill in the blanks with the simple past tense or the past perfect.

1. By the time the teacher caught the cheater, the student already _____ the classroom. (leave)

2. By the time the United States _____ the war, the soldiers had grown tired of fighting. (win)

3. Last week, I _____ the answer when the teacher asked the question. (know)

4. By 1948, World War II _____ . (end)

5. By the time Joan got to class, the teacher _____ the homework. (collect)

6. The class always _____ on time last week. (begin)

7. When Jackie Robinson was recognized for his talent as a baseball player, no Black _____ on a professional baseball team. (ever/play)

8. When Sandra O'Connor was appointed to the Supreme Court, no woman _____ a part of the Supreme Court before. (be)

9. After hearing the sad news, he _____ away with tears in his eyes. (run)

10. When Neil Armstrong _____ on the moon, no human had ever walked there before. (walk)

11. When John F. Kennedy was killed, he _____ as president for only three years. (serve)

12. He _____ her in 1982 before she left for New York. (see)

13. The Soviet Union _____ its space exploration before the United States sent a satellite to the moon. (already/start)

VERBS: THE PASSIVE CONSTRUCTION

Compare the active and passive constructions below.

ACTIVE	John	wrote	the essay.
PASSIVE	The essay	was written	by John.

The direct object in the active construction becomes the subject in the passive. Often, the subject in the active construction is kept as an agent in the passive, as in the phrase *by John* in the previous example.

The verb forms in the passive construction are composed of the auxiliary verb *be* in the appropriate tense and the past participle of the main verb.
Examples:

Past	They were scolded.
Future	He will be scolded.
Present Progressive	We are being scolded.

Although the active construction is used more frequently in English than the passive, there are certain situations when the passive is more effective. The passive construction is often used in the following situations:

1. The speaker considers the performer of the act expressed by the verb unimportant or not essential to the meaning he wishes to convey.
   Harvard was founded in 1636.
   The United Nations Charter was signed in 1945.
   George was wounded in the war.

2. The speaker or writer wants to emphasize the receiver of the activity expressed by the verb:
   The man was hit by a speeding car.
   The notebook was given to me by the teacher.

3. The speaker wishes to make a statement seem objective or impersonal.
   It is believed that the political situation is critical.
   It is thought by experts that the project will fail.

EXERCISE 1

Write "P" if the sentence contains a passive construction and "A" if the sentence contains an active construction.

1. _____ My car engine was repaired this morning.

2. _____ Henry is fixing my car now.

3. _____ The passive construction is often used in textbooks.

4. _____ Sound was introduced to the movies in 1927 by Warner Brothers.

5. _____ The essay assignment was turned in too late.

6. _____ We never cheat on exams.

7. _____ Quang went to the dentist yesterday.

8. _____ The grammar lessons are easy.

9. _____ Peace was achieved with great difficulty.

10. _____ English is spoken in many parts of the world.

11. _____ The baby was delivered at 2:00 A.M.

12. _____ The film was developed quickly.

13. _____ The murderer has escaped from prison.

14. _____ At this moment, the waiters are serving dinner.

15. _____ Everyone likes Jaime.

EXERCISE 2

Change the following sentences from the active to the passive construction.

1. The mailman delivered the mail late.
2. Shakespeare wrote *Romeo and Juliet*.
3. A shark bit the child.
4. Miguel took the dog for a walk.
5. Frank Lloyd Wright built my house.
6. María planted the flowers several years ago.
7. The violinist played the song well.
8. Kent gave me this present.
9. Barbara will sign the contract soon.
10. We hold meetings once a week.

11. The plumber repaired the broken toilet.

12. The teacher gave Jaime the reward.

13. Abraham Lincoln, the sixteenth president of the United States, hated slavery.

14. Dr. Martin Luther King, Jr. desired equal rights for all people.

15. José has already served the dinner.

VERBS: GERUNDS AND INFINITIVES

Gerunds

The gerund consists of a verb + *ing* (such as *writing* and *listening*).

1. Gerunds are similar in function to nouns and, like nouns, can occur in subject or object position.
   Subject Position: *Swimming* on a hot day can be fun.
   Object Position: We enjoy *singing*.

2. Use the word *not* to make the gerund negative.
   Would you mind not sitting here?

3. Gerunds can occur after the preposition *to*, as in *get accustomed to, get used to,* and *look forward to.* In this case, *to* is not a part of an infinitive.
   I'm looking forward to improving my education.

4. Gerunds can also serve as objects of prepositions.
   The thought of eating cake made the poor child smile.

5. Possessive nouns (such as *the boys'*) and possessive pronouns (such as *my* and *your*) often come before gerunds.
   Mike's singing was off-key.
   They looked forward to your coming.

6. Gerunds can be preceded by *for* to indicate purpose.
   A bowl is a dish for eating soup.

7. The following is a list of verbs and expressions that can be followed by a gerund. They are grouped together by meaning.

appreciate
enjoy
like*

favor
prefer*

anticipate
contemplate
look forward to
miss
regret

can't stand (bear)*
detest
dislike
hate
resent

begin*
continue
keep (on)
start*
take turns

finish
give up
quit
stop

acknowledge
admit (to)

escape
evade

consider
intend
suggest
try*

discuss
dream about
talk about
think about

include
omit

avoid
delay
postpone
put off

can't help (can't resist)
resist

get (be) accustomed to
get (be) used to

be committed to
be opposed to
insist on
object to
deny

mind (don't mind)
tolerate

be busy
be engaged in

have a good (hard) time
have difficulties
have fun
have problems

*These verbs can also be followed by an infinitive.

Infinitives

The infinitive consists of *to* + a verb (such as *to sing, to dance*). Its purpose is similar to that of nouns.

1. Infinitives often occur after adjectives such as *easy, necessary, possible, difficult, nice, fortunate, happy, lucky, afraid, sad, ready, determined.*

    It is easy to learn to dance.
    I am ready to go home.

2. *In order to* preceding a verb indicates a reason for purpose.
   I called [in order] to invite you to dinner.

3. The following is a list of verbs and expressions that can be followed by an infinitive.

aim	agree	allow	It's difficult (hard)
arrange	consent	give permission	It's easy
advise	decline	have permission	It's interesting
cause	refuse	permit	It's nice
convince			It's possible
encourage	offer	claim	
expect	promise	pretend	can't stand (bear)*
forbid			hate*
force	attempt	appear	like*
get	fail	seem	prefer*
invite	manage		want
order	try*	be able	would like
persuade		know how	
plan		learn	begin*
prepare		teach	start*
remind			
require			be left
tell			remain
urge			
warn			

*These verbs can also be followed by a gerund.

EXERCISE 1

Circle the best answer.

1. The student is tired of _____ (studying, to study).

2. He insisted on _____ (seeing) (to see) the principal.

3. Hank wants _____ (taking) (to take) a day off work next week.

4. He looks forward to _____ (painting) (paint) the old house.

5. I considered _____ (taking) (to take) dance lessons.

6. The doctor advised his patient _____ (seeing) (to see) a dentist.

7. How fortunate I am _____ (knowing) (to know) you.

8. Michael quit _____ (hitting) (to hit) his younger brother.

9. The counselor convinced me _____ (taking) (to take) eighteen units this semester.

10. Ernesto is thinking about _____ (going) (go) to the beach this week.

EXERCISE 2

Circle the letter of the best answer.

1. Paul discussed _____ to the ranch with his father.

   a. go   b. that he goes   c. to go   d. going

2. John appears _____ happy.

   a. be   b. to be   c. is   d. seems

3. I'd like _____ this winter.

   a. to be ski   b. ski   c. to ski   d. that I ski

4. The parents avoided _____ the child the truth.

   a. telling   b. to be telling   c. to tell   d. that they tell

5. I dislike _____ at fancy restaurants.

   a. eating   b. eat   c. that I eat   d. to eat

6. I hope he has a great time _____ .

   a. travel   b. to travel   c. travels   d. traveling

7. The young woman was jealous of Rosa's _____ .

   a. to sing   b. singing   c. sing   d. sings

8. The teacher appreciated her _____ on time.

   a. coming   b. to come   c. comes   d. come

9. He persuaded the gifted writer _____ the book.

   a. write   b. to write   c. writing   d. writes

10. Kim forced her brother _____ his mind.

   a. making up   b. to make up   c. makes up
   d. that he make up

VERBS: MODAL AUXILIARIES

Modal auxiliaries are special kinds of verbs that

- change the meaning of the verb they precede
- never have verb endings (*-s, -ing, -ed*)
- are followed by a simple form of a verb (without an ending [*-s, -ing, -ed*])

1. We make a sentence with a modal negative by adding *not*.
   He might *not* sing.

2. We make a question by placing the modal auxiliary before the subject.
   Should he sing?

3. We make a modal auxiliary continuous with *be* + verb + *ing*.
   He *should* be singing.

4. *To* is not used after a modal auxiliary.
   She *can* sing.
   Exception: She *ought to* sing.

5. Notice that *cannot* is written as one word.
   I *cannot* go.

Modals and Meaning

To review the meanings of modals, refer to the chart. Note that some modals can express the same meaning.

I *may* sing. = I *might* sing. (possibility)

CHART OF MODALS AND RELATED IDIOMS BY MEANING

MEANING	PRESENT	FUTURE	PAST
Ability, physical	can be able to	— be able to	could be able to
Ability, learned	can be able to know how to	— be able to know how to	could be able to know how to
Possibility, ability	can be able to	can/could be able to	could be able to
Potential	—	can	could have (not realized)
Suggestion	—	can could	could have (not realized)
Permission	may can be permitted to be allowed to	may can be permitted to be allowed to	— could be permitted to be allowed to
Necessity	must have to	must have to	— have to
Prohibition	must not	must not	—
Lack of necessity	not have to	not have to	not have to
Advice	should ought to had better be supposed to	should ought to had better be supposed to[a]	should have ought to have — be supposed to
Possibility (maybe)	may might could	may might could	may have might have could have
Deduction	must	—	must have
Preference	would rather	would rather	would rather have
Opportunity not taken	—	—	could have
Impossibility	—	—	couldn't have
Condition	would	would	would have

[a]For *be supposed to* in the future, we use the verb *be* in the present tense:
He's supposed to be here tomorrow.

OTHER USES OF MODALS

1. Request for permission:

$$\left.\begin{array}{l}\text{May}\\\text{Can}\\\text{Could}\end{array}\right\}\quad\text{I use your pen?}$$

2. Offer:

I'll mail your letter for you.

3. Promise:

If you'll elect me to be your mayor, I'll improve your city.

4. Refusal:

I won't go. = I refuse to go.

5. Request:

$$\left.\begin{array}{l}\text{Would}\\\text{Will}\\\text{Could}\\\text{Can}\end{array}\right\}\quad\text{you close the door?}$$

Would you mind* closing the door?

6. Want:

I would like to be a doctor.

7. Invitation:

Would you like to go to the movies with me?

EXERCISE 1

Explain the difference in meaning between the sentences in the following groups.

Example: a.   He cannot skate. = He does not have the ability to skate.
            b.   He must not skate. = He is not allowed to skate.

---

*Responding "Yes, I mind" means "no." It is an angry response. To grant the request, we say, "No, I don't mind," "Not at all," "Of course not."

1. a. You cannot use the computer.
   b. You should not use the computer.
   c. You must not use the computer.
2. a. You should talk more softly.
   b. You ought to talk more softly.
   c. You have to talk more softly.
3. a. She must see her doctor soon.
   b. She might see her doctor soon.
   c. She had better see her doctor soon.
4. a. His research must be exact.
   b. His research might be exact.
   c. His research could be exact.
5. a. He might know how to do it.
   b. He should know how to do it.
   c. He must know how to do it.

EXERCISE 2

The following sentences contain errors related to the use of modal auxiliaries. Correct them. Note that there is more than one correct answer for some of these sentences.

1. John can seldom <u>writes</u> effective essays.
2. He had to <u>adapted</u> to life in the United States.
3. My mother never let me stay out late because she was scared that something <u>may</u> happen to me.
4. Without the right kind of motivation, I <u>could</u> not graduate from college next year.
5. Last year she <u>must</u> learn algebra.
6. Henry is not very punctual so he <u>must</u> not arrive on time tomorrow afternoon.
7. The murderer might slowly and steadily <u>creeps</u> to the door before opening it.
8. I'm not sure why you got such a bad grade on the last test. You <u>should</u> not have studied enough.
9. Three years ago, Ma <u>must</u> go to Europe.
10. I can't find my car keys. I might have <u>leaves</u> them at home.

SUBJECT-VERB AGREEMENT

In English, verbs agree with their subjects.

SINGULAR	PLURAL
A flower grows.	Flowers grow.
The student writes a book.	The students write books.

1. A verb agrees with the subject, not with the complement. A complement is a word that refers to the same person or thing as the subject of the sentence. It follows a linking verb, such as *be*.

   The students' main problem *is* grammar difficulties.

   In the previous sentence, the subject is *problem*, which is singular. The subject is not *difficulties*. Rather, *difficulties* is the complement. Therefore, the verb takes the singular form *is*. If the sentence is reversed, it reads:

   Grammar difficulties *are* the students' main problem.

   The subject is now the plural noun *difficulties*, and *problem* is the complement. The verb now takes the plural form *are*.

2. Prepositional phrases have no effect on a verb.

   A man *with two large guns* hides behind the fence.

   In that sentence, the subject (*man*) is singular. The prepositional phrase *with two large guns* has no effect on the verb (*hides*), which remains singular. Consider the following sentence:

   One of the students is unhappy.

   The singular verb *is* agrees with the singular subject *one*, not with the plural object of the preposition (*students*).

3. The following indefinite pronouns are singular and require singular verbs. (These pronouns are called indefinite because they do not refer to a specific person or to a definite thing, as do subject pronouns such as *he, she,* or *it*.)

   anybody, anyone, anything
   each, each other
   either, neither
   everybody, everyone, everything
   nobody, no one, nothing
   somebody, someone, something

   Everybody loves children.
   Each of these students receives the minimum wage.
   Either of those books is appropriate.

Notice that in the last two sentences, the verbs agree with the singular subject *each* and *either*. The verbs are not affected by the plural nouns in the prepositional phrases *of these students* or *of those books*.

4. When *each, every* or *any* is used as an adjective, the subject it modifies requires a singular verb.

   Every car and motorcycle needs license plates.
   Each cafe and restaurant is inspected by the Board of Health.

   Notice that the adjectives *every* and *each* make the verbs in the sentences singular even though each sentence has more than one subject.

5. Words such as *athletics, economics, mathematics, physics, statistics, measles,* and *news* are usually singular, despite their plural form.

   Statistics is a difficult subject.
   The news is interesting.

6. Treat collective nouns as singular unless the meaning is clearly plural. Collective nouns such as *jury, committee, audience, crowd, class, troop, family,* and *couple* name a class or a group. In the United States, collective nouns are usually treated as singular since they emphasize the group as a unit. Occasionally, when there is some reason to draw attention to the individual members of the group, a collective noun may be treated as plural.

   The audience is pleased with the performance.
   The audience clapped their hands.

7. The phrase *the number* is treated as a singular while the phrase *a number* is treated as a plural.

   The number of college-age students is increasing.
   A number of students are going to the play.

8. Subjects joined by *and* usually take plural verbs.

   Michael and Marie like to play together.
   The Browns and Mr. Nguyen go to France often.

9. When parts of a subject are joined by *or* or *nor*, the verb agrees with the closest noun.

   Neither the duck nor the chickens have been purchased.
   Either the car or the trucks are scheduled for repair next week.
   Either the trucks or the car is scheduled for repair next week.

10. The verb agrees with the subject even when the normal word order is inverted.

   There are many reasons to study. (The subject is *reasons*.)
   On the floor are some books. (The subject is *books*.)

EXERCISE 1

Some of the sentences in this exercise contain subject-verb agreement errors. Others are correct as written. If the sentence contains a subject-verb agreement error, cross out the incorrect verb, and write the correct verb in its place. If the sentence is correct, write a C next to the sentence number.

_____ 1. Each of Mary's dresses are washable.

_____ 2. Does anyone want this piece of cake?

_____ 3. At this resort, a guest with the right connections get the choice room.

_____ 4. The result of his actions was a divorce.

_____ 5. In most states, every man and woman over eighteen is free to marry without parental consent.

_____ 6. Her main concern right now are plans for the party.

_____ 7. Her secret in the beauty contests was never revealed to the other contestants.

_____ 8. Any soldier, sailor, airman, and marine with an honorable discharge have various benefits.

_____ 9. Everybody in the front three rows gets to come on stage.

_____ 10. The most important subject in the exams was derivation of square roots.

EXERCISE 2

In the following sentences, underline the subject and then circle the correct verb.

1. Television (interfere, interferes) with my homework.
2. One of my favorite aunts (arrive, arrives) in town today.
3. Examinations usually (occur, occurs) at the semester's end.
4. The speakers (express, expresses) their views very well.
5. This pile of books (belong, belongs) in the bookcase.
6. (Does, Do) the Browns want to go out tonight?
7. Running and shoving at the pool (are, is) forbidden.
8. Reading two books each day (is, are) just too much.
9. Smoking for ten years really (establish, establishes) the habit.
10. College (is, are) important.

11. He (agree, agrees) with me.
12. The local hospitals (employ, employs) a lot of people.
13. Driving three hundred miles (exhaust, exhausts) me.
14. Whatever you want to do (is, are) fine with me.
15. Complaining and whining (is, are) going to get you nowhere.
16. The seasons of the year (revolve, revolves) mechanically.
17. Hard work (impress, impresses) everybody.
18. One of my best friends (is, are) here.
19. All the women in town (admire, admires) our woman mayor.
20. Departments of this school (lose, loses) many students each year.

EXERCISE 3

Underline the subject of each sentence or clause and locate the corresponding verb. If the verb does not agree with the subject, cross out the verb and write the correct form in the blank to the left. If the sentence is correct as given, write C in the blank to the left.

_____ 1. The difference between twins are often surprising.

_____ 2. Both the drinks and the dessert was left off the bill.

_____ 3. Each of the puzzles require thirty minutes to solve.

_____ 4. Neither of us enjoy the outdoors.

_____ 5. There is only three original songs in the band's repertoire.

_____ 6. The price of every one of the houses in our neighborhood is beyond reach.

_____ 7. The cabinet for the stereo components are made of oiled oak.

_____ 8. The subject I want to write about are the effects of acid rain on the environment.

_____ 9. Delaware's two senators and one representative is its only representation in Congress.

_____ 10. Among the crowd was three pickpockets.

_____ 11. Neither the ring nor the watch were stolen.

_____ 12. The pieces of the grandfather clock was spread over the floor.

_____ 13. Three kinds of film is sold at the shop.

_____ 14. When are the committee members going to meet?

_____ 15. If the audience fail to applaud, the play will close.

_____ 16. The family eat together every night.

_____ 17. The first thing that I saw at the festival were the cheerful faces of the crowd.

_____ 18. One of the students falls asleep each morning in class.

_____ 19. Neither the books nor the record is his.

_____ 20. The number of students are not large.

SENTENCE FRAGMENTS AND RUN-ONS

A sentence fragment is an incomplete sentence that has been punctuated so that it looks like a sentence. Sentence fragments usually begin with a capital letter and end with a period but do not provide the full meaning of a sentence. Although fragments often appear in literature, they are not acceptable in academic prose. A complete sentence must have a subject and a predicate.

1. Dependent clauses cannot stand alone. They must be preceded or followed by independent clauses (which have both a subject and a predicate). Dependent clauses begin with words called subordinators (such as _who, which,_ and _that,_ as well as _after, although, because, before, even if, in order that, once, since, though, unless, until, when, where,_ and _while_).

    Fragment:
    We should not forget. _That we have lots of time._

    Complete Sentence:
    We should not forget that we have lots of time.

    Fragment:
    After the plane had left without us and we sat in the airport. My sister began to cry.

    Complete Sentence:
    After the plane had left without us and we sat in the airport, my sister began to cry.

2. Verbal phrases cannot stand alone. Verbal phrases include infinitives, gerunds, and participles.

    Fragment:
    The students lined up in front of the door. _To respond to the teacher._
    (infinitive fragment)

Complete Sentence:
To respond to the teacher, the students lined up in front of the door.
Fragment:
Responding to the teacher. The students lined up in front of the door. (gerund fragment)
Complete Sentence:
Responding to the teacher, the students lined up in front of the door.
Fragment:
Pleased by the teacher. The students lined up in front of the door. (participle gerund)
Complete Sentence:
Pleased by the teacher, the students lined up in front of the door.

3. Prepositional phrases cannot stand alone. They are composed of prepositions (such as *in, on,* and *at*) and their associated words. They do not include subjects and predicates.

    Fragment:
    I could not see anything. *Through the fog.*

    Complete Sentence:
    I could not see anything through the fog.

4. Noun phrases cannot stand alone since they lack verbs. Noun phrases are composed of nouns together with any adjectives, phrases or clauses which modify the nouns.

    Fragment:
    The children crying for food on the next corner. Should be fed.

    Complete Sentence:
    The children crying for food on the next corner should be fed.

Run-on Sentence/Comma Splice

A run-on sentence is composed of two sentences written together without the correct punctuation to separate them.

Run-on Sentence (Incorrect):
We can see changes, but not improvements the quality of life has not improved.

Correct Sentence:
We can see changes, but not improvements. The quality of life has not improved.

EXERCISE 1

Correct each of the sentence fragments in the following passage by creating new sentences or combining the fragments with other sentences.

What we know about the Aztecs comes from three sources: Aztec "picture books," diaries, and records kept by the Spaniards. And the objects found by archaelogists.

Humans lived in Mexico as early as 11,000 B.C. Indians wandered from north to south. Looking for food. By 6,500 B.C. many of the Indians had settled in the Valley of Mexico. Some of the early Indians were the Olmec, the Zapotec, the Maya, the Toltec, the Miztec and the Chichimec. Most were farmers. Who worked hard. Their main crop was maize.

About 1200, the Tenocha people moved. Into the Valley of Mexico. After many battles with their neighbors. They settled on an island in the middle of Lake Texcóco—"The Lake of the Moon." From this island, they built the powerful nation called the Aztec. However, according to Aztec records. The history is different.

EXERCISE 2

Write "C" (correct) if the paragraphs in this exercise do not contain any run-on sentences or sentence fragments. Write "I" (incorrect) if the paragraphs do contain run-on sentences and sentence fragments. Underline the sentence fragments and run-on sentences.

1. _____ All reptiles have backbones, breathe with lungs, and have scales on the outside of their bodies. Only reptiles are cold-blooded. They are no warmer than the air around them. When the air becomes extremely cold. They are cold. When the air is warm, they are warm.

2. _____ Most reptiles live in warm places. They cannot live where it is cold all of the time they often live in tropical areas. Such as Florida.

3. _____ Baby reptiles hatch from eggs. Some reptiles keep their eggs in their bodies until they are ready to hatch. Then, the babies are born.

4. _____ Baby reptiles look much like their mothers and fathers. Growing very quickly, they often change colors. As they grow up.

5. _____ One kind of reptile is the turtle. There are many kinds of turtles. Some are land turtles and some are water turtles. Mud turtles live in mud.

RELATIVE CLAUSES

Relative clauses describe or identify nouns.

1. The relative clause follows the noun.

Noun	*Relative Clause*
people	who have big cars
books	that have interesting pictures

2. The relative pronouns *who(m)*, *that*, and *which* introduce relative clauses.

3. A relative clause can modify the object of the main clause.

    I have a horse <u>which</u> *I ride a lot.*

    Note that it is incorrect to say *I have a horse which I ride <u>it</u> a lot.*

4. A relative clause may modify the subject of the main clause.

The horse	<u>that</u> *I bought* <u>which</u> *I bought*	is very pretty.
The teacher	<u>that</u> *I respect* <u>who</u> *I respect* <u>whom</u> *I respect*	is excellent.

5. The relative pronoun may replace an object noun or a subject noun.
    I have a horse which has a beautiful mane. (*Which* replaces the subject. *The horse* has a beautiful mane.)

    I have a horse which I ride a lot. (*Which* replaces the object. I ride *the horse* a lot.)

    Note: *Whom* is used in formal circumstances when the relative pronoun replaces a living object. *Who* is used more commonly in informal situations and in spoken language.

6. *Whose,* a possessive form of *who,* can be used to introduce a relative clause.

    There are many children. Their writing is good.

    There are many children <u>whose</u> *writing is good.*

7. Relative clauses can be *restrictive* or *nonrestrictive.* Restrictive relative clauses are a necessary part of the sentence. When the relative clause is taken out, either the sentence does not make sense or it is false. Restrictive clauses are *not* set off by commas because the commas are unnecessary to make clear what specific noun is being referred to.

    All men *who beat their wives* should be put in prison.

    All men should be put into prison. (not true)

8. Nonrestrictive relative clauses provide additional information which is not necessary in the sentence. When they are taken out, the sentence is still true. Commas always precede and follow these types of relative clauses.

    Spanish, *which is the language of millions of people,* is the national language of Mexico.

    Spanish is the national language of Mexico. (true)

EXERCISE 1

Fill in the blanks with an appropriate relative clause.

    1. A taxi driver is a person _____ .

    2. A student is a person _____ .

    3. A pair of scissors is a device _____ .

    4. A teacher is a person _____ .

    5. A sewing machine is a machine _____ .

    6. A gardener is a person _____ .

    7. A cook is a person _____ .

    8. A lawn mower is a machine _____ .

    9. A knife is a utensil _____ .

    10. A waiter is a person _____ .

EXERCISE 2

Tell which sentences have a nonrestrictive relative clause. Punctuate those sentences. Follow the example given.

Example: Taiwan which is an island in the Pacific Ocean is highly industrialized.

Nonrestrictive: Taiwan, which is an island in the Pacific Ocean, is highly industrialized.

1. Richard Nixon who was from California was impeached.
2. All artists who are not paid are called amateurs.
3. Alaska which is the northernmost state in the United States was purchased from Russia in 1867 for only seven million dollars.
4. The players that play together as a team usually win.
5. In soccer, the team that does not kick off in the first half of the game gets to kick off at the start of the second half.
6. José Martínez who is a good student always receives good grades.
7. Mike saw George López who graduated last spring.
8. He lives in Oslo which is the capital of Norway.
9. My favorite play is The Merchant of Venice which was written by Shakespeare.
10. The Suez Canal which is about 103 feet long is located in Egypt.

PARALLEL STRUCTURES

Sentences often employ parallel words, phrases and clauses to make the writing more concise and readable.

> We should finish our homework after we *eat dinner, watch television,* and *discuss the day's events.* (parallel verb forms)

1. Words using the same grammatical structure should be used in all parts of the parallel structure.
   - Correct:
     I can see *the ocean, the mountains,* and *the valley* from my window.
   - Incorrect:
     I can see *the ocean, the mountains* and *look at the valley* from my window.

2. Sometimes parallel structures appear inside of pairs of correlative conjunctives (which include *either . . . or, both . . . and, neither . . . nor,* and *not only . . . but*).
   - Parallel (Correct):
   Either Thuy *will visit* her mother, or she *will finish* her homework.
3. In academic prose, it is important not to omit repeated words in parallel constructions when these words assure clear and grammatically correct sentences.

EXERCISE 1

Underline the parallel structures in the sentences that follow. Explain why they are parallel structures in the space provided. Follow the example given next.

Example:

<u>Take it</u> or <u>leave it</u>.   Both are verb phrases.

1. Carl preferred to do his own cooking, cleaning, and scrubbing.
   _____

2. On a sunny day, we can see both the bay and the mountains.
   _____

3. This week, the senators may vote to protect our environment, or they may vote to increase defense spending.
   _____

4. She ate cold cereal for breakfast and cold pizza for lunch.
   _____

5. Early to bed, early to rise makes a man healthy, wealthy, and wise.
   a. _____
   b. _____

EXERCISE 2

The following sentences fail to use parallel structures appropriately. Write an accurate revision of each of the sentences using correct parallel structures. Do not worry if your revision changes words of the original sentence. Follow the example:

> Some children hate mushrooms and for others it's spinach that they hate.
> *Revision:* Some children hate mushrooms and others hate spinach.

1. The teacher asked the children to be calm and for them to be quiet.
2. This company makes neither high-quality products, nor that last.
3. Bill preferred doing his own landscaping and to clean the house by himself.
4. We ate dinner in a meadow overlooking the river and watching the sunset.
5. A college is a place for fostering friendships, for developing an understanding of values and beliefs, and to meet others with similar interests.
6. Our research department conducts experiments, and we can produce new products.
7. They ate many kinds of foods at the picnic—watermelon, strawberries, fried chicken and they ate hot dogs.

PARTICIPLES ENDING IN -ING AND -ED

Some participles are formed by adding *-ing* to the verb and some participles are formed by adding *-ed* to the verb.

PARTICIPLES

	+ *ed*	+ *ing*
interest	interested	interesting

1. Adjectives that end with the suffix *-ing* describe or characterize the thing to which they refer. The suffix *-ing* is also related to cause.

   > My vacation in Spain was exciting. (The word *exciting* describes my vacation.)
   > Engineering is interesting. (The word *interesting* describes engineering.)
   > Failing the class is disappointing. (My failure to pass the class causes disappointment.)
   > Eating worms is disgusting. (The action of eating worms causes disgust.)

2. The suffix *-ed* describes a person's response to or feeling about something.

   > We were bored by the lecture.
   > (Our response to the lecture was one of boredom.)

   > She was frightened by the mouse.
   > (Her feeling about and response to the mouse was that of fear.)

   The following is a partial list of adjectives that end in *-ing* and *-ed*.

-ING	*-ED*
amusing	amused
boring	bored
disappointing	disappointed
disgusting	disgusted
exciting	excited
frightening	frightened
interesting	interested
overwhelming	overwhelmed
pleasing	pleased
surprising	surprised

EXERCISE 1

Fill in the blanks with the correct adjective.

1. John is _____ in the job. (interesting, interested)

2. The students found the concert _____ . (entertaining, entertained).

3. The New Yorker has some _____ (amusing, amused) cartoons.

4. The lecture is _____ (fascinating, fascinated).

5. The gift that José gave Tuan was very _____ (pleasing, pleased).

6. John was _____ (boring, bored) by the lecture.

7. Nobody likes to be around John because he is _____ (boring, bored). He never says anything interesting.

8. Jan is _____ (pleasing, pleased) with her new radio.

9. It is _____ (surprising, surprised) that the professor failed the student.

10. I was _____ (disappointing, disappointed) that Joanna could not meet me after class.

Appendix C: Style and Organization

PARAGRAPHS

Paragraphs often contain a topic sentence, developing sentences (which support the topic sentence), and a concluding sentence.

The Topic Sentence

Topic sentences provide a central focus in a paragraph and state the main idea. They can be positioned early or late in the paragraph. However, they are most commonly located at the beginning. When they are positioned in the first sentence of the paragraph, as in the following example, every sentence that follows adds some new example or detail to support the statement made in the topic sentence. Good topic sentences make a point and give an idea which is worth developing further.

Example:

  <u>Mornings</u> <u>are</u> <u>difficult</u> <u>for</u> <u>me</u>. When I hear my alarm ring at 7:00 A.M., I usually grumble. I'm groggy and grumpy. After cursing the weather, I grab the morning paper and eat my morning breakfast. I become irrationally angry with the news and shout at whoever is nearby. If I'm lucky, my family forgives me for my behavior since they understand that mornings are tough on me.

The Developing Sentences

The *developing sentences* need to address the idea presented in the topic sentence and no other ideas. Sometimes you will need to have many developing sentences and other times just a few. If the idea in your topic sentence is simple, you may be able to cover the topic with one or two sentences, but if the idea is complex, you may need to write many sentences.

The Concluding Sentence(s)

When a paragraph stands alone, there is often a concluding sentence. In general, the conclusion in your paragraph is one sentence which brings the ideas in your paragraph to a close. It lets the reader know that you have finished discussing the topic.

EXERCISE 1

Read the following paragraph. Identify the topic sentence and conclusion.

  The first few months of a romance are the best. A new love's habits are endearing at the beginning; only later do they become annoying. New lovers find joy during those first few months in discovering new things about each other; however, the thrill of discovery wears off after hearing a story one hundred times. During the early stages, star-struck lovers marvel at how well they "fit" together. As time passes and as each changes in different ways, the "fit" may be more like a straitjacket. Luckily, most couples do experience these first few months of pure joy; that "perfect" beginning provides the foundation which allows them to survive the following twenty years!

EXERCISE 2

Add topic sentences to the following paragraphs.

1. In industry, X-rays are used to inspect materials and products in order to discover defects (problems) in them. Museums use X-rays to examine paintings to identify the artist of the period. Sometimes a second painting is discovered under the first. X-rays can be used in almost any situation where someone wants to see inside something that cannot be penetrated by light.

2. Among the ancient people who wrestled were the Egyptians. There are ancient Egyptian wall paintings over 5,000 years old which show Japanese wrestlers. Chinese sculptures from previous centuries also show wrestlers in action.

3. California gave the land to the Federal Government in 1906, and it become part of Yosemite National Park. The park, founded in 1864, now covers about 760,000 acres. More than a million and a half visitors come to Yosemite each year to see the great waterfalls, strange rock formations, and rugged mountains.

EXERCISE 3

The following topic sentences are weak because they are so vague. Rewrite the sentences so that they become more specific and can be addressed in one paragraph.

1. Education is very important.
2. Disneyland is a park in California.
3. Engineering is an excellent major.
4. Smoking is bad.

THESIS STATEMENTS

The thesis statement is similar to a topic sentence; however instead of controlling a single paragraph, the thesis statement controls an entire essay. In contrast, topic sentences normally treat one aspect or subcomponent of the thesis statement.

1. Like good topic statements, good thesis statements have the following characteristics:
   - they name the topic of the text;
   - they establish the writer's view of the topic;
   - they express a significant view; and
   - they suggest how the topic might be developed.

   Consider the sample thesis statement that follows:

   > Because of the political corruption of his colleagues and the mood of the nation, Richard Nixon was forced to lie about Watergate. (This thesis statement names the topic [Richard Nixon], the writer's position [that he was forced to lie about Watergate], and forecasts two supporting points [reasons why Nixon lied].)

2. In addition, thesis statements may provide the reader with a preview of the kinds (and order) of main supporting points.

3. Thesis statements must focus on a topic limited enough to be covered within the length limits of the intended essay.

EXERCISE 1

The following theses are faulty. Revise them so that they: (1) focus on a limited topic; (2) establish a definite point of view; and (3) express a significant point of view. Follow the example given.

Example:

- Faulty Thesis:
  I like dogs.
- Revised Thesis:
  My dog, Rover, has helped me in many ways.

1. This essay discusses my feelings about marriage.
2. Education has helped many people.
3. Elvis Presley was famous.
4. College has changed me.
5. It's a good idea to help the poor.
6. My home town is a nice place.
7. Abortion is a controversial issue.
8. Childhood can be fun.
9. I have many memories which have affected my life.

EXERCISE 2

Write thesis statements for six of the following topics.

1. your attitude towards college
2. one of your friends
3. what makes a good student
4. your biggest problem at college
5. an improvement the United States needs
6. your reasons for coming to school
7. your opinion of friendship
8. what you would like to be doing five years from now
9. your biggest fear

QUOTATIONS

Do not use *dropped quotations.* Dropped quotations are those which are introduced with little warning. To avoid surprising your reader when you use quotations, employ signal words in your writing which prepare the reader for what is to come. Signal phrases often include the author's name and appropriate background information.

DROPPED QUOTATION

The language of television commercials is often repetitive. "We are going to repeat and repeat, these commercials say, and we are going to grate on your nerves—and you are going to remember us."

QUOTATION WITH SIGNAL PHRASE

The language of television commercials is often repetitive. According to Michael J. Arlen, a television critic for *The New Yorker* and popular author, "At times, this [repetitive] sales approach has been given various fine-sounding methodological names by advertisers, but essentially it is the voice of the small boy who wants something: I want, I want, I want, I want—and finally you give it to him."[1]

[1]Arlen, Michael J. Three views of women. From *The View from Highway 1* by Michael J. Arlen. Copyright 1974, 1975, 1976 by Michael J. Arlen. Originally appeared in *The New Yorker.*

1. To avoid repetition and monotony, vary your signal phrases, as in these examples:
   - In the words of linguist Peter Farb, "..."
   - Burnham answers these objectives with the following analysis: "..."
   - Ronald Reagan claims, "..."
   - As Noam Chomsky has noted, "..."
   - President George Bush offers an odd argument for this view: "..."
   - Raimes, a dedicated teacher, points out, "..."

   When the signal phrase includes a verb, it is important to choose one that is appropriate. By choosing an appropriate verb, such as the ones in the list that follows, you can make sure that your source's ideas are understood.

acknowledges	comments	endorses	reasons
adds	compares	grants	refutes
admits	confirms	illustrates	rejects
agrees	contends	implies	reports
argues	declares	insists	responds
asserts	denies	notes	suggests
believes	disputes	observes	thinks
claims	emphasizes	points out	writes

2. It is not necessary to quote an entire sentence from a source. When you want to quote a word or expression, make sure that you weave a part of a source's sentence into your own sentence and that the whole statement is grammatically correct.

   Lionel Tiger argues that our society "has shifted to a pattern of serial polygamy," a system in which people have more than one spouse, one at a time, but one after another.

3. To shorten a quoted passage, you can use ellipses (three periods with spaces between) to show that you have left out words. The sentences that remain must be grammatically correct.

   In a recent article, Paul Robinson, a Stanford professor, argued that "the worst thing on TV is educational TV ... since it corrupts the very notion of education and renders its victims uneducatable." (218)

   When you want to omit a full sentence or more, use a period before the three ellipsis dots.
   Ordinarily, do not use ellipses at the beginning or at an end of a quotation.

4. When you quote more than four typed lines of prose, you should set off the quotation by indenting it ten spaces from the left margin. Use the normal right margin and do not single-space. Long quotations should be introduced by a sentence which contains background information about the quotation. Such long quotations are normally followed by a colon. Quotation marks are unnecessary because the indented format tells readers that the quotation appears word for word.

Michael Harrington (1928-1989), a professor of political science at Queens College, New York, explains why poor people in the United States are largely invisible:

> The traveler comes to the Appalachians in the lovely season. He sees the hills, the streams, the foliage—but not the poor. Or perhaps he looks at a run-down mountain house and, remembering Rousseau rather than seeing with his eyes, he decides that 'those people' are truly fortunate to be living the way they are and that they are lucky to be exempt from the strains and tensions of the middle class.[2]

EXERCISE 1

Complete the following statements by using an appropriate verb:

1. President George Bush recently _____ , "Taxes will never be raised."

2. George Spindler, an anthropologist at Stanford University, _____ that "education in the United States fails to meet the needs of American children."

3. William Shakespeare _____ , "fashion wears out more apparel than the man."

4. Plumb, a professor of history at Harvard, fervently _____ that the family is dying.

5. Edward T. Hall, a well-known anthropologist who teaches at Northwestern University, _____ in his book, The Hidden Dimension, that Arabs and Americans cannot understand one another because they behave differently during conversations.

[2]Harrington, Michael. 1962. The invisible poor. In *The Other America* by Michael Harrington. Macmillan Publishing Company.

6. Graves _____ that American schools should emphasize critical thinking.

7. "Several major steps are involved in summarizing a paragraph," _____ Connie Shoemaker.

8. Higgins _____ , "Computers are essentially stupid."

9. Lee _____ , "When President Park died, the Korean people mourned uncontrollably."

10. *The World Book Encyclopedia* _____ , "Certain regions of China, India and Russia have always been those hardest hit by famine."

Note: There is more than one correct answer for these items. Correct your answers with your instructor.

Appendix Exercise Answers

ANSWER KEY: APPENDIX B

What follows are the answers to the grammar exercises in Appendix B.

Countable and Uncountable Nouns

PAGE 291, EXERCISE 1

1. books
2. advice
3. homework
4. novels
5. grammar
6. traffic
7. information
8. vocabulary
9. violence
10. luck
11. clothing
12. computers
13. knowledge
14. noise
15. gossip

PAGE 292, EXERCISE 2

1. is
2. has
3. is
4. is
5. is
6. is
7. is
8. are
9. is
10. was
11. are
12. was
13. is
14. is
15. bothers

Pronoun Reference

PAGE 295, EXERCISE 1

1. You cannot use the pronoun *they* here because the subject of the sentence, *many people,* has already been stated. *They* is redundant.
2. I—*Maria and I* are in the subject position in the sentence. Therefore, a subject rather than an object pronoun is needed.
3. they—In this case, *they* refers to Mary and Jane.
4. I—*Kim and I* are in the subject position in the sentence. Therefore, a subject rather than an object pronoun is needed.

5. me—The pronoun follows the preposition *to*. Therefore, an object pronoun is required. Subject pronouns such as *I* cannot follow the preposition *to*.
6. themselves—*themself* does not exist in standard English.
7. mine—*mines* does not exist in standard English.
8. it—The pronoun refers to the uncountable noun, *research*. Uncountables are referred to by singular pronouns.
9. her—The pronoun agrees in gender with the subject, *mother*.
10. our—A possessive adjective is used when it precedes a gerund.

PAGES 295–296, EXERCISE 2

1. me
2. him and me
3. mine
4. I
5. themselves

6. him
7. hers
8. you and me
9. themselves
10. his

PAGE 296, EXERCISE 3

1. my
2. him
3. my
4. you
5. it [that it is, in fact, Odysseus] or him
6. she
7. she
8. they
9. they
10. they

PAGES 297–298, EXERCISE 1

Definite Articles

1. the
2. the, the
3. ф
4. the, the
5. ф

6. ф
7. The
8. The
9. The
10. ф

PAGE 298, EXERCISE 2

1. Gold is an important metal.
2. The/A cat named Chester chased the mouse.
3. I am studying the/a book that is about geology.
4. I always exercise in the morning.
5. Did you see the man who is sitting next to José?

6. I always buy the/o gas at Joe's Gas Station.
7. I went to bed at midnight.
8. I drank the/o lemonade that Gia made.
9. I drank some tea. The tea was too hot.
10. He always strives to obtain wisdom.

Articles with Proper Nouns

PAGE 300, EXERCISE 1

1. Spanish
2. Mr. Helman
3. Mr. Helman, English
4. English, Literature of the World, Stanford University
5. Tuesday, December
6. Mr. Helman, Pepsi-Cola
7. Algebra
8. Algebra, English
9. English
10. Mr. Helman
11. Main Street
12. Mr. Helman

PAGES 300–301, EXERCISE 2

1. Japan
2. the United States, China, and South Korea
3. the Atlantic Ocean
4. the Hawaiian Islands
5. the Great Depression, the Japanese
6. the United States, Germany, France, Italy, and Great Britain
7. the East, the West
8. the United States
9. the United States, Japanese, the Japanese, English
10. the North Pole, the South Pole

Verb Tense: Simple Present and Present Progressive

PAGE 304, EXERCISE 1

1. tastes
2. prefers
3. are trying
4. am graduating
5. is working
6. owns
7. writes
8. know
9. tells
10. fight

PAGES 304–305, EXERCISE 2

1. sings
2. is majoring
3. equals
4. is going
5. cries
6. impresses
7. perceive
8. is earning
9. are reviewing
10. is flying

Verb Tense: Simple Past and Present Perfect

PAGE 309, EXERCISE 1

1. c
2. c
3. d
4. c
5. a
6. a
7. c
8. a
9. d
10. c

PAGES 309–310, EXERCISE 2

1. left
2. went
3. has wanted
4. has improved
5. was
6. have not returned
7. studied
8. flew
9. has saved
10. lived
11. studied
12. visited
13. has used
14. have had
15. has doubled
16. saw
17. left

Verb Tense: The Past Perfect

PAGES 311–312, EXERCISE 1

1. C
2. C
3. I
4. I
5. I
6. C

PAGE 312, EXERCISE 2

1. had left
2. won
3. knew
4. had ended
5. had collected
6. began
7. had ever played
8. had been
9. ran
10. walked
11. had served
12. saw or had seen
13. had already started

Passive Constructions

PAGE 314, EXERCISE 1

1. P	6. A	11. P
2. A	7. A	12. P
3. P	8. A	13. A
4. P	9. P	14. A
5. P	10. P	15. A

PAGES 314–315, EXERCISE 2

1. The mail was delivered late by the mailman.
2. *Romeo and Juliet* was written by Shakespeare.
3. The child was bitten by a shark.
4. The dog was taken for a walk by Miguel.
5. My house was built by Frank Lloyd Wright.
6. The flowers were planted by María.
7. The song was played well by the violinist.
8. This present was given to me by Kent.
9. The contract will be signed by Barbara soon.
10. The meetings are held by us once a week.

11. The broken toilet was repaired by the plumber.
12. The reward was given to Jaime by the teacher.
13. Slavery was hated by Abraham Lincoln, the sixteenth president of the United States.
14. Equal rights for all people was desired by Dr. Martin Luther King, Jr.
15. The dinner has already been served by José.

Gerunds and Infinitives

PAGES 317–318, EXERCISE 1

1. studying
2. seeing
3. to take
4. painting
5. taking
6. to see
7. to know or knowing
8. hitting
9. to take
10. going

PAGE 318, EXERCISE 2

1. d
2. b
3. c
4. a
5. a
6. d
7. b
8. a
9. b
10. b

Modal Auxiliaries

PAGES 321–322, EXERCISE 1

1. a. You do not know how to use the computer.
      You are unable to use the computer.
   b. It is not advisable for you to use the computer.
   c. You are not allowed to use the computer.

2. a. It is a good idea for you to talk more softly.
   b. It is advisable for you to talk more softly.
   c. You are required to talk more softly.

3. a. It is imperative that she see her doctor soon.
      She is required to see her doctor soon.
   b. It is possible that she will see her doctor soon.
   c. It is imperative that she see her doctor soon.
      She is required to see her doctor soon.

4. a. His research is surely exact. His research is required to be exact.
   b. His research is possibly exact.
   c. His research is possibly exact.

5. a. It is possible that he knows how to do it.
   b. He probably knows how to do it. It is advisable for him to know how to do it.
   c. He surely knows how to do it. He is required to know how to do it.

PAGE 322, EXERCISE 2

1. write
2. adapt
3. might
4. cannot
5. had to
6. might
7. creep
8. must
9. had to or must have
10. left

Subject-Verb Agreement

PAGES 325–327,

Exercise 1	Exercise 2	Exercise 3
1. error, *are* should be *is*	1. interferes	1. is
2. C	2. arrives	2. were
3. error, *get* should be *gets*	3. occur	3. requires
4. C	4. express	4. enjoys
5. C	5. belongs	5. are
6. error, *are* should be *is*	6. Do	6. C
7. C	7. are	7. is
8. error, *have* should be *has*	8. is	8. is

9. C	9. establishes	9. are
10. C	10. is	10. were
	11. agrees	11. was
	12. employ	12. were
	13. exhausts	13. are
	14. is	14. C
	15. are	15. fails
	16. revolve	16. eats
	17. impresses	17. was
	18. is	18. C
	19. admire	19. C
	20. lose	20. is

Sentence Fragments and Run-Ons

Exercise 1 (PAGE 329)

What we know about the Aztec comes from three sources; Aztec "picture books," diaries, and records kept by the Spaniards, and the objects found by archaeologists.

Humans lived in Mexico as early as 11,000 B.C. Indians wandered from north to south looking for food. By 6500 B.C. many of the Indians had settled in the Valley of Mexico. Some of the early Indians were the Olmec, the Zapotec, the Maya, the Toltec, the Miztec and the Chichimec. Most were farmers who worked hard. Their main crop was maize.

About 1200, the Tenocha people moved into the Valley of Mexico. After many battles with their neighbors, they settled on an island in the middle of Lake Texcóco—"The Lake of the Moon." From this island, they built the powerful nation called the Aztec. However, according to Aztec records, the history is different.

Exercise 2 (PAGES 329-330)

1. Incorrect
   When the air becomes extremely cold. (sentence fragment)
2. Incorrect
   They cannot live where it is cold all of the time they often live in tropical areas. (run-on sentence)
   Such as Florida. (sentence fragment)
3. Correct

4. Incorrect

   <u>As they grow up</u>. (sentence fragment)
5. Correct

Relative Clauses

Exercise 1 (other answers are possible)   (PAGE 331)

1. who drives a taxi
2. who studies
3. which/that cuts
4. who teaches
5. that/which sews
6. who gardens
7. who cooks
8. that/which cuts the lawn/grass
9. that/which cuts
10. who waits on tables/who serves food

Exercise 2   (PAGE 332)

1. *Nonrestrictive:* Richard Nixon, who was from California, was impeached.
2. *Restrictive:* All artists who are not paid are called amateurs.
3. *Nonrestrictive:* Alaska, the northernmost state in the United States, was purchased from Russia in 1867 for only seven million dollars.
4. *Restrictive:* The players that play together as a team usually win.
5. *Restrictive:* In soccer, the team that does not kick off in the first half of the game gets to kick off at the start of the second half.
6. *Nonrestrictive:* José, Martínez, who is a good student, always receives good grades.
7. *Nonrestrictive:* Mike saw George López, who graduated last spring.
8. *Nonrestrictive:* He lives in Oslo, the capital of Norway.
9. *Nonrestrictive:* My favorite play is <u>The Merchant of Venice</u>, which was written by Shakespeare.
10. *Nonrestrictive:* The Suez Canal, which is about 103 feet long, is located in Egypt.

Parallel Structures

Exercise 1 (PAGE 333)

1. Carl preferred to do his own <u>cooking</u>, <u>cleaning</u>, and <u>scrubbing</u>. All three of these words are gerunds.
2. On a sunny day, we can see both <u>the bay</u> and <u>the mountains</u>. Both *bay* and *mountains* are nouns.
3. This week, <u>the senators may vote to protect our environment</u>, or <u>they may vote to increase defense spending</u>.
   These two independent clauses both consist of subject + modal auxiliary + verb phrase.
4. She ate <u>cold cereal for breakfast</u> and <u>cold pizza for lunch</u>.
   Both expressions consist of the word, *cold,* followed by a noun which is modified by a prepositional phrase.
5. <u>Early to bed, early to rise</u> makes a man <u>healthy</u>, <u>wealthy</u> and <u>wise</u>.
   a.   The first two underlined expressions consist of the adverb, *early,* followed by an infinitive (to + Verb).
   b.   The next three underlined words are all adjectives.

Exercise 2 (PAGE 334)

1. The teacher asked the children to be calm and quiet.
2. This company makes neither high-quality nor lasting products.
3. Bill preferred doing his own landscaping and housekeeping.
4. We ate dinner in a meadow overlooking the river and watched the sunset.
5. A college is a place for fostering friendships, for developing an understanding of values and beliefs, and for meeting others with similar interests.
6. Our research department conducts experiments and produces new products.
7. They ate many kinds of foods at the picnic—watermelon, strawberries, fried chicken and hot dogs.

Participles Ending in /-ing and /-ed

Exercise 1 (PAGE 336)

1. interested
2. entertaining
3. amusing

4. fascinating
5. pleasing
6. bored
7. boring
8. pleased
9. surprising
10. disappointed

ANSWER KEY: APPENDIX C

Paragraphs

PAGE 338, EXERCISE 1

1. *Topic sentence:* The first few months of a romance are the best.
2. *Conclusion:* That "perfect" beginning provides the foundation which allows them to survive the following twenty years!

PAGE 339, EXERCISE 2 (Other answers are possible.)

1. X-rays are used in several ways.
2. Wrestling is one of the oldest known sports.
3. Yosemite Valley was developed into a major park over the past 100 years.

PAGE 339, EXERCISE 3 (Other answers are possible.)

1. The education I received at college has affected my ability to earn a living.
2. A trip to Disneyland can provide an enjoyable experience for children.
3. Engineering is an excellent major for those students with a strong background in math.
4. Smoking can damage a person's health.

Thesis Statements

PAGE 340, EXERCISE 1

There is no single correct answer for this exercise. Check your answers with your teacher. The following revised thesis statements should provide you with suggestions.

1. This thesis statement is too broad. Moreover, it does not address a definite point of view.
   Revised Thesis: Marriage encourages individuals to lose their identities.
2. This thesis statement is too broad.
   Revised Thesis: Education has helped me to earn more money, make friends, and attain satisfaction.
3. This thesis statement is not significant. Everyone knows that Elvis Presley was famous.
   Revised Thesis: Elvis Presley was famous because of his charisma, not his singing ability.
4. The thesis statement is too general.
   Revised Thesis: College has matured me by making me more independent, reliable, and self-sufficient.
5. This thesis statement is too general.
   Revised Thesis: Educating the poor can improve today's economy.
6. This thesis statement is too general and not very significant. (Many people like their home towns.)
   Revised Thesis: My home town, Vincent, is the best place to raise children.
7. This thesis statement fails to give the writer's point of view.
   Revised Thesis: Women should have the right to make their own decision regarding abortion.
8. This thesis statement is too broad and insignificant. (Many people think of childhood as having its fun moments.)
   Revised Thesis: Childhood is not always fun for children who grow up homeless.
9. This thesis statement is too broad and insignificant. (We all have memories.)
   Revised Thesis: Memories of my work picking grapes as a young boy inspired me to seek a good education.

PAGE 341, EXERCISE 2

There is no single correct answer for this exercise. Check your answers with your teacher.

Quotations

PAGES 343 - 344, EXERCISE 1

There is more than one correct answer for these items. Check your answers with your instructor.